# Ethical Decision Quality

*Building an Ethical Decision Culture*

By

**Ali E. Abbas**

Ethical Decision Quality: Building an Ethical Decision Culture

By Ali E. Abbas

This book first published 2023

Ethics International Press Ltd, UK

British Library Cataloguing in Publication Data

A catalogue record for this book is available from the British Library



Print Book ISBN: 978-1-80441-220-6

eBook ISBN: 978-1-80441-221-3

## Dedication

To my mother and family

Awareness
Stakeholders
Motives
Formulation
Environment
Tolerances and Trade-Offs
Reasoning and Rationalization
Well-Being
Information
Alternatives
Cognitive Biases
S
A
M
F
E
T
R
W
I
A
C
Ethical Decision Quality

## Disclaimer

An extensive amount of literature, data gathering, and media sources have been compiled while writing this book. The data is presented with precise references and citations to illustrate, with numerous examples, how the elements of ethical decision quality and the fundamental organizational impediments were conceived. The book does not judge the truth or falsity of the publicly available media articles or other citations in the public record.

# Contents

# Preface

How do you assess the ethical quality of decisions? What are the impediments to ethical decision quality in an organization? And how do you build an organization's ethical decision culture? This book will address these questions by drawing conclusions and insights based on numerous media articles, documentaries, movies, and case studies.

Several factors inspired the writing of this book. The first was the observation that organizational decision-making and ethics have often been treated as different topics. This separation impacts the quality and rigor of decision-making methods that are incorporated into the analysis of ethical situations, as well as the ethical quality of the analysis of many decision-making processes. Decision-making under uncertainty can be a challenging task without relying on appropriate tools and processes. There is no reason to believe that decisions involving ethical considerations are simpler or require less rigor.

The field of decision analysis provides a wealth of tools to help decision-makers achieve clarity of action. For example, decision analysis highlights situations where individuals become reluctant to changing a course of action because of the sunk cost bias even if a change is necessary and even if the inaction has ethical implications. Further, if you judge a decision only by the outcome that is received, then you would be falling into a well-known decision trap of failing to recognize the difference between a decision and its outcome; and this judgment may also have ethical implications. And if you operate on behalf of others using a risk tolerance that is too high, you may be exposing stakeholders to unwanted risk and loss of value. On the other hand, if you operate with a risk tolerance that is too low, you may be leaving good deals on the table and losing value to stakeholders. Despite these (and many other) well-known tools in the field of decision-making, decision analysis has yet to be fully integrated into the teachings of ethics.

On an organizational level, teaching ethics without a focus on decision making principles and the need to capture uncertainty, can render the teaching irrelevant to corporate decisions and can steer the direction of the analysis toward deterministic reasoning, which overlooks uncertainty and ignores a wealth of knowledge on traps, biases, and normative decision-making methods.

The *New York Times* and the *Wall Street Journal* published articles questioning whether ethics courses are useless and whether business schools can teach students to be virtuous.[1]

On the other hand, teaching decision-making without a focus on ethics ignores the ethicality of the chosen alternatives. The tools of decision analysis are insensitive to the morality of their application. For example, you can use decision analysis to decide on the best way to rob a bank, and the decision tools you incorporate will help you determine the best strategy to achieve your purpose. You can also knowingly use information that is not credible in the analysis or deliberately not take into account any opposing information. Or you can use a flawed method of decision-making that yields outcome-predetermined analysis. The analysis is insensitive to the ethicality of the information you enter. It is therefore essential to integrate ethics into the teaching of decision analysis.

A second impetus for writing this book was the observation that "what is ethical" and "what is legal" (or "what is compliant with corporate policy") are widely confused, which further complicates ethical decision-making. When operating within the bounds of the legal system, organizations place much more emphasis on recommendations made by the legal team than on the ethical implications of the decision. And while organizations have what is referred to as "ethics officers," many are, in effect, compliance officers that enforce corporate policy even if it violates some ethical principles. It is therefore essential to create distinctions highlighting the impacts of focusing solely on the legal system or compliance while making decisions. A method to determine the best decision alternative must consider the ethical, legal, and prudential aspects of a decision.

A third reason for writing this book was the need for a method to assess the ethical quality of decisions, either in real time or through a survey of past choices. A scan of thousands of media articles about poor decision-making that led to ethical collapses in for-profit and not-for-profit

1 https://www.nytimes.com/1989/11/25/opinion/ethics-courses-useless.html; https://www.wsj.com/articles/SB106365505376228100

organizations revealed repeatable elements that were impacted during the decision-making process. Following this observation, there was a need to categorize the findings and present a method to assess the ethical quality of decisions. "*Ethical decision quality*" (or EDQ) is coined for this purpose. All of the ethical collapses that were observed during the data gathering of this book resulted from failures in one or more elements of ethical decision quality.

A fourth reason for writing this book was the observation that, besides ethics and decision training, there is a need to identify (and minimize) impediments to ethical decision-making inherent within organizations. The data gathered showed that, in many cases, it was a few organizational mindsets and leadership actions that impacted the ethical quality of decisions. A characterization of these common mindsets and leadership actions that impeded ethical decision quality is provided.

The observed patterns also identified ways by which ethics can be taught and practiced to better fit within the context of organizational decision-making. In response to the queries from the *New York Times* and the *Wall Street Journal* about the efficacy of ethics training in organizations, the findings reveal that besides ethics training, several additional layers are needed: (1) a layer that understands, identifies, and audits the elements of ethical decision quality; (2) a layer that identifies and minimizes organizational traps, mindsets and structures that impede ethical decision quality; (3) leadership commitment to building a legal, ethical, and prudential decision-making environment; and (4) a commitment to avoiding common managerial decisions that impede ethical decision quality. The term "*building an ethical decision culture*" is coined for this purpose.

While writing this book, I often reflected on whether the patterns that had already been categorized, while repeatable, were general enough to capture the essence of collapses in a broad range of industries, cultures, and enterprises. But those periods would quickly end because another scandal would occur, and its patterns would fit precisely within the patterns that had already been categorized. These new occurrences would confirm that the results were generalizable and that the recent scandals were predictable.

*Ethical Decision Quality: Building an Ethical Decision Culture* is structured as follows:

Part 1 presents many real-life examples of decisions made by organizational administrators. The main objectives of this part are to provide motivation for why a method to assess the ethical quality of decisions is needed. Not all portions of the examples in Part 1 include ethical violations. Some examples were introduced merely to compare what different corporate administrators did in similar situations. Subtitles are inserted within the examples to highlight the repeat patterns observed during the data gathering. Reflection points are also presented for brainstorming alternate routes that could have been pursued, reflecting on the situation from different perspectives, or identifying patterns, traps, or common impediments to ethical decision quality.

Part 2 presents the elements of ethical decision quality and reflects on the weak elements of the decisions made in part 1 before the ethical collapses occurred. The elements discussed in this part provide a method to assess the ethical quality of a decision in real time or through a survey of past decisions.

Part 3 identifies common impediments to ethical decision quality that were gleaned from the data-gathering phase of this book. One action item that evolved was the need to create more awareness about what is legal and ethical. This book discusses the implications of focusing solely on the legal aspects of a decision. The term *"legally unethical"* is coined for this purpose. I hope this term becomes more common in mainstream language. Another action item is the need to create awareness about the difference between ethics and compliance. While many organizations have what is referred to as "ethics officers," they are, in effect, compliance officers that work closely with the legal department to enforce organizational policies that may themselves be unethical.

Part 4 of the book explains how to build an "ethical decision culture," which nurtures ethical decision-making across the organization and minimizes the common impediments to ethical decision quality.

This book is written for anybody interested in learning about ethical decision-making. It can be used in classroom discussions that combine ethics and organizational decision-making. It is also particularly relevant for corporate managers.

Besides its use by managers, this book can also be used by individuals during job interviews by asking about the organization's stance on ethical decision quality and its ethical decision culture during the interview process and before accepting a job offer.

I hope you enjoy reading this book and that it can help improve the ethical quality of your decisions and the ethical decision culture within your organization.

Ali Abbas

# Part 1

# A Short While Ago, in a Galaxy Not Too Far Away

# Chapter 1

# Our Founding Fathers Wrote an Important Document

*We hold these truths to be self-evident,*
*that all men are created equal,*
*that they are endowed by their Creator*
*with certain unalienable Rights,*
*that among these are Life,*
*Liberty and the pursuit of Happiness.*

**Figure 1.1.** *Portrait of Dr. Benjamin Franklin*

## 1.1. The Founding Fathers characterized fundamental human rights

A short while ago, five authors (John Adams, Benjamin Franklin, Thomas Jefferson, Roger Sherman, and Robert Livingston) were tasked with writing an important document[2]. After some edits and debates, it was approved

2 https://www.archives.gov/founding-docs/declaration-transcript

by the Continental Congress on July 4, 1776 announcing the separation of thirteen states from Britain. The document starts with the phrases,

> *We hold these truths to be self-evident, that all men are created equal, that they are endowed by their Creator with certain unalienable Rights, that among these are Life, Liberty and the pursuit of Happiness.*

**Reflection**

Cambridge Dictionary defines "unalienable" as "something that cannot be taken away from you or denied"[3]. The founding fathers identified some unalienable rights that are endowed upon individuals at birth.

1) What actions have some people done in the past to take these rights away from others?

2) What other rights have been identified in various constitutions or human rights declarations? Hint: For one example, conduct a search on the United Nations "Declaration of Human Rights".

## 1.2. Ethical tolerances: They tolerated violations of the unalienable human rights when they did not have support from the delegates

A draft of the Declaration of Independence had a clause about slavery. The clause read,

> *He has waged cruel war against human nature itself, violating its most sacred rights of life and liberty in the persons of a distant people who never offended him,*
> *captivating and carrying them into slavery in another hemisphere, or to incur miserable death in their transportation thither.*[4]

This clause did not resonate well with the Southern delegates (and some of the Northern delegates) who were profiting from the slave trade.

---

[3] https://dictionary.cambridge.org/us/dictionary/english/inalienable-right

[4] https://www.npr.org/2015/07/03/419824340/scrapped-declaration-of-independence-passage-denounced-slavery

As a result, the paragraph was dropped. After another eighty-seven years, a Civil War, the Emancipation Proclamation, and the Thirteenth Amendment slavery ended.

## 1.3. One of the authors consistently included uncertainty in reasoning about the future

Dr. Benjamin Franklin (shown in figure 1.1), one of the authors, always allowed for uncertainty and unanticipated consequences in his writings. He mentioned, as an example, rather jokingly, on November 13, 1789 about the Constitution.

> *Our new Constitution is now established,*
> *everything seems to promise it will be durable;*
> *but, in this world, nothing is certain except death and taxes.*

Dr. Franklin remained optimistic about forming a republic, not a monarchy, but still considered uncertainty in his responses to this question. Historical records of the events of the last day of the convention noted on September 18, 1787,

> *A lady asked Dr. Franklin: Well Doctor, what have we got a republic or a monarchy—*
> *A republic, replied the Doctor if you can keep it.*

**Reflection**

1) Is it helpful to allow room for uncertainty when reasoning about the future?

2) Are there biases that make you believe something you desire is more likely to occur? Yes. The desirability bias is the tendency to believe the likelihood of something you desire is higher. Note that Franklin was cautious about asserting the prospect he desired would occur without simultaneously providing a condition for which it would not occur. He was less affected by this bias than many others.

## 1.4. Franklin noted an obligation to update belief in the light of new information

Dr. Benjamin Franklin also observed the importance of updating beliefs and that there is an obligation to change opinions and to act in the light of new information. He mentioned,

> *I confess that there are several parts of this constitution which I do not at present approve, but I am not sure I shall never approve them: For having lived long, I have experienced many instances of being obliged by better information, or fuller consideration, to change opinions even on important subjects, which I once thought right, but found to be otherwise.*

**Reflection**

Can you think of situations where not acting on new information can harm others?

## 1.5. He noted the effects of prejudices, local interests, and selfish views that impede ethical decision-making in a group

Dr. Franklin noted the impact of motives, prejudices, local interests, selfish views, and errors of the opinion of various individuals when writing the Constitution.

> *I doubt whether any other convention we can obtain may be able to make a better Constitution . . . for when you assemble a number of men to have the advantage of their joint wisdom, you inevitably assemble with those men all their prejudices, their passions, their errors of opinion, their local interests, and their selfish views. From such an assembly, can a perfect production be expected?*

## 1.6. He rationalized acts because there were no better ones available, and they were best for the public good

Dr. Franklin rationalized his consent to the Constitution because, among other things, he expected no better and that it was of interest to the public good.

> *Thus, I consent to this Constitution because I expect no better and because I am not sure that it is not the best. The opinions I have had of its errors I sacrifice to the public good.*

## 1.7. He used state-of-the-art decision-making methods (that were available at the time)

In 1780, Joseph Priestley asked Benjamin Franklin for help with a decision. His response is present in the Library of Congress[5], where he (correctly) noted that he could not tell Priestly what to do but how he (Franklin) made decisions. Dr. Franklin also noted that decision-making is difficult and comes with challenges. He replied,

> *In the Affair of so much Importance to you, wherein you ask my Advice, I cannot, for want of sufficient Premises, advise you what to determine, but if you please, I will tell you how.*
>
> *When these difficult Cases occur, they are difficult chiefly because while we have them under Consideration, all the Reasons pro and con are not present to the Mind at the same time; but sometimes one Set present themselves, and at other times another, the first being out of Sight. Hence the various Purposes or Inclinations that alternately prevail and the Uncertainty that perplexes us.*

## 1.8. He recognized our cognitive limitations in recalling all details of a decision at once

Benjamin Franklin also recognized our cognitive limitations and inability to recollect all the information at once. He wrote,

---

5 https://founders.archives.gov/documents/Franklin/01-19-02-0200

*To get over this, my Way is to divide half a Sheet of Paper by a Line into two Columns, writing over the one Pro, and over the other Con.*

*Then during three or four Days Consideration I put down under the different Heads short Hints of the different Motives that at different Times occur to me for or against the Measure.*

He offered guidance on how to reduce the complexity of the problem:

*When I have thus got them all together in one View, I endeavour to estimate their respective Weights; and where I find two, one on each side, that seem equal, I strike them both out: If I find a Reason pro equal to some two Reasons con, I strike out the three. If I judge some two Reasons con equal to some three Reasons pro, I strike out the five; and thus proceeding I find at length where the Ballance lies; and if after a Day or two of farther Consideration nothing new that is of Importance occurs on either side, I come to a Determination accordingly.*

Benjamin Franklin offered a method that first lists the pros and the cons. This goes on for three or four days until he is able to recollect the most important elements. He then simplifies the complexity of the situation by canceling the pros and cons of equal importance. When a pro is as important as a con, the two items cancel, and you can simplify the problem by not having to think about them. Sometimes a pro can cancel two or more cons or vice versa. When pros and cons have been canceled, there is less complexity and more clarity about the best alternative because we have fewer items to consider.

## 1.9. He acknowledged the limitations of his proposed decision reasoning

Benjamin Franklin acknowledged that while his method provides clarity in some situations, it does not entail the precision of algebraic quantities that may be required. He understood the limitations of his method. He continued,

*And tho' the Weight of Reasons cannot be taken with the Precision of Algebraic Quantities, yet when each is thus considered separately and*

> *comparatively, and the whole lies before me, I think I can judge better and am less likely to take a rash Step; and in fact, I have found great Advantage from this kind of Equation, in what may be called Moral or Prudential Algebra.*

And since then, the field of decision analysis and reasoning under uncertainty has developed significantly.

**Reflection**

Can you think of the ethical implications of using decision-making methods without mentioning their limitations?

Can you think of the ethical implications of using flawed methods of decision-making?

## 1.10. He observed the impacts of cognitive biases on decision-making

Benjamin Franklin understood the effects of biases (and particularly cognitive dissonance) long before the phenomenon was coined by the scientific community. The Benjamin Franklin effect is a proposed psychological phenomenon described by Franklin as follows:

> *He that has once done you a Kindness will be more ready to do you another, than he whom you yourself have obliged.*

The idea is that a person who has done you a favor, even if they did not like you previously, will be more willing to do you more favors. Franklin explained how he used that phenomenon to his advantage against a rival legislator in Pennsylvania:

> *Having heard that he had in his library a certain very scarce and curious book, I wrote a note to him, expressing my desire of perusing that book, and requesting he would do me the favour of lending it to me for a few days. He sent it immediately, and I return'd it in about a week with another note, expressing strongly my sense of the favour. When we next met in the House, he spoke to me (which he had never done before), and with*

*great civility; and he ever after manifested a readiness to serve me on all occasions, so that we became great friends, and our friendship continued to his death.*

**Reflection:**

Can you think of the ethical implications of exploiting individuals' cognitive biases?

# 200+ Years Later . . .

# Chapter 2

# Bill Gates, Microsoft, and the Most Influential Foundation in History

*I have an obligation to return my resources*
*to society in ways that have the greatest*
*impact for reducing suffering and improving lives.*

—Bill Gates's personal value trade-offs in 2022

**Figure 1.2.** *Bill Gates made six predictions in January 1998.*

## 2.1. In 1998, Bill Gates made six predictions at Stanford—five of them came true

In January 1998, I asked Bill Gates in Memorial Auditorium at Stanford University three questions (figure 1.2):

1. Where do you expect to see Microsoft in the next five years?

2. What do you think about Microsoft's competitive advantage and current competition?

3. What are your views that Netscape has just been offered for free in response to Internet Explorer being bundled with the Windows operating system?

This event occurred amid news that an investigation into the bundling of

Internet Explorer with Windows was underway. It was not the first time that an investigation into Microsoft's business decisions had been conducted: In 1992, the Federal Trade Commission began an inquiry into whether Microsoft was using its monopoly power in the PC operating system market.[6] The investigation was closed with an agreement from Microsoft not to tie other Microsoft products to the sale of Windows. However, Microsoft remained free to integrate additional features into the operating system.

Bill Gates responded to my three questions. Many individuals in his place might have said, "Oh, there has been an investigation, so I cannot answer that." He could have said that, but he did not. His responses are below.

## 2.2. In response to the three questions, Bill Gates made six predictions

**Prediction 1:** Gates replied, *"Windows and Office will still be our main products."* He was right!

**Prediction 2:** In response to competition, Gates added, *"If we slow down and don't do a good job, the companies that are most likely to replace us are companies whose names we don't know today—start-up companies who would take a new approach of doing something in a different way, the same way that Microsoft did when it came into business."* He was right! Microsoft has not been replaced by a company whose name was known at the time, nor does there appear to be any company capable of replacing Microsoft in the near future.

**Prediction 3:** Bill Gates said, *"The internet will be more mainstream."* He was right!

**Prediction 4:** Gates took a shiny silver-looking personal digital assistant (PDA) from his pocket and said, *"Devices like these will become more popular. They will change the way we do business and see the internet."* This was about a decade before the birth of the iPhone. He was right!

**Prediction 5:** Gates added that it wouldn't be long until computers will respond to spoken words. *"Speech will become a standard part of the interface,"* making them simpler to operate and more accessible. He was right!

---

6 https://en.wikipedia.org/wiki/United_States_v._Microsoft_Corp.

**Prediction 6:** In response to the question about Internet Explorer bundled with Windows, Gates replied,

> *As far as browsers go, basically, nobody has ever paid for a browser.*

He then asked an auditorium full of students,

> *Did anybody here pay for a browser?*

When nobody raised their hand, he added,

> *I am sorry, you should get a refund. It's a little bit of an accounting trick that they ever allocated money in that direction because you could always download the thing, and they would never come back to you after ninety days and say, "Hey, the ninety days are out, and you should pay money for this thing."*

Gates added this assertion:

> *Browsers have always been a feature, not a product.*

Bill Gates then predicted what would happen with the legal system.

> *The Department of Justice (DOJ) will soon come to the realization that their actions would lead to a suboptimal product.*

And regarding government actions leading to a crippled product, he added,

> *We are quite confident that won't happen.*

**Reflection**

Compare Bill Gates' statement "*We are quite confident that won't happen*" to Benjamin Franklin's statement "*[I]n this world, nothing is certain except death and taxes*".

## 2.3. What is the importance of thinking about the future and unanticipated consequences?

In response to my third question about competition, Bill Gates added,

> *There is competition out there, lots of competition. We've got Sun, who thinks the PC is an evil thing. We've got IBM, who still likes to sell high-priced computers. We've got any number of companies.*

He also added,

> *Nobody thought we would be the ones to redefine how computing would work and make it so you can exchange different hardware and still run the same software on those machines. That was just heresy. People would have laughed at that idea.*

Gates further added,

> *It is not clear that anybody would have even worked with us if they had known that would be the eventual impact of running standards like our operating system on those machines.*

This last statement is an example of what we shall refer to as "unanticipated consequences." It also demonstrates how different people have different beliefs and perspectives about the future.

**Reflection:**
**Can you ignore uncertainty when thinking about the future?**

- How would you rate Bill Gates's predictions compared with others in the industry then?
- Was reasoning with uncertainty important for technology companies in that environment? Is it necessary today?
- Is thinking about the future important for ethical decision-making?

## 2.4. Can the government affect decision-making (for better or worse)?

Bill Gates received another question about how he felt when he got up every morning, knowing that the Department of Justice was investigating him. Gates replied, "*One of the privileges of success in this country is government scrutiny.*" He added that investigating the computer industry was more interesting than other sectors, such as bread, and he asked,

> *If you were the DOJ, would you investigate bread or computer software?*

He added that there was a certain irony in the government's actions against Microsoft because the software industry was the most competitive in the country, and it created jobs. Gates added,

> *The question is whether the DOJ wants us to cripple our products or not. We have to do a better job at articulating what we are doing and creating public awareness.*

## 2.5. Can different stakeholders have different perspectives about the same situation?

There were many stakeholders with different perspectives in this situation.

**Bill Gates:** Make a better, cheaper product. A browser was a feature of a product, not a product by itself. Government intervention might cripple the product.

**Netscape:** Given the user base, the bundling of Internet Explorer with the Windows operating system meant that Netscape would probably be out of business. This marked the beginning of overtaking the browser market from Netscape. Netscape was eventually sold to America Online (AOL)[7].

**Consumers:** They would appreciate not having to pay for a browser, as Gates said, "*Did anybody here pay for a browser? I am sorry, you should get a refund.*" Consumers would also appreciate a better and cheaper product. However, consumers might have concerns about price gouging after/if a firm becomes a monopoly.

---

7 https://time.com/3857628/aol-1985-history/

**Other companies:** Microsoft could be a growing threat to their business. Gates said, *"Nobody would have worked with us if they knew the impacts of our operating system."*

**Government and the legal system:** Antitrust violations are illegal.

## 2.6. Can the environment impact your response? Gates's deposition made the judge laugh in court

Five months later, in May 1998, the Department of Justice and the district attorneys of twenty states sued Microsoft for using its monopoly power. Bill Gates's deposition by the Department of Justice was on August 28, 1998, several months after the presentation at Stanford. Gates's deposition, which his legal team may have influenced, gave the world a different image of Bill Gates than the one they were accustomed to and responses that were different in nature from the responses at Stanford.

CNN reported,

> *Gates's deposition transcript made the judge laugh in court.*[8]

The following is a sample exchange with David Boies, the attorney for the Department of Justice.[9] We shall refer to David Boies in a future chapter. The conversation here relates to an email Bill Gates had sent about the importance of the internet browser share to Microsoft. Compare Bill Gates's willingness to respond to questions in the deposition with his readiness to respond at Stanford.

*Importance: High*

> *Boies: Okay. Let me ask you to look at Exhibit 401. This is a message from you to Mr. Ballmer and Mr. Chase with a copy to Mr. Maritz and some other people also given copies dated August 15, 1997, at 4:07 p.m. on the subject of IBM and Netscape, correct?*
>
> *Gates: Uh-huh.*

---

8 http://edition.cnn.com/TECH/computing/9811/17/judgelaugh.ms.idg/

9 https://www.washingtonpost.com/wp-srv/business/longterm/microsoft/documents/gates0902p2.htm

*Boies: And you type in here "Importance: High."*

*Gates: No.*

*Boies: No?*

*Gates: No, I didn't type that.*

*Boies: Who typed in "High"?*

*Gates: A computer.*

*Boies: A computer. Why did the computer type in "High"?*

*Gates: It's an attribute of the e-mail.*

*Boies: And who set the attribute of the e-mail?*

*Gates: Usually, the sender sends that attribute.*

*Boies: Who is the sender here, Mr. Gates?*

*Gates: In this case, it appears I'm the sender.*

*Boies: Yes. And so you're the one who set the high designation of importance, right, sir?*

*Gates: It appears I did that. I don't remember doing that specifically.*

**The conversation continues:** *I don't know what you mean "concerned."*

*Boies: What non-Microsoft browsers were you concerned about in January of 1996?*

*Gates: I don't know what you mean "concerned."*

*Boies: What is it about the word "concerned" that you don't understand?*

*Gates: I'm not sure what you mean by it.*

*Boies: Is—*

*Gates: Is there a document where I use that term?*

*Boies: Is the term "concerned" a term that you're familiar with in the English language?*

*Gates: Yes.*

*Boies: Does it have a meaning that you're familiar with?*

*Gates: Yes.*

**The conversation goes on:** *Internet browser share does not involve other companies.*

*Boies: Now, when you were referring there to Internet browser share, what were the companies who were included in that?*

*Gates: There's no companies included in that.*

*Boies: Well, if you're winning browser share, that must mean that some other company is producing browsers and you're comparing your share of browsers with somebody else's share of browsers; is that not so, sir?*

*Gates: You asked me if there are any companies included in that and now—I'm very confused about what you're asking.*

*Boies: All right, sir, let me see if I can try to clarify. You say here, "Winning Internet browser share is a very, very important goal for us." What companies were supplying browsers whose share you were talking about?*

*Gates: It doesn't appear I'm talking about any other companies in that sentence.*

*Boies: Well, sir, is a market share something that is compiled only for one company? I understand if a company has a monopoly, that may be so, but in an usual situation where a company does not have a monopoly, share ordinarily implies comparing how much of a product one company has with how much of a product another company has, correct?*

*Gates: Yes.*

*Boies: Now, when you were talking about Internet browser share here, what companies were you talking about?*

*Gates: You're trying—you seem to be suggesting that just because share involves comparing multiple companies, that when I wrote that sentence, I was talking about other companies. It doesn't appear that I'm talking about other companies in that sentence. I've really read it very carefully, and I don't notice any other companies in there.*

*Boies: Oh, you mean you don't see any other company mentioned in that sentence; is that what you're saying?*

*Gates: The sentence doesn't appear to directly or indirectly refer to any other companies.*

*Boies: When you refer to an Internet browser share here, sir, what is the share of?*

*Gates: Browser usage.*

*Boies: Of course, you don't say "browser usage" here, do you, sir?*

*Gates: No, it says "share."*

*Boies: Now, let's say that you meant browser usage because that's what your testimony is. What browser usage were you talking about in terms of what your share of browser usage was? What browsers?*

*Gates: I'm not getting your question. Are you trying to ask what I was thinking when I wrote this sentence?*

*Boies: Let me begin with that. What were you thinking when you—*

*Gates: I don't remember specifically writing this sentence.*

*Boies: Does that mean you can't answer what you were thinking when you wrote the sentence?*

*Gates: That's correct.*

**Reflection: Motives, environment, and decision-making**

- Compare Bill Gates's responses during the deposition with his answers at Stanford eight months earlier. What could have influenced the responses during the testimony?
- Do you believe Gates's strategy during the deposition was impacted by a legal team? Was it affected by the environment? Or the high stakes involved?
- Environments: Are there environments that you believe would make people act differently than they would have in a different setting? Could coercive environments impact responses?
- Bill Gates used the names of many companies in his talk at Stanford. But he did not mention the word "Netscape." Instead, he used either "the thing" or "the browser." Can the responses during the deposition shed light on why Bill Gates did not use the word "Netscape" during the presentation at Stanford?

## 2.7. The legal verdict

Bill Gates's sixth prediction at Stanford turned out to be wrong. Following the depositions in August and September of 1998, the judge concluded that Microsoft had violated multiple sections of the Sherman Antitrust Act (an act formed in 1890)[10] and that Microsoft had used its monopoly power to collapse its rival, Netscape, by giving its browser for free. The Department of Justice deemed the browser a product, not a feature of the operating system.

**Reflection: Legal vs. ethical**

While integrating Internet Explorer into the Windows operating system was deemed a violation of the legal system, would consumers be harmed by a free browser that was integrated into the operating system instead of paying for a browser that is not integrated?

---

[10] Sherman Antitrust Act (1890), approved July 2, 1890. The Sherman Antitrust Act was the first federal act that outlawed monopolistic business practices.

- Are there aspects of a monopoly that could benefit consumers even though they are deemed illegal? Are there aspects of a monopoly that could harm consumers?
- What actions of organizations with a dominant market share (or a monopoly) do you consider unethical?
- Has the government ever made legislation incentivizing firms to manufacture products by limiting their competition? Hint: conduct research on the Orphan Drug Act.
- Are government officials up-to-date on the latest technological advances when they legislate? Do they need to be? Can you give examples?

## 2.8. Can biases affect predictions? Can they affect decision-making?

Out of all the predictions that Bill Gates gave, there was one that he presumably desired most, and it was also the one about which he said that they were pretty confident won't occur: the last one. And it was also the only prediction out of the six that was wrong.

Are humans subject to any internal biases that make us believe that something we desire is more likely to occur? Yes. Absolutely! This is called the "optimism bias" or "desirability bias." This bias also explains why individuals working on political campaigns believe that their candidate is more likely to win. This bias also explains why some people now use the term "cautiously optimistic," although they end up being subject to that bias anyway.

And there are many other biases that can also play a role in our perception of a situation. The confirmation bias, for example, demonstrates that we attend to information that supports our views about a situation and that we put much less weight on other information that contradicts our views. It is possible that Bill Gates may have discounted contradictory information about what might happen at the time.

## 2.9. Are there other biases that could have been triggered by the legal team?

Yes, of course. While we cannot ascertain that the last prediction was provided by a legal team, we can certainly assume that Gates had legal counsel, probably one of the best legal teams in the country. A legal team that was also subject to a desirability bias. A legal team that may also be subject to other biases, such as the "overconfidence bias," which makes us overestimate our abilities or our forecasts; and this bias could have been amplified because of the 1992 investigation into Microsoft, which had been closed.

Further, if Gates had multiple detailed conversations with his attorneys about the mechanisms for addressing the investigation, which we can presume he did, and if this information was readily available in his memory at the time, then it is possible that the perception of the likelihood of success would increase. This is known as the "availability bias," and it is especially relevant to predictions when information is readily available in our minds. The more available the information about an event, the higher the probability that we believe it will occur.

## 2.10. Science matters: Microsoft's commitment to core competence, R&D, and academia

Back to the auditorium at Stanford, Bill Gates received other questions, two of which will be highlighted here for comparison with other companies in future chapters. The first was about Microsoft's commitment to research and development and what role it is playing in Microsoft's future. And the second was about Microsoft's acquisition of other companies.

In response to the first question, Gates said,

> *We are making these investments in research because we believe that they will allow us to make better products.*

Gates added,

> *Sometimes we fund things that are fairly unusual. We have hired some very world-class theoretical mathematicians to think about models of computational complexity. We don't give them schedules or deadlines. We*

> *let them go out to do what they want. It is fun to have those people there . . . They are incredibly bright people.*

Gates added that this was a long-term investment that might still need to materialize. Further, Microsoft started a research center in the Bay Area and another research center in Cambridge. Gates noted,

> *If you multiply a low probability by a big benefit of it happening, you get something great.*

**Reflection: Bill Gates used "probability multiplied by benefit" in his reasoning**

- Note that Bill Gates was using probability to characterize the uncertainty, and he was using probability multiplied by benefit as a criterion for rationalizing the investment. We shall refer back to this notion in our discussion of ethical reasoning.
- Compare this method of reasoning with Benjamin Franklin's method of pros/cons two hundred (plus) years earlier. Can the pros/cons method be used when there is uncertainty about the outcomes? Is it as precise as a probability assignment?

## 2.11. Microsoft's vision for its series of acquisitions: Long-term and value-added

Since 1987 and up to the talk at Stanford, Microsoft had purchased an average of about six companies a year.[11] Some were successful, others were not, and some (such as Intuit in 1994) did not go through due to antitrust concerns. Microsoft also purchased Expedia.com as well as several other companies.

In response to a question about the vision for these purchases and whether these companies would ever catch up to be the core business, the response was "*It will be tough for them to catch up or match our classic business . . . They can be contributors.*" Gates added further that "*the payoff is not in the near*

[11] https://en.wikipedia.org/wiki/List_of_mergers_and_acquisitions_by_Microsoft

*term"* and that *"we have to believe the internet will pick up."* Further, Microsoft could add value to these products. *"We used software to improve Barney doll. We can make it far more engaging than TV and computer."*

## 2.12. Two years later: The birth of the most influential foundation in history

Shortly after that, the Bill & Melinda Gates Foundation was born[12]. It is the most impactful charitable foundation in history. In 2018, the foundation was the largest private donor to the World Health Organization (WHO), the second being the United States.

### A change in perception can occur after a major event

The Gates Foundation works in countries to eradicate diseases like malaria, improve education, and tackle poor sanitation. The BBC reported that Bill and Melinda Gates were inspired to do more work after learning about how millions of children in less-developed countries die of preventable diseases each year.[13] The couple has donated more than $36 billion of their own wealth.

### Bill Gates's personal value trade-offs: Personal wealth vs. societal benefit

Besides the previous contributions to the foundation, in July 2022, Gates made a significant announcement in an interview with Anderson Cooper. CNN stated,

> *Bill Gates funnels $20 billion to foundation and plans to drop off list of wealthiest people.*[14]

He added that he will eventually "drop off" the world's richest list. Gates mentioned,

[12] https://www.gatesfoundation.org/about/our-story
[13] https://www.bbc.com/news/world-us-canada-56979480
[14] https://www.cnn.com/2022/07/13/business/bill-melinda-gates-foundation/index.html

*I have an obligation to return my resources to society in ways that have the greatest impact for reducing suffering and improving lives.*

## The Gates Foundation attracted other major donors

In 2006, Warren Buffett made a lifetime pledge of more than $30 billion to the foundation. Together with Warren Buffett, Bill and Melinda Gates launched the Giving Pledge campaign in 2010 to encourage other people to donate the majority of their wealth to good causes.

**Reflection**

- Personal trade-offs: Was Bill Gates obliged by the legal system to donate any of his personal wealth?
- Motives: In 2023, do you believe Bill Gates is motivated by being the richest person in the world?
- Would it be okay if Bill Gates donated some of Microsoft Corporation's research and development money or the employees' retirement funds to help with virtuous causes, such as eradicating malaria, improving education, and tackling poor sanitation? Does being ethical require you to do that?
- In 2023, does Bill Gates prefer more money to less? In 2023, if someone offered to donate either $500 or $5 billion to the Gates Foundation, which do you think Bill Gates would prefer? Why? Is being motivated by more money unethical?

## Jeff Bezos's personal value trade-offs: Climate change and unifying humanity

CNN reported that Amazon founder Jeff Bezos made a lifelong pledge to give away the majority of his $124 billion net worth.[15] Bezos told CNN that he would devote the bulk of his wealth to fighting climate change and to supporting people who can unify humanity.

---

[15] https://www.cnn.com/2022/11/14/business/jeff-bezos-charity/index.html

## 2.13. Bill Gates made another two predictions about the future. One of them came true!

Bill Gates has since made two other predictions, and it is reasonable to assume that neither of them is subject to a desirability bias; in fact, they are nothing to be desired.

The first prediction was during a TED Talk he gave in 2015,[16] explicitly mentioning that the world is not ready for a pandemic . . . He was right!

The second prediction was an effort that started from projects within the Gates Foundation. In his book, Gates predicts, *"If nothing else changes, the world will keep producing greenhouse gases, climate change will keep getting worse, and the impact on humans will, in all likelihood, be catastrophic."*[17] Gates further notes that "'if nothing else changes' is a big If" and believes that things can change. Tick . . . tick . . . tick . . .

**Reflection: Trade-Offs between the present and the future**

Some decisions, like climate change involve making changes in lifestyle or manufacturing methods to realize a better and more sustainable future, possibly for other generations. Do you believe people are more willing to make changes that will yield present or future benefits?

[16] https://www.ted.com/talks/bill_gates_the_next_outbreak_we_re_not_ready?language=dz

[17] Bill Gates, *How to Avoid a Climate Disaster* (2021). https://www.penguinrandomhouse.com/articles/how-to-avoid-a-climate-disaster-excerpt/

# Chapter 3

# Valeant Pharmaceuticals

*I think we didn't find anything they were doing that was illegal, and that's the thing that's startling about this.*

—Congresswoman Claire McCaskill, from the Netflix documentary *Dirty Money*

**Figure 1.3.** *Left to right: Michael Pearson (CEO), Howard Schiller (CFO), and Bill Ackman (chairman of the board)*

## 3.1. Motives? Short-term increase in stock price

Valeant was a struggling drug company worth $2.1 billion when Michael Pearson, a former McKinsey executive, joined as CEO. During Pearson's tenure from 2008 to 2016, the stock price increased from $13.24 to $252. The company was valued at $85.6 billion.[18] Michael Pearson garnered Wall Street admiration at the time. But how did he do it? What were the consequences? And what was the environment that enabled it?

[18] https://www.theglobeandmail.com/globe-investor/valeant-passes-rbc-as-canadas-largest-company-by-market-value/article25642880/#:~:text=Valeant%20Pharmaceuticals%20International%20Inc.%2C%20the,on%20the%20Toronto%20Stock%20Exchange.

## 3.2. The environment: Can the legal system encourage a monopoly?

The Orphan Drug Act was passed in 1983 to incentivize pharmaceutical companies to invest in developing "orphan" drugs for rare diseases (diseases that affect fewer than two hundred thousand Americans). The US Food and Drug Administration noted the findings of Congress:

> *[D]rugs for these diseases and conditions are commonly referred to as "orphan drugs"; because so few individuals are affected by any one rare disease or condition, a pharmaceutical company which develops an orphan drug may reasonably expect the drug to generate relatively small sales in comparison to the cost of developing the drug and consequently to incur a financial loss;*
>
> *there is reason to believe that some promising orphan drugs will not be developed unless changes are made in the applicable Federal laws to reduce the costs of developing such drugs and to provide financial incentives to develop such drugs; and it is in the public interest to provide such changes and incentives for the development of orphan drugs.*[19]

The incentives offered by the Orphan Drug Act include

> *[a] 7-year marketing exclusivity to sponsors of approved orphan products, a tax credit of 50 percent of the cost of conducting human clinical testing, and research grants for clinical testing of new therapies to treat orphan diseases.*
>
> *Exclusive marketing rights limit competition by preventing other companies from marketing the same version of the drug, unless they can prove clinical superiority.*[20]

---

[19] https://www.fda.gov/industry/designating-orphan-product-drugs-and-biological-products/orphan-drug-act-relevant-excerpts

[20] https://oig.hhs.gov/oei/reports/oei-09-00-00380.pdf

**Reflection: Government-enforced monopoly?**

- Compare the legal system's stance regarding limiting competition in the Orphan Drug Act with their stance in the Sherman Antitrust Act in Microsoft's antitrust case.
- What was the government's rationale to limit competition for orphan drugs and not for Microsoft?

## 3.3. Europe follows

Similar legislation in Europe, known as market exclusivity, was introduced to offer incentives for orphan drugs.[21] The incentive awarded by the European Commission to a drug with an orphan designation includes

> *[o]rphan medicines benefit from ten years of market exclusivity once they receive a marketing authorization in the European Union (EU).*
>
> *This measure is intended to encourage the development of medicines for rare diseases, by protecting them from competition from similar medicines with similar indications, which cannot be marketed during the exclusivity period.*

**Reflection: Incentives and unintended consequences**

- Can incentives have unanticipated consequences? Is there a need to consider uncertainties following a chosen alternative?
- Brainstorm additional alternatives that the government could have selected to address this situation.

## 3.4. Unanticipated consequences of government incentives?

Following the Orphan Drug Act, pharmaceutical companies raised the prices of orphan drugs. But they did not just increase the prices of newly

[21] https://www.ema.europa.eu/en/human-regulatory/post-authorisation/orphan-medicines/market-exclusivity-orphan-medicines

developed drugs under the Orphan Drug Act incentives. They also increased the prices of drugs that had been around for over sixty-two years.

The *New York Times* tweeted and later reported that, in 2015, the price of a sixty-two-year-old drug called Daraprim jumped from $13.5 to $750 overnight.[22] The *New York Times* also wrote about similar price increases with another company: "The $6 Million Drug Claim: New treatments for rare diseases are changing the lives of patients, but the price can reach millions of dollars for a single person."[23]

America's Health Insurance Plans (AHIP), which represents nearly 1,300 companies offering health insurance to more than 200 million Americans, noted that many drugs that are not orphan related are given an "orphan" designation by drug companies:[24]

> *A sample of 45 orphan drugs available between 2012 and 2014 showed that almost half of these drugs' usage was for non-orphan diseases.*[25]

And it was not just the *New York Times* reporting about the drug price increases or the significant revenues that pharmaceutical companies were making. Bloomberg also reported the issue: "When the Patient Is a Gold Mine: The Trouble with Rare-Disease Drugs."[26] It also questioned how a treatment that helps fewer than eleven thousand people makes so much money for Alexion.

## 3.5. Valeant's motives? Short-term gain? Compare with Microsoft

Back to the Valeant stock price increase from $13.24 to $252 and how it achieved it. The chosen alternative was to increase drug prices significantly. But you would have to find drugs without competition to raise prices.

---

22 https://www.nytimes.com/2015/09/21/business/a-huge-overnight-increase-in-a-drugs-price-raises-protests.html?smid=tw-nytimes&smtyp=cur

23 https://www.nytimes.com/2019/08/25/health/drug-prices-rare-diseases.html

24 https://www.ahip.org/news/press-releases/drug-prices-for-rare-diseases-skyrocket-while-big-pharma-makes-record-profits

25 https://www.ahip.org/resources/orphan-drug-utilization-and-pricing-patterns-2012-2014

26 https://www.bloomberg.com/news/features/2017-05-24/when-the-patient-is-a-gold-mine-the-trouble-with-rare-disease-drugs

Otherwise, demand would decrease, and nobody would buy your product. However, if you select a drug with a government-supported monopoly or one that the Orphan Drug Act protects, then you automatically have limited competition.

But there was another problem: the time needed to develop an orphan drug and the corresponding price increase would not enable a stock price increase within such a short time frame—it takes time to develop new drugs. And so there was a need for an additional mechanism to achieve fast growth. Congresswoman McCaskill explained this mechanism in the Netflix documentary *Dirty Money*:

> *They found a drug that had a monopoly. They bought the company, stripped out all the R&D in the company, made no changes to the drug, and then jacked the price up 300, 400, 500, 700 percent. And the American people were left holding the bag.*

On average, pharmaceutical companies spend about 18 percent of their revenue on the research and development of new drugs. Valeant spent only about 3 percent. Valeant's primary source of growth was not the development of new drugs, but rather mergers and acquisitions and the corresponding increase in drug prices.

## 3.6. Valeant's attitude toward R&D: Science doesn't matter. Compare with Microsoft

*Forbes* magazine noted that Valeant Pharmaceuticals and, by extension, its billionaire CEO, Michael Pearson, had released several presentation slides arguing that the investment in R&D in the drug industry is wasteful and loses money.[27] In a TV interview with Bloomberg, Mike Pearson noted,

> *We've looked at the return on research and development in total. Um, for the last decade or so, it has not been positive for the industry.*

---

[27] https://www.forbes.com/sites/matthewherper/2014/06/12/valeant-pharmas-arguments-about-drug-research-are-misleading-and-wrong/?sh=cb980ad57550

**Reflection**

Compare Valeant's focus on R&D with Bill Gates's statements in 1998:

> *We are making these investments in research because we believe that they will allow us to make better products.*
>
> *The payoff is not in the near term.*

## 3.7. Perspectives from different stakeholders

Think of the different perspectives of the various stakeholders in this situation.

- **Valeant:** We are maximizing shareholder return.
- **Consumers:** Consumers who had health insurance through their jobs were shielded from drug price increases. However, they felt the burden of the price increases only when they left their jobs.
- **Government:** The government feels that pharmaceutical companies misused privileges given to them.
- **Political campaigns:** Price increases by pharmaceutical companies also made their way to presidential campaigns. Former First Lady Hillary Clinton, who was running for president, tweeted,

  *Hillary Clinton @HillaryClinton*

  *Price gouging like this in the specialty drug market is outrageous. Tomorrow I'll lay out a plan to take it on. -H*

- **Legal system:** So far, nothing is illegal. Congresswoman McCaskill noted, *"I think we didn't find anything they were doing that was illegal, and that's the thing that's startling about this."*
- **Acquired companies:** Valeant made a series of acquisitions that cost over $30.8 billion. Companies were purchased for a premium price to enable fast acquisition.

- **Hospitals:** The *Wall Street Journal* (*WSJ*) reported that drug price increases added an $8.6 million deficit to the Cleveland Clinic budget. Like many other clinics, the Cleveland Clinic first administers the drugs to a patient in need, hoping to recover the cost from the patient care. But they ended up with a loss, necessitating to cut costs in other areas to make up for it.[28]

- **Rest of society:** Insurance premiums nationwide increased, affecting all US health insurance holders. US insurance premiums have gone up by 43 percent since 2008.

**Reflection**

- Was the act of increasing orphan drug prices by pharmaceutical companies illegal?

- Is increasing the price of a product by a company unethical?

- Is the act of increasing the price of a drug that is protected by a government-incentivized monopoly unethical? Are there certain expectations the government wanted the pharmaceutical companies to abide by under this act? Were the expectations spelled out clearly?

## 3.8. Valeant's ethical trade-offs and tolerances: Shareholders vs. stakeholders

Between 2010 and 2015, Valeant increased the monthly price of Syprine from $652 to over $21,000.[29] The stock price rose, but as a result, there was significant harm to others.

Bethany McLean, a well-known journalist, noted the divergence for Valeant between what is good for investors and what is good for society.[30] We shall refer to the amount of harm to stakeholders that an organization is willing to tolerate to maximize its profit as its "ethical trade-off."

---

28 https://www.wsj.com/articles/pharmaceutical-companies-buy-rivals-drugs-then-jack-up-the-prices-1430096431
29 https://www.collins.senate.gov/newsroom/soaring-prices-decades-old-drugs
30 https://www.vanityfair.com/news/2016/06/the-valeant-meltdown-and-wall-streets-major-drug-problem

**Reflection**

- Compare Bill Gates's personal value trade-offs within the Bill & Melinda Gates Foundation with those of Valeant's corporate value trade-offs.
- Is it unethical to increase value for shareholders? Under what conditions could the actions be deemed unethical?

## 3.9. Top-bottom value slogans of the form "We are the champions of morality"

During that time, Valeant Pharmaceuticals International's mission statement mentioned their core values:

> *Improving people's lives with our health care products*[31]

**Reflection**

- Were there other values that better reflected what Valeant was actually doing?
- Why do you believe Valeant had this slogan?

## 3.10. Escalation of commitment to fraud

Following the significant price increases of drugs, insurance companies stopped honoring many reimbursements of prescriptions made for some pharmaceutical companies. As a result, pharmaceutical companies and clinics carried a risk of no refund after the drug was administered. In response, Valeant formed a start-up company called Philidor, whose publicized purpose, as presented in some media presentations on Valeant's old files, was as follows:

> *Philidor dispenses Valeant medications before adjudication of the reimbursement may be finalized. Patients get their medicines more quickly and Valeant takes the risk for non-reimbursement.*[32]

[31] https://www.comparably.com/companies/valeant-pharmaceuticals-international/mission

[32] http://ir.valeant.com/~/media/Files/V/Valeant-IR/reports-and-presentations/10-26-15-investor-presentation.pdf

The risk of no reimbursement was shifted to Philidor. But because Valeant owned Philidor, it still carried the risk of no refund by its holdings of Philidor. In its Securities and Exchange Commission (SEC) filings, however, Valeant did not disclose its affiliation with Philidor and the corresponding risk that it bears. This omission of facts enabled Valeant to present higher profit projections than it otherwise could have made had it reported the risk. And as a result, the stock price continued to increase based on Valeant's projections. Further, some Valeant executives also engaged in a kickback scheme that led to their personal profit.

**Reflection**

Are there acts of deception, harm, or theft in not disclosing the relationship with Philidor? Who are the affected stakeholders?

## 3.11. Crisis management strategies: Before and after pressure builds up

### If the media finds out, but you feel you can get away with it: Fast to deny

Soon after that, the media found out. In an interview with CNBC, Michael Pearson said there were many allegations in the press, but nothing had been proven. The board chair, Bill Ackman, noted,

> *The bottom line for us is we are very confident both in the management, in Mike Pearson, and the larger team, and the board of directors. We are not currently seeking any board representation.*

### Pressure builds up, and you cannot get away with it: Fire CEO and bring friends

Soon after, pressure built up. Ackman ultimately fired Pearson. The Netflix documentary *Dirty Money* noted,

> *Ackman took control of the board. He fired Pearson. He got people to the board who were all friends of his, and then the stock continued going down.*

Bethany McLean noted,

> *This whole thing made a mockery of this idea that a company with this august hedge fund on is board was a well-managed company because it was all just a complete "swear word" show . . . a shit show. It really was. It was a disastrous . . . uh . . . couple of weeks that have to go down in history as the worst management in crisis management ever.*

## Legal system gets involved: Initial reaction—obstruct depositions

A Senate committee called the Aging Committee was formed. The committee deposed Michael Pearson. In response, he decided he would not attend his deposition. He later changed course after the committee threatened him to be in contempt. The Senate web page reported,

> *Valeant Chief Executive Officer (CEO) Michael Pearson today reversed course and will now be deposed by the Senate Special Committee on Aging as part of its continuing investigation into pharmaceutical drug pricing.*
>
> *Last week, Mr. Pearson failed to comply with a Congressional subpoena requiring him to attend a deposition. After his failure to appear, Aging Committee Chairman Susan Collins and Ranking Member Claire McCaskill scheduled a Business Meeting of the Committee to consider a contempt resolution for Mr. Pearson.*[33]

**Reflection**

Why would someone want to avoid a deposition?

## 3.12. The verdict

The Justice Department posted on its web page,

> *Today, we charge corporate fraud at Valeant Pharmaceuticals. Gary Tanner, a former Valeant executive, and Andrew Davenport, the CEO of*

[33] https://www.aging.senate.gov/press-releases/valeant-ceo-reverses-course-senate-special-committee-on-aging-to-depose-michael-pearson

*Philidor, allegedly concocted a fraudulent scheme to illegally use Philidor as a vehicle for personal profit and self-dealing. Their alleged kickback scheme illegally converted Valeant shareholder money into their own personal nest eggs.*[34]

The SEC investigation reported,

*Valeant, among other things, misstated revenue transactions and included erroneous revenue allocations. . . . Much of that growth came from sales to Philidor, a mail-order pharmacy Valeant helped establish, fund, and subsidize.*

*Valeant improperly recognized revenue relating to Philidor sales and did not disclose its unique relationship with or risks related to Philidor in SEC filings and earnings and investor presentations. Valeant ended its ties to Philidor in October 2015 and restated its 2014 financial statements in April 2016, reducing the revenue that was improperly recognized.*[35]

**Reflection**

Can you identify elements of deception, harming, or stealing by Valeant?

## Additional consequences

Fines were also introduced. The SEC noted on its web page on July 31, 2020,

*The Securities and Exchange Commission today announced that Bausch Health, formerly Quebec, Canada-based Valeant Pharmaceuticals, agreed to pay a $45 million penalty to settle charges of improper revenue recognition and misleading disclosures in SEC filings and earnings presentations.*

*Three former executives—the chief executive officer, chief financial officer, and controller—also agreed to pay penalties to settle charges against them.*

---

[34] https://www.justice.gov/usao-sdny/pr/former-valeant-executive-and-former-philidor-ceo-charged-manhattan-federal-court

[35] https://www.sec.gov/news/press-release/2020-169

Shortly after, Valeant lost more than 90 percent of its value, more than $80 billion; and Valeant's stock price fell to $8 per share, a 97 percent drop from its peak.

# Chapter 4

# Enron Corporation

*You have been fantastic to the Bush family. I don't think anybody did more than you did to support George. And of course, at this stage in my life and Barbara's too, that's what really matters: your family and your friends.*

—Former president George H. W. Bush to an Enron executive

**Figure 1.4.** *Former president G. W. Bush with Kenneth Lay*

## 4.1. Some chronological facts

In July 1985, Kenneth Lay founded Enron, a natural gas pipeline company. In August 2000, Enron was the seventh-largest publicly held corporation in the United States, with a market valuation of $70 billion and a stock price of $90.75. In November 2001, Enron shares plummeted to less than $1; and in December 2002, Enron filed for chapter 11 bankruptcy protection.

About twenty thousand Enron employees lost their jobs, $2 billion was lost in retiree funds, $1.2 billion was lost in employee retirement funds, several Enron executives were charged with fraud and received jail time, and Arthur Andersen (Enron's accounting firm) ceased to exist, and its eighty-five thousand employees lost their jobs. What happened? What decisions were made? And what factors contributed to this downfall?

## 4.2. The environment: Friends and family; It's all in the family

Enron's former chief executive, Kenneth Lay, was a close friend of former president Bush Sr. He was also a friend of former president G. W. Bush. Figure 1.4. shows a meeting between then-president G. W. Bush and Kenneth Lay.

Democracynow.org reported about this relationship:

> *Enron founder Ken Lay and his family rank among President Bush's biggest financial backers of his political career. The family donated about $140,000 to Bush's political campaigns in Texas and for the White House. The president personally nicknamed Ken Lay "Kenny Boy." Overall Enron employees gave Bush some $600,000 in political donations.*[36]

An example of the relations between the Bush family and Enron was displayed in Bush Sr.'s message to Richard Kinder[37], an Enron executive who was leaving Enron:

> *Rich, you have been fantastic to the Bush family. I don't think anybody did more than you did to support George. And of course, at this stage in my life and Barbara's too, that's what really matters: your family and your friends.*

**Reflection**

Think of the implications of this relationship in terms of it being a deterrent for stakeholders to express any concerns about Kenneth Lay. Think of the impact of this relationship on outside investment banks and their willingness to support and tolerate unethical acts from Enron to engage with them in profits.

---

[36] https://www.democracynow.org/2006/5/26/enron_the_bush_connection
[37] https://www.forbes.com/profile/richard-kinder/?sh=1411a2e2f62b

## 4.3. Valhalla scandal: Deleting evidence, ethical tolerance, and risk tolerance

In 1987, Kenneth Lay was chief executive of Enron Oil. The company had traders betting on whether oil prices would go up or down. The traders made significant amounts of money for Enron, but two of them (the company's president, Louis Borget, and the treasurer, Tom Mastroeni) also transferred some of the trade profits they made for Enron into their personal bank accounts. The traders were able to cover up this diversion of funds by destroying daily trading records so nobody else would know how much profit had materialized.

**Reflection**

Can you identify acts of deception, harming, or stealing? Can you identify the motives that led to these acts?

## 4.4. Fast to cover up, slow to acknowledge

When this practice was discovered, the traders first denied any wrongdoing and presented falsified bank accounts to the Enron board. Later, they admitted that they had diverted some of the corporate profits they made from Enron trading into their personal accounts.

## 4.5. Environments supporting high-risk trades

Auditors brought in to inspect the situation advised Kenneth Lay that the traders were gambling beyond their limits and were exposing Enron Oil to financial risk. Lay decided to keep things "as is" because this was the only part of the company that was making profits despite the diversion of profits into personal bank accounts that had occurred. Enron sent a telex to Borget:

> *Please keep making us millions.*[38]

A few months later, they took out $90 million and gambled with Enron's reserves. Borget was charged with (and convicted of) fraud and spent a year in jail.

---

[38] *Enron: The Smartest Guys in the Room* https://www.imdb.com/title/tt1016268/

**Reflection**

- What levels of risk should a company operate with? We shall refer to this as "risk tolerance."
- What level of profit generated by employees would make a board close its eyes on the fact that the traders had diverted corporate earnings into personal accounts and that they had destroyed trails of trading activities? We shall refer to this as "ethical tolerance."
- Notice the pattern of deleting records that is prevalent with many ethical collapses.
- Are there any biases that increase the tendency for keeping things "as is" instead of taking action?

## 4.6. Environment: Using connections with politicians for deregulation

Kenneth Lay relied on his relations with the government to push for energy deregulation. ABC News reported about the mechanism by which they achieved this:

> *Enron made a decision that they needed government to go their way and they put the money out to make sure that happened.*[39]

The Center for Public Integrity noted,

> *There was no company in America closer to George W. Bush than Enron.*

The Public Policy Institute of California (PPIC) noted,

> *[The] company's goal in backing Bush and other politicians was to encourage further deregulation of the energy industry.*[40]

The *Guardian* described the mechanism by which Enron approached politicians as

---

[39] https://abcnews.go.com/Politics/story?id=121269&page=1
[40] https://www.ppic.org/wp-content/uploads/content/pubs/report/R_103CWR.pdf

> *Enron was just trying to help.*[41]

It further noted,

> *New evidence suggests the company may also have promoted deregulation so enthusiastically because it knew it could fix the system to its own advantage.*

Under pressure from energy companies, in 1996, California passed legislation to deregulate electricity. Competitive markets for the wholesale of electricity began in April 1998.

**Reflection**

Observe the similarities between Enron, Theranos and FTX (discussed in a future chapter) when lobbying for legislation.

## 4.7. Top-bottom slogans of the form "We are the champions of morality"

During that time, Kenneth Lay gave the pretense of a high moral value at Enron. He mentioned,

> *Enron is a company that deals with everyone with absolute integrity. We want people to leave the transaction with Enron thinking that they've been dealt with in the highest possible way as far as integrity and truthfulness.*

## 4.8. Bringing on the external consultants

In August 1990, Enron hired Jeffrey Skilling. Skilling had been providing consulting services to Enron while at McKinsey & Company. Jeffrey Skilling changed the focus of Enron to become a stock market for natural gas instead of a natural gas pipeline company. By 1992, Enron became the largest buyer and seller of natural gas in North America. In December 1996, after the deregulation of electricity markets, Enron promoted Skilling to president and COO of the company, reporting to Enron's chief executive officer and chairman, Kenneth Lay.

---

[41] https://www.theguardian.com/business/2005/feb/05/enron.usnews

## 4.9. Using hypothetical future value accounting for deception

One of the main features of Enron's scandal was its "mark-to-market" accounting practice, which relied on future value projections instead of materialized profit and loss. This mechanism enabled Enron to "cook the books" and make their profits appear higher, which led to an increase in stock price. Arthur Andersen signed off on the mark-to-market accounting system, and the SEC approved it. Arthur Andersen's fees were reported to be $1 million per week.

**Reflection**

- Compare this strategy of giving a pretense of higher profits with that conducted by Valeant.
- What motives could have led Arthur Andersen to sign off on this accounting system?

## 4.10. Organizational transgression toward internal stakeholders

Skilling initiated an annual employee performance system called the Performance Review Committee (PRC). The review was on a scale of 1 (the best) to 5 (the worst), with an outcome-predetermined performance such that about 10 percent would get a 5 (and get fired) each year.

**Reflection**

Think about the implications of this review committee on collaborations and teamwork, on the well-being of individuals, and on their tolerance to unethical acts conducted by leadership if they were perceived as being on the "good side" of leadership. Think of the implications of this system on building a yes-man culture within Enron.

## 4.11. Conformity bias manifestations

Conformity bias is the tendency of individuals to change their behavior to better fit within the environment. The documentary *Enron: The Smartest Guys in the Room* noted,

> *When Jeff got Lasik on his eyes, everybody at Enron got Lasik, so nobody was wearing glasses.*

## 4.12. Deception: Cook the books, cover up the losses

In one instance, when Enron suffered losses, Merrill Lynch stepped in to help with the cover-up. In 1999, Merrill Lynch gave Enron a loan; but on the books, it was recorded that Merrill Lynch bought power barges from Enron (located in Nigeria). This transaction would conceal loans taken by Enron, conceal Enron's losses, and further present the loan as income. This transaction enabled Enron to cover up losses for that quarter and further helped increase the stock price.

## 4.13. Escalation: Cover up the losses, ignore conflicts of interest

In 1999, Andrew Fastow, Enron's chief financial officer (CFO), devised a scheme to further cover up Enron's losses. Leveraged by Enron stock, he formed two limited partnerships to buy Enron's poorly performing assets. Fastow received an exemption from conflict-of-interest rules by the board of Enron because he had a personal financial stake in these companies. Fastow also secured a deal with Enron to cover his personal losses. This system enabled Enron to hide its losses in its quarterly balance sheets. It was also a mechanism to raise money for Enron by investors willing to invest in a company that solely did business with Enron. This scheme enabled Enron to cover debt and losses of $30 billion.[42]

---

[42] https://en.wikipedia.org/wiki/Andrew_Fastow

## 4.14. Contributing to political campaigns

In January 2000, George Bush named Kenneth Lay as an advisor to his presidential transition team; and in September 2000, Kenneth Lay contributed more than $290,000 to George Bush's election campaign.

## 4.15. Jumping on the deception bandwagon: Cover-up of losses

Many other financial institutions dealing with Enron invested in Fastow's companies, further contributing to the cover-up of Enron's losses and benefiting from the investments backed by Enron stock. These institutions included Merrill Lynch, JPMorgan Chase, and Deutsche Bank.

**Reflection: Contributors to a bandwagon environment?**

- Could the perception of having close relations with the presidential family have contributed to the bandwagon of the cover-ups?
- What were the motives of various individuals in this setup?
  - Kenneth Lay? Money? Short-term benefit? Connections with the presidential family?
  - Fastow?
  - Jeffrey Skilling?
  - Bankers?

## 4.16. Using the media to enable deception

At the same time that all this cover-up was occurring, *Fortune* magazine chose Enron for six years in a row (1995–2000) as the most innovative company in the United States. Enron also made news when it gave Alan Greenspan, the Federal Reserve chair, the Enron Award for Distinguished Public Service.

## 4.17. Deception extends to more stakeholders

At a time when executives knew that the company could not sustain itself, many Enron executives off-loaded their stock. Kenneth Lay sold $300 million worth of stock, Jeff Skilling sold stock for $200 million, and others (including Enron executive J. Clifford Baxter) sold stock for $35 million. At the same time, Enron executives led employees to believe they should keep buying Enron stock for retirement accounts.

In a video that appeared later, employees asked Skilling,

> *Should we invest all of our 401(k) in Enron stock?*

Skilling replied, "Absolutely!"

## 4.18. Stress environments and "do whatever it takes" to make profit

Enron traders noticed that when the demand was higher than the supply, the electricity prices increased. So they came up with the idea of creating artificial shortages by shutting down power plants. This idea soon triggered an energy crisis in California in 2000 and 2001, with many blackouts and electricity prices selling by three hundred to four hundred times the amount they normally would. The shortages helped Enron make $1.6 billion. Utility bills skyrocketed as households could not pay for the increased electricity price.

Some tapes revealed a conversation between an Enron trader and an individual at a power plant, urging him to shut down to increase electricity prices.[43]

> *Enron trader to power plant employee: Hey, this is David up at Enron. There's not much demand for power at all here. If we shut it down, can you bring it up in three or four hours?*
>
> *Power plant employee: Oh, yeah.*
>
> *David: Why don't you just go ahead and shut her down then, if that's okay?*
>
> *Power plant employee: Okay.*

[43] *Enron: The Smartest Guys in the Room*

## 4.19. Pressure builds up but feeling you can get away with it: Fast to deny

Anger and frustration at the increasing energy prices increased. Demonstrators with "You Robbed Us" signs were waiting outside a town hall meeting in California where Skilling spoke. A demonstrator threw a blueberry pie in the face of Jeffrey Skilling while he was sitting with the panel. Skilling was quick to deny any involvement and replied,

> *Consumers in California are angry, and they should be. And if we had anything to do with this, then we are the stupidest people in the world.*

## 4.20. Using politicians to enable ethical violations

Enron had a fear that energy deregulation would collapse in the wake of the blackouts and the California crisis. This would have deprived Enron of the profits of trading on high electricity prices. Consequently, Kenneth Lay met with then Vice President Dick Cheney and argued against the imposition of price caps in California by the federal government. Following the meeting, Cheney mentioned to the press,

> *There's not a lot you can do. You can't manufacture kilowatts in the White House.*

President G. W. Bush then followed,

> *They know full well my administration's belief that price controls will not solve the problem.*[44]

Soon after, the Federal Energy Regulatory Commission (FERC)—a commission led by the man Kenneth Lay had personally recommended for the job—refused to intervene. Later, a Democratic Senate then forced FERC to impose regional price caps.

---

44 https://georgewbush-whitehouse.archives.gov/news/releases/2001/06/text/20010618-4.html

## 4.21. Crisis management strategies

### Media finds out

On March 5, 2001, Bethany McLean published an article in *Fortune* magazine titled "Is Enron Overpriced?" She explained that investors were clueless about how Enron earned and reported its profit.

### SEC inquiry: Feeling you can get away with it? Cover up, deny amid slogans of "We are the champions of morality"

The SEC inquired into the acts of Enron. Kenneth Lay held a meeting shortly after in which he said,

> *Fastow dealt with this in the most ethical and appropriate manner possible.*

At the same time, and only a few blocks away, Arthur Andersen had begun destroying Enron files.

### Pressure builds up: Replace Fastow; "We are the champions of morality"

Soon after, the Enron board discovered that Fastow had made $45 million from his ventures. Fastow was fired. Kenneth Lay said he was not aware of what was going on. "*Clearly, one person betrayed our trust. I was not aware of it to the extent that I did not know what he was doing.*"

### Rationalizations: What we are doing is in the best interest of the shareholders

Depositions by Congress and investigations by SEC began. In response to what occurred, Jeffrey Skilling mentioned,

> *I did not do anything that was not in the best interest of the shareholders of the company.*

**Can the legal system aid violations by offering protection for not speaking?**

Representative Jim Greenwood asked Fastow, *Were your actions consistent with your fiduciary duties to Enron and its shareholders or with commonsense notions or corporate ethics and propriety?*

Fastow replied, *Mr. Chairman, on the advice of my counsel, I respectfully decline to answer the questions based on the protection offered to me under the United States Constitution.*

## 4.22. Impacts and unanticipated consequences

In February 2004, the SEC issued a press release:

> *Washington, D.C., Jeffrey Skilling, Enron Corp.'s former President, Chief Executive Officer, and Chief Operating Officer*
>
> *Feb. 19, 2004 — The Securities and Exchange Commission today announced that it has charged Jeffrey with violating, aiding, and abetting violations of, the antifraud, lying to auditors, periodic reporting, books and records, and internal controls provisions of the federal securities laws.*[45]

Court documents revealed,

> *From at least 1999 through late 2001, Skilling, Causey, and others manipulated Enron's publicly reported financial results and made false and misleading public statements about Enron's financial condition and its actual performance. As a result of their scheme to defraud, Skilling, Causey, and others made millions of dollars, by unlawful insider trading and other means, at the expense of Enron shareholders, the investing public, and Enron employees.*[46]

Consequences:

- Skilling originally received a sentence of seventeen and a half years but was released on February 22, 2019, in agreement to give $42 million to victims of the Enron fraud.

[45] https://www.sec.gov/news/press/2004-18.htm
[46] https://www.sec.gov/litigation/complaints/comp18582.htm

- Sixteen Enron execs, including Skilling, were sentenced to prison.
- Kenneth Lay passed away before his guilty verdict was appealed.
- Two Enron traders from the office where the tapes were made admitted to manipulating energy prices and pled guilty in court.
- Cliff Baxter committed suicide.
- Enron filed for bankruptcy, twenty thousand employees lost their jobs, Enron employees lost $1.2 billion in retirement funds, and Enron retirees lost $2 billion in retirement funds.
- Arthur Andersen was found guilty of obstructing justice for shredding documents and was subsequently dissolved.
- Merrill Lynch executives were convicted of fraud in the Nigerian power barge case.
- The Public Policy Institute of California reported the excess amount customers had to pay for electricity: "*Although total energy costs for wholesale power were $7.4 billion in 1999, they were about $27 billion per year from 2000 through 2001, burdening California consumers and businesses with almost $40 billion in added costs.*"[47]
- The outages and energy price crisis led to the ousting of Gray Davis, California's Democratic governor, and paved the way for Arnold Schwarzenegger to become California's governor. New laws, including the Sarbanes-Oxley regulations, were put into effect to prevent these issues from occurring again in similar situations but also had unanticipated consequences in excluded small investors from investment opportunities.

[47] https://www.ppic.org/wp-content/uploads/content/pubs/report/R_103CWR.pdf

# Chapter 5

# Theranos

*For the media, Elizabeth Holmes' story proved irresistible: a bright young woman revolutionizing blood testing, in Silicon Valley no less.*
*—Brit McCandless Farmer,*

writing for CBS News, May 20, 2018[48]

**Figure 1.5**. *Elizabeth Holmes with former president Bill Clinton, former Secretary of State Madeleine Albright[49], and Jack Ma[50], founder of Alibaba*

---

48 https://www.cbsnews.com/news/was-the-media-duped-by-elizabeth-holmes-theranos/

49 https://history.state.gov/departmenthistory/people/albright-madeleine-korbel

50 https://www.forbes.com/profile/jack-ma/?sh=53bb7f2e1ee4

## 5.1. Elizabeth Holmes made a prediction about the future. She was wrong!

In 2015, Elizabeth Holmes was named to *Forbes* magazine's American billionaire list with a 50 percent stake in the start-up Theranos. Holmes was named the $4.5 billion woman, making her the world's youngest female self-made billionaire. In 2015, Elizabeth Holmes was asked what she was most certain about in 2025. She replied,

> *Every person would have access to their health information, and nobody would ever have to say goodbye too soon.*

On November 18, 2022, Elizabeth Holmes was sentenced to 135 months (eleven years, three months) in federal prison for defrauding investors in Theranos of hundreds of millions of dollars.

## 5.2. Ignoring the science and academia recommendations

Elizabeth Holmes arrived at Stanford University in 2002. Her father had worked as vice president for Enron Corporation and was laid off along with numerous others following the Enron scandal. A vision of wanting to invent something had been in Holmes's dreams since high school. At Stanford, she had an idea of changing how blood testing worked: building a patch that would scan for infectious diseases and release antibiotics. Phyllis Gardner, a professor at Stanford, explained to her that the patch would not work because the antibiotics described needed to be given at higher doses than a patch could deliver.[51]

**Reflection**

- Was the alternative of blood testing using a single drop of blood and releasing antibiotics feasible then?
- Should you abandon your idea if someone told you it would not work based on scientific reasoning?

---

[51] https://www.businessinsider.com/stanford-professor-phyllis-gardner-on-theranos-and-elizabeth-holmes-2019-3

- After exploring the feasibility of the alternative from several sources, what should you do if you find out that the alternative is not feasible?
- Can the focus on solely achieving your objectives cloud your judgment?
- Are there biases that can make you ignore information that does not appeal to your vision?
- Did Holmes have the scientific knowledge to follow her passion? Is having the scientific knowledge needed to pursue your goals a necessity? What else would be required?

## 5.3. Following your passion without the core knowledge to determine the feasibility of an alternative

Holmes proceeded with another idea of testing, but without the antibiotic release. Her vision was to conduct a series of blood tests using only one drop of blood. Holmes convinced her parents to take money set aside for her Stanford education to help her start a company. She dropped out of Stanford and started to reach out to potential venture capitalists before the prototype was ready.

### Reflection

- Is it unethical to reach out for funding before a prototype is ready?
- In your view, did Holmes believe she would be successful? Would she have dropped out of Stanford if she felt she would not be successful?
- Could Holmes's dropping out of Stanford have been influenced by the story of Bill Gates or Mark Zuckerberg? Are there biases that make people follow suit?

## 5.4. Escalation resulting from pressure: Do whatever it takes to get the job done?

In 2006, Holmes had a meeting with Novartis. Larry Ellison set up the appointment. She had a promise of support from Ellison if Novartis in Switzerland was interested in the working prototype, Theranos 1. The stakes were high, and she was under pressure to perform. As demonstrated in the miniseries *The Dropout*, the device stopped working the night before the demo, and they were up all night trying to get it to work. When they were unsuccessful, they showed Novartis prerecorded tests and results during the demo but told people at Novartis that these results were being acquired in real time from a blood sample. Following the demo, they were able to secure funding from Novartis. Round B funding for Theranos ended at $165 million.[52]

**Reflection**

- Can you identify any elements of deception that occurred during this demo?
- What was the motive?
- How do you believe Holmes rationalized it to herself?
- What would you have done if you were in Holmes's situation?
- What would you have done if you had witnessed that situation as an employee?
- What factors might deter you from speaking up?
- What level of deception would you allow before speaking up?

## 5.5. Ethical tolerance: Organization vs. employee

When Henry Mosley, Theranos's CFO, learned that the Novartis demo involved a prerecorded lab test, he confronted Holmes about the ethics of

---

[52] Netflix documentary *Dirty Money*

the situation and the integrity of the revenue projections given to investors. Holmes first downplayed the issue and then fired Mosley for not being a "team player."

## 5.6. Action in the light of new information: Escalation of commitment

In many cases, decision analysis requires thinking about downstream decisions and the need to act in the light of new information. If information that the product is not feasible is revealed, what do you do when you find out? In August 2007, Holmes used the prototype, Theranos 1, in a study with Pfizer involving terminal cancer patients in Nashville, Tennessee. The prototype was still not ready, but patients were being subjected to the tests.

**Reflection**

- In comparison with Valeant's reasoning that medical breakthroughs take a long time to develop, do you believe Elizabeth Holmes thought she could deliver?
- If the test results could jeopardize the lives and safety of patients, would you tolerate this situation?
- Are there biases that could make individuals continue doing what they are doing even if new information reveals that a new course of action is necessary? Yes. One example is the sunk cost bias, which we shall refer to in a future chapter.

## 5.7. Action in the light of new information: It's all in the family

Holmes told Sunny Balwani, an individual she was dating then, that she had faked the demonstration. He told her not to tell anyone. When the Pfizer contract did not go through, the board wanted to replace Holmes as CEO. She convinced them to keep her after telling them that she would get a chief operating officer who would also invest $13 million in Theranos. In September 2009, Sunny Balwani joined Theranos as chief operating officer.

Holmes and Balwani did not reveal to other stakeholders that they were dating.

**Reflection: Motives leading to unethical acts?**

- What motives do you believe led Balwani to join Theranos?
- What would you have done if you were in this situation and were told that a prerecorded test was shown to Novartis?

## 5.8. The culture of secrecy, cover-up, and controlling information enables fraud

Holmes and Balwani maintained a culture of secrecy within Theranos. Employees in one department were forbidden from discussing their projects with employees in other departments. Everybody had to sign nondisclosure agreements (NDAs) that prohibited them from talking about Theranos.[53]

### Secrecy enables escalation and further deception

Holmes's vision was to scan for hundreds of potential diseases with a device called the Edison that could test with only a few drops of blood taken with a finger prick. However, there were two problems with the feasibility of this idea: The first was that the samples taken were too small for all the advertised tests. As a result, the "few drops of blood" would need to be diluted, lowering the tests' accuracy. The second problem was that the tests conducted could interfere with one another within the small space allocated for them in the device.

While the Edison never worked properly, Holmes continued to boast about its success and promote it to investors and in TED Talks. In 2012, Holmes cut a deal with Walgreens (without having a working prototype) to set up "minilabs" in their pharmacies. When faced with this new situation, Holmes and Balwani used conventional testing devices from other vendors.

---

53 https://www.vanityfair.com/news/2016/07/theranos-culture-of-secrecy-comes-back-to-haunt-it

They used traditional vials of blood from patients to deliver conventional test results while promoting them as Theranos technology.[54]

## Legal system laws regarding information in private vs. public companies

The legal system has different transparency requirements for public and private companies. When Holmes was asked why they had not released any information about the product, she responded,

> *We don't need to explain ourselves to competitive companies.*

And when asked about her plans for an initial public offering (IPO), Holmes replied,

> *We believe there is value in being a private company: you do not have to reveal what you are doing until it is done.*

CCTV cameras were installed throughout the Theranos workplace. Theranos leadership was monitoring employees' keystrokes. Some individuals reported that they would email another colleague and then get a response from Sunny Balwani, who was not on the original email.

**Reflection**

- Why do you believe there was a culture of secrecy at Theranos?
- Why do you believe leadership was keen on monitoring conversations and emails?

## 5.9. Bandwagons, using the media to enable fraud, and conformity

Elizabeth Holmes is an example of how the media created an icon out of a person and how it unintentionally enabled fraud. CBS News reported,

[54] https://www.usatoday.com/story/money/2022/07/07/elizabeth-holmes-theranos-sunny-balwani-convicted/10007246002/

> *For the media, Elizabeth Holmes' story proved irresistible: a bright young woman revolutionizing blood testing, in Silicon Valley no less.*[55]

In the same article, Katy Textor of *60 Minutes* reflected, *"I think using the media was part of the Theranos strategy."*

In September 2013, following the launch of the 4s model, the *WSJ* published an article titled "Elizabeth Holmes: The Breakthrough of Instant Diagnosis; A Stanford dropout is bidding to make tests more accurate, less painful—and at a fraction of the current price."[56]

The article presented a glowing profile of Elizabeth Holmes following the partnership with Walgreens. Holmes was soon on the front covers of *Fortune, Forbes, Inc.*, and *T* magazines.

In 2015, the *New York Times* reported how Elizabeth Holmes was named *Glamour*'s "Woman of the Year."[57] *Time* magazine placed Elizabeth Holmes on its list of one hundred luminaries, and CNBC compared Elizabeth Holmes to Steve Jobs:

> *World's youngest female billionaire—next Steve Jobs?*[58]

*Inc.* magazine also made the comparison in its article titled "Why the Next Steve Jobs Will Be a Woman: A rising tide of female founders will produce the next iconic entrepreneur."[59]

Holmes also wore a black turtleneck similar to the one Steve Jobs wore. In a future chapter, we shall refer to "conformity bias," where individuals conform to expectations or the environment.

Also, Holmes had connections with media mogul Rupert Murdoch, from whom she raised funds. When news about the deception ultimately broke,

---

55 https://www.cbsnews.com/news/60-minutes-was-the-media-duped-by-elizabeth-holmes-theranos/
56 https://www.wsj.com/articles/SB10001424127887324123004579055003869574012
57 https://www.nytimes.com/2021/11/18/technology/elizabeth-holmes-theranos-trial.html
58 https://www.cnbc.com/2015/09/23/worlds-youngest-female-billionaire-next-steve-jobs.html
59 https://www.inc.com/magazine/201510/kimberly-weisul/will-the-next-steve-jobs-be-a-woman.html

*Inc.* magazine had a follow-up article: "It Turns Out Elizabeth Holmes Was a Massive Fraud, and the Media Helped Create Her: How the media helped create the legend of Elizabeth Holmes and enabled her fraud in the process."[60]

The *Guardian* released the article "How Theranos Used the Media to Create the Emperor's New Startup."[61]

**Reflection**

Think of the environment in a company with that level of secrecy, where people had limited information about other departments and whose CEO was getting that level of media attention. Would you feel that any complaint made by an employee about deception or fraud in this environment would change anything?

## 5.10. High-ranking politicians on the board

Elizabeth Holmes's board profile was a culmination of America's most elite figures. The BBC reported,

> *US Treasury Secretary George Schultz, media tycoon Rupert Murdoch and America's richest family, the Waltons, were among her backers.*[62]

In addition, the board included Henry Kissinger and William Perry, to name a few. Further, Holmes had an impressive list of investors, including Larry Ellison, the Walton family of Walmart, and the family of former secretary of education Betsy DeVos.

## Only in America?

Henry Kissinger, former US secretary of state and also a Theranos board member, wrote about Elizabeth Holmes in an article in *Time* magazine, saying that she was a visionary that was turning an undergraduate dream

[60] https://www.inc.com/dustin-mckissen/elizabeth-holmes-was-a-massive-fraud-our-click-driven-media-helped-create-her.html
[61] https://www.theguardian.com/commentisfree/2018/jun/03/theranos-elizabeth-holmes-media-emperors-new-startup
[62] https://www.bbc.com/news/business-58336998

into a global reality, that she had a "fierce and single-minded dedication with great charm," and also that

> *[h]er story could happen only in America.*[63]

General James Mattis, also a board member, wrote to Holmes in March 2013: *"I'm a strong believer in what you have designed/built and hope we can get it in the theater soon to test it."*[64] Business Insider reported about the influence and power of the board in an article titled "How Elizabeth Holmes Convinced Powerful Men Like Henry Kissinger, James Mattis, and George Shultz to Sit on the Board of Now Disgraced Blood-Testing Startup Theranos."[65]

Former secretary of defense, William Perry, who was also on the board, told the *New Yorker* about Holmes:

> *She has sometimes been called another Steve Jobs, but I think that's an inadequate comparison. She has a social consciousness that Steve never had. He was a genius; she's one with a big heart.*[66]

In 2015, when Elizabeth Holmes was said to be America's youngest female self-made billionaire, she appeared onstage with former US president Bill Clinton to talk about the future of equality and opportunity. Mr. Clinton said to Holmes, "*You founded this company twelve years ago, right? Tell them how old you were.*" Holmes replied, "*I was nineteen.*" Holmes also appeared on a panel with Joe Biden, who was vice president at the time they met.

Figure 1.5 shows Elizabeth Holmes with former president Bill Clinton, former secretary of state Madeleine Albright, and Jack Ma, the founder of Alibaba.

---

63 https://time.com/collection-post/3822734/elizabeth-holmes-2015-time-100/

64 https://www.npr.org/2021/09/23/1040033127/mattis-elizabeth-holmes-theranos-trial

65 https://www.businessinsider.com/theranos-former-board-members-henry-kissinger-george-shultz-james-mattis-2019-3

66 https://www.theverge.com/22656190/theranos-elizabeth-holmes-wire-fraud-trial-founder-myth

**Reflection**

- Consider the effects of having high-ranking politicians on your board. Can it enable fraud? Can it deter whistleblowers? Can it lead to more escalation and doing whatever it takes to get the job done?

- How would you explain the statements made by so many distinguished American politicians about Holmes? Are there biases that make so many people follow the same trend? Was it a bandwagon? Was it wanting to be part of what was perceived to be a breakthrough? Was it wanting to support the cause?

## 5.11. Lobbying for legislation: Ms. Holmes, you are magnificent!

Holmes went on to lobby the Arizona House of Representatives for a change in the legal system advocating for laboratory testing without a physician's order.

> *Elizabeth Holmes to the Arizona House Health Committee: Giving people the right will, by definition, begin the process of enabling them to engage in their health.*
>
> *House of Representative: Ms. Holmes, you are magnificent!*

Soon after, House Bill 2645 passed. It includes the following:

> *A person may obtain any laboratory test from a licensed clinical laboratory on a direct access basis without a health care provider's request or written authorization if the laboratory offers that laboratory test to the public on a direct access basis without a health care provider's request or written authorization.*[67]

[67] https://www.azleg.gov/legtext/52leg/1r/bills/hb2645s.pdf

## 5.12. Feeling you can get away? Deny and leverage the board to enable deception

In 2012, Theranos approached Lieutenant Colonel David Shoemaker about deploying the device in the military. Shoemaker expressed concern about the technology and launched an inquiry with the Food and Drug Administration (FDA) about its use without FDA clearance. Elizabeth Holmes followed up with an email to General James Mattis to dispel the military reviewer's "blatantly false information." Mattis, who was on the board of Theranos, convinced Colonel Shoemaker that a more limited experiment was allowed.[68]

## 5.13. Ignore the science: Accuracy of information detectors for syphilis test

The *Mercury News* reported about the accuracy of the Theranos syphilis tests: In one run, the sensitivity of the test was 0.65. This means that if one hundred people who have syphilis tested, sixty-five would be told they have the disease, and the other thirty-five would be told they did not have it. In another run, the sensitivity was 0.8. Yet Theranos claimed the sensitivity was 0.95. They did this by ignoring many false tests in the samples they produced.

The tests also showed that 20 percent of the people who tested (whether or not they had syphilis) were reported to have the disease. Yet national statistics in the United States show that thirty thousand people a year, or 0.009 percent of the population, get it.[69]

**Reflection**

If the chance that a person has syphilis is 0.009 and if 20 percent of the people who test (whether or not they have it) receive a positive test indication, what must be the sensitivity of the test? What implications do these results have on giving false-positive or false-negative indications?

---

68 https://www.washingtonpost.com/news/wonk/wp/2015/12/02/internal-emails-reveal-concerns-about-theranoss-fda-compliance-date-back-years/

69 https://www.mercurynews.com/2018/10/18/theranos-whistle-blower-speaks-out/

We shall refer back to this question in the section "Ethical Information" when discussing updating information.

## 5.14. Enabling fraud with top-bottom slogans about morality

In an interview, Elizabeth Holmes said about Theranos,

> *We are the only lab company that is actually really focused on leading with transparency.*[70]

In an interview with Ken Auletta, General Mattis was asked about the first words that come to his mouth when he thinks of Elizabeth Holmes. He responded,

> *First is integrity, uh, competence. And competence is both technical, scientific, but also focused on human rights in the most classical sense of what human rights are about. And all of a sudden, you have the ability to know if someone is ill or not. I mean, literally, within minutes of taking... you know, a drop of blood. And I mean she is really a revolutionary in the true sense.*

In the same spirit of preaching morals, Elizabeth Holmes also told employees of Theranos,

> *What higher purpose in life is there than to be part of this change?*

Elizabeth Holmes mentioned to Charlie Rose in an interview on June 3, 2015,

> *If today were my last day on this Earth and I could say that the people who've gone through hell in being able to just get the test done that they need to get, I've done something in this world that has made it a little bit of a better place, right?*

---

[70] https://www.youtube.com/watch?v=PvznWSEKoEE

## 5.15. Leveraging the legal team to encourage deception? Avoiding/delaying subpoena

Ian Gibbons, a Theranos scientist, received a subpoena regarding Holmes's contributions to the Theranos filed patents. He panicked and was concerned that he would be sued by Theranos if he released information during the deposition because of an NDA he had signed with the company. The Theranos legal team worked with Gibbons to avoid the subpoena by citing medical reasons. Gibbons committed suicide shortly after with an overdose of prescription drugs.

## 5.16. Crisis management

### A. Media finds out

Several whistleblowers from Theranos approached the *Wall Street Journal* after quitting their jobs in 2014. The whistleblowers included Adam Rosendorff, Erika Cheung, and Tyler Shultz (grandson of board member George Shultz).

On October 16, 2015, the *WSJ* published an article by John Carreyrou titled "Hot Startup Theranos Has Struggled with Its Blood-Test Technology: Silicon Valley lab, led by Elizabeth Holmes, is valued at $9 billion but isn't using its technology for all the tests it offers."[71]

The article reported that Theranos was using its own technology on only a very small number of the 240 tests that it performed and, further, that the majority of its tests were done with traditional vials rather than the few drops of blood as advertised.

### Feeling you can get away with it? Deny, attack source of information, and champion morality and integrity

Upon the publication of the *WSJ* article, Elizabeth Holmes was quick to deny and attack the source of information amid slogans of integrity. At the *WSJ* tech conference in Laguna Beach, California, Holmes said,

[71] https://www.wsj.com/articles/theranos-has-struggled-with-blood-tests-1444881901

*We know what we're doing, and we're very proud of it. We know the facts. We know the integrity of what we've done.*

CNN reported about Elizabeth Holmes's reaction: "*Elizabeth Holmes slams Theranos critics.*"[72]

The Hulu series *The Dropout* shows a scene where Elizabeth Holmes is attacking the author of the *WSJ* article:

*Well, it's sexism. Yeah, this reporter clearly has an issue with women. Yeah. Women in power. That's right. John Carreyrou.*[73]

Theranos also filed a complaint against Tyler Shultz (one of the whistleblowers) in court, with allegations that he revealed trade secrets and that he was a disgruntled former employee.[74]

When the *WSJ* approached Theranos for comment, Theranos hired David Boies's law firm (yes, the same David Boies with Bill Gates) to help block the release of the article. In his book, *Bad Blood*, John Carreyrou described efforts by Mr. Boies and his firm to intimidate and terrify the whistleblowers and referred to those efforts as those of "thugs."

### B. Using biases to enable fraud: "Us vs. them" bias

HuffPost reported about four ways Holmes manipulated her employees:

1. *You're changing the world.*
2. *It's on you.*
3. *We're all in this together.*
4. *It's us versus them*[75]

The "us vs. them" mechanism triggers several biases that make individuals

[72] https://www.cnn.com/2022/01/04/tech/elizabeth-holmes-rise-and-fall/index.html
[73] https://tvshowtranscripts.ourboard.org/viewtopic.php?f=1262&t=52248
[74] https://www.mercurynews.com/2018/10/18/theranos-whistle-blower-speaks-out/
[75] https://www.huffpost.com/entry/elizabeth-holmes-office-employees_l_5c92abe3e4b01b140d351b6f

find common ground in defending the team and attacking the opponent even if the team is at fault. It often leads to group polarization, where the group becomes exaggerated in its hostility toward the opponent. In one meeting, Sunny Balwani told Theranos employees,

> *Remember, these are the guys who are after us, and they are attacking the work that you guys are doing. Are you ready? One, two, three, f— — you!*

The Theranos workforce yelled back the expletive, swearing allegiance to Theranos and clapping in aggressive enthusiasm.

**Reflection**

Are there other biases that can be exploited in the manipulation of employees?

### C. Feeling you cannot get away with it, but pressure has not built up: Change procedures unethically slow

A few weeks after the publication of the *WSJ* article, the Food and Drug Administration released a report saying that Theranos needed to validate its technology properly. On January 25, 2016, the Centers for Medicare & Medicaid Services (CMS) sent Theranos a letter saying its California lab had failed to comply with federal standards and that

> *[t]he deficient practices of the laboratory pose immediate jeopardy to patient health and safety.*

The SEC also began conducting an investigation. In response, Walgreens said it would not send any lab tests to Theranos's California lab. Theranos was quick to respond that "*the survey . . . does not reflect the current state of the lab.*"

On January 28, 2016, Walgreens issued this statement:

> *In light of the letter dated Jan. 25 from the Centers for Medicare and Medicaid Services (CMS) to Theranos, Inc., Walgreens said today that it has informed Theranos that it must immediately cease sending any clinical laboratory tests provided through Theranos Wellness Centers at*

*Walgreens to the Theranos lab in Newark, Calif., for analysis. In addition, Walgreens is suspending Theranos laboratory services at its Palo Alto, Calif., store, effective immediately.*[76]

The attorney general of Arizona also began an inquiry. On April 18, 2017, Theranos settled with the CMS in an agreement to a $30,000 fine and agreed not to operate a clinical laboratory for two years. Another settlement was made with the attorney general of Arizona to pay $4.65 million to refund the 175,000 Arizonans who purchased a blood test from Theranos between 2013 and 2016.

### D. Pressure builds up: Change leadership

After the settlement, Theranos released a statement that the settlement was in fact in alignment with its revised business model and that the new focus was on miniature automated testing platforms such as its miniLab.

In May 2016, Balwani stepped down and left Theranos. Theranos also voided two years of blood tests. The company also added three new board members: Fabrizio Bonanni, a former executive vice president of Amgen; William Foege, a former CDC director; and Richard Kovacevich, a former Wells Fargo CEO.

## 5.17. Consequences: Multiple lawsuits, SEC, and settlements

In November 2016, Walgreens sued Theranos for breach of contract and sought to recover the $140 million it invested into the company. The lawsuit was settled in August 2017. In May 2017, Theranos settled a lawsuit brought by investor Partner Fund Management, who sought to recoup a $96 million investment it made in the company in 2014.

In November 2016, the *WSJ* published the article "Theranos and David Boies Cut Legal Ties: Famed litigator disagrees with Theranos over strategy for handling investigations of company."[77]

---

[76] https://www.businesswire.com/news/home/20160128006274/en/Walgreens-Informs-Theranos-Cease-Newark-Calif.-Lab

[77] https://www.wsj.com/articles/theranos-and-david-boies-cut-legal-ties-1479514351

In March 2018, the SEC charged Elizabeth Holmes and Sunny Balwani with fraud. This charge was settled when Holmes agreed to a fine of $500,000 and to being barred from serving as an officer or director in any publicly traded company for the next ten years. The SEC released the following statements:

*Theranos and Holmes have agreed to settle the fraud charges levied against them. Holmes agreed to pay a $500,000 penalty, be barred from serving as an officer or director of a public company for 10 years, return the remaining 18.9 million shares that she obtained during the fraud, and relinquish her voting control of Theranos.*

*If Theranos is acquired or is otherwise liquidated, Holmes would not profit from her ownership until—assuming redemption of certain warrants—over $750 million is returned to defrauded investors and other preferred shareholders.*[78]

## 5.18. Stakeholders: Investors, doctors, patients, and Elizabeth Holmes

On June 14, 2018, the Department of Justice charged Holmes and Balwani with fraud.[79] Their indictment describes these different perspectives:

### Fraud to doctors by omission and commission regarding capability of product

*Holmes and Balwani used advertisements and solicitations to encourage and induce doctors and patients to use Theranos's blood testing laboratory services, even though, according to the government, the defendants knew Theranos was not capable of consistently producing accurate and reliable results for certain blood tests. Holmes and Balwani defrauded doctors and patients (1) by making false claims concerning Theranos's ability to provide accurate, fast, reliable, and cheap blood tests and test results, and (2) by omitting information concerning the limits of and problems with Theranos's technologies.*

---

[78] https://www.sec.gov/news/press-release/2018-41

[79] https://www.justice.gov/usao-ndca/us-v-elizabeth-holmes-et-al

### Fraud to investors

> *Defendants also allegedly made numerous misrepresentations to potential investors about Theranos's financial condition and its future prospects. For example, the defendants represented to investors that Theranos conducted its patients' tests using Theranos-manufactured analyzers; when, in truth, Holmes and Balwani knew that Theranos purchased and used for patient testing third party, commercially available analyzers.*

## 5.19. Intent is the critical issue

Before the verdict, multiple media outlets discussed the issue of intent.[80] Did Elizabeth Holmes cover up the defects in Theranos technology to defraud investors while also endangering the lives of patients? Reuters reported, *"Holmes' intent was the 'critical issue' in the case."*[81] We shall refer back to the issue of intent in "Ethical Awareness."

**Reflection**

- In your view, would Holmes have maintained her shares in Theranos if she believed that she would not be successful? Would she have dropped out of Stanford?
- Regardless of the stance taken by the legal system and whether or not Holmes kept her shares, can you identify acts of deception, theft, or harm by Elizabeth Holmes?

## 5.20. The legal verdict

According to the Justice Department,

> *Elizabeth A. Holmes was sentenced on Friday, November 18, 2022, to 135 months (11 years, 3 months) in federal prison for defrauding investors in*

---

80 https://apnews.com/article/technology-business-health-san-jose-conspiracy-ba9b2e4d4bdca0be4ec2d310ae2957aa

81 https://www.reuters.com/legal/government/elizabeth-holmes-fraud-trial-over-theranos-draws-close-2021-12-16/

*Theranos, Inc. of hundreds of millions of dollars.*[82]

*Ramesh "Sunny" Balwani was sentenced on Wednesday, December 7, 2022, to 155 months (12 years, 11 months) in federal prison for fraud that risked patient health by misrepresenting the accuracy of Theranos blood analysis technology and defrauded Theranos investors of millions of dollars.*[83]

*In addition to the 155-month prison term, U.S. District Judge Davila sentenced Balwani to three years of supervision following his release from prison.*

## Impacts on stakeholders and different perspectives

Elizabeth Holmes's perspective (and part of her defense) was that if they had enough time, they would have been able to complete the product successfully. Further, Holmes did not sell her share of Theranos throughout this whole time (compare with Enron executives).

Investors lost about $700 million: The DeVos family lost about $100 million, Rupert Murdoch lost about $125 million, and the Walton family lost $150 million.

In terms of employees, about eight hundred people lost their jobs.

In terms of patients, about 7.8 million inaccurate test results were produced. Those tests included a false HIV positive, a false cancer diagnosis, and a false indication of a miscarriage.

Female entrepreneurs in Silicon Valley reported that they now struggle to find investors. Ian Gibbons, a Theranos scientist, committed suicide.

CNBC released an article titled "Boies Schiller Law Firm Loses Several Attorneys Over Issues Involving Harvey Weinstein, Elizabeth Holmes, Founder's Kids."[84]

---

82 https://www.justice.gov/usao-ndca/pr/elizabeth-holmes-sentenced-more-11-years-defrauding-theranos-investors-hundreds

83 https://www.justice.gov/usao-ndca/us-v-elizabeth-holmes-et-al

84 https://www.cnbc.com/2021/09/10/boies-schiller-loses-lawyers-over-controversies-involving-theranos-harvey-weinstein.html

# Chapter 6

# Volkswagen (in America)

*It should first be decided whether we are honest.*
*If we are not honest, everything stays as it is.*

—Oliver Schmidt, former Volkswagen (VW) executive
who was sentenced to seven years in prison

## 6.1. The environment: Regulation limiting the use of a product

In 2003, diesel-powered vehicles accounted for about 4 percent of California motor vehicles, but they produced about 60 percent of the directly emitted particulate matter.[85] In 2003, the potential cancer risk associated with exposure to diesel particulate matter was greater than the combined risks of all other toxic air contaminants. Diesel engines also emit nitrogen oxide (NOx) that damages the human respiratory system,[86] as well as sulfur oxides that pose several health threats. To mitigate these hazards, the California Air Resources Board (CARB) implemented a risk-reduction plan to reduce Californians' exposure to diesel emissions.[87] The program, among other emission control strategies, calls for low-sulfur diesel fuel and NOx aftertreatment.

## 6.2. Lobbying politicians for diesel incentives: Presentation, perspective, and frame

In 2000, VW, Mazda, and several other companies who had an interest in using diesel fuel formed the Diesel Technology Forum to lobby for the increased use of diesel engines in the United States.[88] They presented the

---

[85] https://ww2.arb.ca.gov/resources/fact-sheets/california-low-sulfur-diesel-fuel-fact-sheet
[86] https://www.epa.gov/no2-pollution/basic-information-about-no2
[87] https://ww2.arb.ca.gov/our-work/programs/diesel-risk-reduction-plan
[88] https://www.reuters.com/article/cbusiness-us-usa-volkswagen-deception-in-idCAKCN0RO2IP20150924; https://europe.autonews.com/article/20150925/COPY/309259985/vw-stunned-u-s-regulators-with-diesel-cheat-confession

initiative as a way to reduce US reliance on imported oil. Following this initiative, President Bush called for new consumer tax credits for energy-efficient hybrid, clean diesel, and fuel cell vehicles in his 2006 fiscal year budget. The energy bill would provide up to $3,400 per vehicle in tax credits to consumers for the purchase of these cars.[89]

## 6.3. Deception to achieve sales goals

In the same year of 2006, a US sales strategy of VW promoted their vehicles to customers in the United States as "clean diesel vehicles" to capitalize on the new tax credits. But there was only one problem with this strategy: VW had no idea how to manufacture a "clean diesel vehicle." The Air & Waste Management Association noted, *"Shortly after the sales campaign was kicked-off, a senior VW official was filmed in 2007 complaining that compliance with CARB's diesel regulations was 'impossible.'"*[90]

## 6.4. Using the media to enable deception

Despite not having a clean diesel vehicle, TV ads about one of VW's vehicles, the new Jetta TDI, were prevalent. In 2008, the Jetta TDI was named "Green Car of the Year."[91] Jetta buyers would receive an income tax credit of $1,300 for using "clean diesel." The Jetta was sold out immediately at VW dealers when it went on sale in 2009.

## 6.5. Top-bottom value slogans of the form "We are the champions of morality"

With the launch of the "clean diesel" sales campaign and while still not having a clean diesel vehicle, Volkswagen's CEO at the time, Martin Winterkorn, made an announcement that their mission was to produce sustainable, reliable, and successful vehicles that would *"win the hearts and minds of the American customers."*

---

[89] https://georgewbush-whitehouse.archives.gov/news/releases/2005/08/20050808-4.html
[90] https://pubs.awma.org/flip/EM-June-2018/haak.pdf
[91] https://www.nbcnews.com/id/wbna27825003

**Reflection**

Do you notice any similarities with media strategies and value slogans adopted by Elizabeth Holmes and Theranos?

## 6.6. Unanticipated consequences: Someone finds out

Meanwhile, in Europe, some regulators were skeptical about how VW could have clean diesel engines in the United States and not in Europe. In 2013, the European Commission conducted a study that ended with the conclusion that European carmakers exploited loopholes in the testing system.[92] A separate study identified significant discrepancies between emission results obtained in the lab and those obtained on the road.[93] In February 2013, the European Commission commissioned a US-based nonprofit organization called the International Council on Clean Transportation in both the lab and driving conditions.[94] The study was conducted with the help of researchers at West Virginia University. The findings showed that the on-the-road emission results of the Jetta were fifteen to thirty-five times higher than the legal limit and that those of the Passat were about ten to twenty times higher.[95] Soon after, the same cars tested by West Virginia University were tested in CARB's test facility east of Los Angeles. There were no irregular emissions during the lab testing. At this point, there was doubt that a "defeat device" was installed in the vehicles.

## 6.7. Presentation in an academic conference: Ignore the science

John German, the director of the International Council on Clean Transportation, presented the findings at an academic conference in San Diego on March 31, 2014.[96] Afraid of being sued, he referred to the vehicles tested

---

92 https://www.reuters.com/article/us-eu-autos-carbon-idINKBN0DG13V20140430
93 https://europe.autonews.com/article/20150925/COPY/309259985/vw-stunned-u-s-regulators-with-diesel-cheat-confession
94 https://www.cnbc.com/2015/09/24/how-volkswagen-fought-epa-on-emissions-cheating-claims.html
95 https://www.scientificamerican.com/article/volkswagen-uses-software-to-fool-epa-pollution-tests/
96 https://www.researchgate.net/publication/267507150_Real-world_exhaust_emissions_from_modern_diesel_cars_A_meta-analysis_of_PEMS_emissions_data_from_EU_EURO_6_and_US_Tier_2_Bin_5ULEV_II_diesel_passenger_cars_Part_1_Aggregated_results

as vehicles A and B.[97] The conference included California regulators, the Environmental Protection Agency (EPA), and employees of Volkswagen.

## 6.8. Crisis management strategies

### Feeling you can get away with it? Unethically fast to cover up/deny/discredit

The first reaction from Volkswagen was that the instruments may need to be calibrated properly and that academics and graduate students running around may have conducted the tests incorrectly.

**Reflection**

Can you identify similarities in the response to that of Theranos?

### CARB does another on-the-road test

CARB did another on-the-road test, and the results showed that emissions while driving were forty times the standard, confirming the earlier study that was conducted by West Virginia University researchers.

**Reflection: Exploring plausible hypotheses before making an accusation?**

Put yourself in this situation. How likely are you at this stage to assume fraud on the side of VW, which also owned Audi and by 2011 had also merged with Porsche? What factors might deter an individual from making a claim against companies once this is discovered? Would fear of being sued play a role?

97 https://www.theguardian.com/business/2015/sep/26/volkswagen-scandal-emissions-tests-john-german-research

## Enabling fraud using a "defeat device"?

Soon after, it was revealed that VW had actually been using special software termed "defeat devices" on their vehicles. The defeat device detects when the vehicle is being tested and then turns on full emission controls. During normal driving (i.e., when the vehicle is not being tested), however, the effectiveness of emission control devices is reduced. As a result, the amount of emission control that is used during normal driving is never tested, and the actual emissions can be 400 percent or even 500 percent higher. It was not just the Jetta or only VW vehicles that had this device, but VW's subsidiaries had it as well.

The EPA reported on its web page that from 2009 to 2016,

> *Volkswagen, Audi, and Porsche installed software on certain diesel vehicles that is designed to detect when the vehicle is undergoing emissions testing.*[98]

The EPA further determined the impact that this defeat device had in terms of sales and emission of excess pollutants:

> *Volkswagen violated the Clean Air Act by the sale of approximately 590,000 diesel motor vehicles equipped with "defeat devices" in the form of computer software designed to cheat on federal emissions tests. The major excess pollutant at issue, in this case, is oxides of nitrogen (NOx), and is a serious health concern.*

## Unethically slow to acknowledge: Feeling you can get away with it? Do nothing

When CARB inquired with VW, Oliver Schmidt, a VW executive, emailed his leadership.

> *It should first be decided whether we are honest. If we are not honest, everything stays as it is.*

The strategy VW chose was to do nothing and to wait. It was decided to not give any explanation in fear that authorities would investigate.[99]

---

98 https://www.epa.gov/vw/learn-about-volkswagen-violations

99 https://www.forbes.com/sites/bertelschmitt/2016/09/25/winterkorn-behind-dieselgate-coverup-new-docs-suggest/?sh=f496d9d477d2

## Feeling you cannot get away with it, but pressure has not built up? Change of procedures or pretense thereof

In December 2014, the EPA announced that VW was going to issue a software fix to solve emission problems from some of its vehicles.[100] In an interview with the BBC, Mr. German said,

> *[VW] swore up and down to the agencies that this would fix the problem. But CARB went out in May [2015] and tested some of the vehicles with the fix and the emissions were still very high. VW tried to offer a lot of other explanations for the high emissions for a very long period of time.*

## Got caught? Admit, change of leadership, "We are the champions of morality"

On September 3, 2015, VW engineers admitted to the EPA that defeat devices had been installed on its cars to deceive US regulators about how much their diesel engines pollute.[101] Oliver Schmidt was transferred to Germany and replaced by Stuart Johnson.

On September 18, 2015, the EPA issued a notice of violation of the Clean Air Act to Volkswagen.[102] The notice alleged that Volkswagen installed defeat devices in its vehicles from 2009 to 2015. These vehicles, in fact, emitted up to forty times more pollution than emissions standards allowed.

In response, VW published a video from then CEO Martin Winterkorn on September 22, where Winterkorn iterated Volkswagen's dedication to cooperating with authorities and to "*do all this with the greatest openness and transparency.*"[103]

[100] https://www.bbc.com/news/business-34519184

[101] https://europe.autonews.com/article/20150925/COPY/309259985/vw-stunned-u-s-regulators-with-diesel-cheat-confession

[102] https://www.epa.gov/vw/learn-about-volkswagen-violations

[103] https://www.crisisshield.co.uk/post/2019/05/15/dieselgate-how-volkswagens-emissions-crisis-response-backfired

## 6.9. Rationalization by governments: Governments would not harm their car industry

Hans Koberstein, editor of *Frontal 21*, explains in the Netflix documentary *Dirty Money* that every European manufacturer was using calibration strategies that had emissions up to 400–500 percent higher than those during laboratory tests. Further, any government in Europe that has a national car industry would not want to rock the boats on this problem by highlighting this emissions gap. They all think,

> *Hmmm, better not to harm our national car industry.*

Further, even if they wanted to set legislation, they can enforce the law only for their own car industry, not others. And so any national government is thinking,

> *Should I harm my national car industry if others won't? No, I will not do this. I am not stupid.*[104]

## 6.10. Impacts on stakeholders

On January 4, 2016, the Department of Justice filed a complaint on behalf of EPA against Volkswagen AG, Audi AG, and Porsche Cars North America for violations of the Clean Air Act.

Shortly after, VW acknowledged it had installed software that deactivated pollution controls on more than 11 million diesel vehicles sold worldwide, exposing numerous people to nitrogen oxide risks. VW settled with a near $15 billion settlement with US regulators and car owners.[105] VW had to buy back 550,000 cars in the United States. In the United States alone, Volkswagen was forced to recall more than 480,000 vehicles and pay about $25 billion in fines.[106] VW's reputation was damaged; and its chief executive, Martin Winterkorn, departed. Oliver Schmidt pleaded guilty to conspiracy and fraud. He was sentenced to seven years in prison and fined

---

[104] Hans Koberstein, editor of *Frontal 21*, from the Netflix documentary *Dirty Money*

[105] https://www.reuters.com/article/us-volkswagen-emissions/volkswagen-emissions-scandal-deepens-as-prosecutors-probe-chairman-idUSKBN1310E9

[106] https://www.theguardian.com/business/2015/sep/26/volkswagen-scandal-emissions-tests-john-german-research

$400,000 for conspiracy to defraud the United States and for violating the Clean Air Act.[107]

## 6.11. Could the legal team have encouraged VW's deception?

The Air & Waste Management Association reported in its EM Magazine in June 2018 about the case of Volkswagen emissions scandal:

> *There is some suggestion that outside legal counsel may have given VW a false sense of security by delivering an unintentionally misleading "reasonable worst case" scenario for VW to base its decisions on.*[108]

Outside legal counsel gave a worst-case scenario of a precedent (a $100 million fuel efficiency case against Hyundai and Kia settled in 2014) that was incomparable to the current situation in the elements of intent, magnitude of incompliance, and an incomparable fact pattern. The report continues,

> *It is impossible for us to know exactly what legal advice VW received (Thank you, attorney-client privilege . . .), but it is interesting to speculate whether VW's internal response would have been different if outside legal counsel had simply said "there is no analog for this, it's uncharted territory" or "here's the worst thing we found, given our different facts, we could easily be facing penalties ten times greater (i.e., US$1 billion-plus)."*

Note that the speculation about whether the outside counsel could have highlighted the possible severe penalties for having a defeat device is irrelevant from an ethical standpoint. Having a defeat device that provides different emission results based on whether it is being tested or not is deception and causes harm to stakeholders.

---

[107] https://europe.autonews.com/article/20171206/COPY/312069936/ex-vw-exec-schmidt-gets-max-7-years-400-000-fine-for-u-s-emissions-violations

[108] W. Haak, "What Compliance Lessons Can We Learn from Volkswagen's Diesel Emissions Scandal?," EM, *The Magazine for Environmental Managers, AWMA*, June 2018.

# Chapter 7

# Wells Fargo

*If you want to find out how strong a company's ethics are, don't listen to what its people say. Watch what they do. This is even more important in our industry because everything we do is built on trust.*

—*The Vision & Values of Wells Fargo* brochure

## 7.1. Environment: Do whatever it takes to meet impossible targets

Can organizational incentives and the desire to do whatever it takes to achieve them induce unethical acts? Yes, absolutely! Can setting impossible targets lead to unethical decision-making that impacts the organization? Yes, absolutely!

The Department of Justice noted,

> *Wells Fargo & Company and its subsidiary, Wells Fargo Bank, N.A., have agreed to pay $3 billion to resolve their potential criminal and civil liability stemming from a practice between 2002 and 2016 of pressuring employees to meet unrealistic sales goals that led thousands of employees to provide millions of accounts or products to customers under false pretenses or without consent, often by creating false records or misusing customers' identities.*[109]

Can the leadership of an organization create an environment that pressures employees to conduct unethical acts and deception? Yes, absolutely! NPR reported,

> *Former employees of Wells Fargo tell NPR that a toxic high-pressure sales culture at the bank drove some workers to deceive customers and open*

[109] https://www.justice.gov/opa/pr/wells-fargo-agrees-pay-3-billion-resolve-criminal-and-civil-investigations-sales-practices

*unauthorized accounts—even in the bank's own headquarters building in San Francisco.*[110]

## 7.2. A culture of deception and organizational transgression tolerated by leadership

Can the leadership of an organization tolerate deception and unethical acts? Yes, absolutely! The Department of Justice noted,

> *Many of these practices were referred to within Wells Fargo as "gaming." Gaming strategies varied widely but included using existing customers' identities—without their consent—to open checking and savings, debit card, credit card, bill pay, and global remittance accounts. From 2002 to 2016, gaming practices included forging customer signatures to open accounts without authorization, creating PINs to activate unauthorized debit cards, moving money from millions of customer accounts to unauthorized accounts in a practice known internally as "simulated funding," opening credit cards and bill pay products without authorization, altering customers' true contact information to prevent customers from learning of unauthorized accounts and prevent Wells Fargo employees from reaching customers to conduct customer satisfaction surveys, and encouraging customers to open accounts they neither wanted or needed. The top managers of the Community Bank were aware of the unlawful and unethical gaming practices as early as 2002, and they knew that the conduct was increasing due to onerous sales goals and pressure from management to meet these goals. One internal investigator in 2004 called the problem a "growing plague."*[111]

## 7.3. Crisis management strategies

### Feeling you can get away with it. Nobody finds out. Do nothing

CNN reported,

---

[110] https://www.npr.org/2016/10/04/496508361/former-wells-fargo-employees-describe-toxic-sales-culture-even-at-hq

[111] https://www.justice.gov/opa/pr/wells-fargo-agrees-pay-3-billion-resolve-criminal-and-civil-investigations-sales-practices

> *Despite knowledge of the illegal sales practices, Community Bank senior leadership failed to take sufficient action to prevent and reduce the incidence of such practices.*[112]

## Top-bottom value slogans of the form "We are the champions of morality"

*The Vision & Values of Wells Fargo* brochure reads,

> *Our ethics are the sum of all the decisions each of us makes every day. If you want to find out how strong a company's ethics are, don't listen to what its people say. Watch what they do. This is even more important in our industry because everything we do is built on trust.*[113]

## Media finds out

The Consumer Financial Protection Bureau (CFPB) posted the following on its website:

> *WASHINGTON, D.C. — Today the Consumer Financial Protection Bureau (CFPB) fined Wells Fargo Bank, N.A. $100 million for the widespread illegal practice of secretly opening unauthorized deposit and credit card accounts. Spurred by sales targets and compensation incentives, employees boosted sales figures by covertly opening accounts and funding them by transferring funds from consumers' authorized accounts without their knowledge or consent, often racking up fees or other charges. According to the bank's own analysis, employees opened more than two million deposit and credit card accounts that may not have been authorized by consumers. Wells Fargo will pay full restitution to all victims and a $100 million fine to the CFPB's Civil Penalty Fund. The bank will also pay an additional $35 million penalty to the Office of the Comptroller of the Currency, and another $50 million to the City and County of Los Angeles.*[114]

---

[112] https://money.cnn.com/2016/09/21/investing/wells-fargo-fired-workers-retaliation-fake-accounts/index.html

[113] https://finance.yahoo.com/news/wells-fargo-just-became-poster-224514610.html?guce_&guccounter=2

[114] https://www.consumerfinance.gov/about-us/newsroom/consumer-financial-protection-bureau-fines-wells-fargo-100-million-widespread-illegal-practice-secretly-opening-unauthorized-accounts/

### Getting caught but feeling you can get away with it: Blame it on employees and have top-bottom value slogans of the form "We are the champions of morality"

Wells Fargo fired 5,300 employees who opened up bank accounts. In a letter to employees dated October 11, 2016, CEO John Stumpf called the employees' actions "*inconsistent with the values and culture we strive to live up to every day.*"

### Pressure builds up: Change leadership

On October 12, 2016, NPR posted,

> *The chairman and chief executive of Wells Fargo & Co., John Stumpf, has resigned effective immediately in the aftermath of a scandal over the bank's past practice of secretly selling services to unsuspecting customers.*[115]

He was succeeded by Timothy J. Sloan.

## 7.4. Recurrence of ethical violations despite a change in leadership?

On February 24, 2020, *Forbes* reported,

> *Wells Fargo, the fourth largest bank in the United States, agreed on Friday to pay $3 billion to settle its long-running civil and criminal probes into the heinous accusations of rampant fraudulent sales practices.*[116]

On September 21, 2022, Congress held a hearing titled "Holding Megabanks Accountable: Oversight of America's Largest Consumer Facing Banks."[117] Chairwoman Maxine Waters noted,

> *As Chairwoman of the Committee on Financial Services, I have sounded*

[115] https://www.npr.org/sections/thetwo-way/2016/10/12/497729371/wells-fargo-ceo-john-stumpf-resigns-amid-scandal

[116] https://www.forbes.com/sites/jackkelly/2020/02/24/wells-fargo-forced-to-pay-3-billion-for-the-banks-fake-account-scandal/?sh=2861410542d2

[117] https://www.congress.gov/117/meeting/house/115151/documents/HHRG-117-BA00-20220921-SD001-U1.pdf

*the alarm about repeat offenders like Wells Fargo. I have held multiple hearings to force Wells Fargo's CEO and other megabank CEOs to answer to the public for their actions. I am disturbed by the fact that some violations in this order occurred or continued since September 2019 when Wells Fargo came under new leadership, which leads me to believe that much, much more needs to be done to rein in Wells Fargo.*

- Between 2011 and 2016, Wells Fargo fraudulently opened millions of unauthorized accounts, costing their customers millions of dollars.

- In September 2016, the CFPB, the Office of the Comptroller of the Currency (OCC), and the Los Angeles city attorney imposed a collective $185 million fine.

- From 2006 to 2016, the bank charged service members illegal fees, failed to disclose their active-duty status in eviction proceedings, and unlawfully repossessed their vehicles, resulting in a $20 million fine and $10 million returned to service members.

- From 2005 to 2016, the bank charged customers for automobile insurance policies they did not need, resulting in some customers going into default and losing their vehicles.

- From 2013 to 2017, Wells Fargo inappropriately charged prospective home loan borrowers fees for extending the period for a mortgage interest rate lock. Together, these abuses led to a collective fine of $1 billion by the CFPB and the OCC.

- In 2017, the OCC and the SEC found that Wells Fargo or its subsidiary failed to comply with anti–money laundering laws. The SEC also found that from 2009 to 2013, Wells Fargo advisers unlawfully sold complex financial products to retail investors, reducing their investment returns.

- Recently, Wells Fargo self-reported that between 2010 and 2018, the bank erroneously denied or failed to offer modifications to customers, resulting in over five hundred people losing their homes.

## Reflection

What factors or mindsets can lead to recurrence of ethical scandals despite a change in leadership?

# Part 2

# The Elements of Ethical Decision Quality

## Summary of Part 2

This part presents the elements of ethical decision quality that can be used to assess the ethical quality of a decision either in real time or through a survey or an audit of past decisions. They can also be used as predictors for ethical collapse when one or more weak elements are present. Our purpose will be to emphasize the effects of each element on ethical decision-making. As we go through each element, reflect on how it may have impacted the quality of ethical decisions in part 1.

The eleven elements of ethical decision quality: 1. **A**wareness. 2. **M**otives. 3. **E**nvironment. 4. **R**easoning and Rationalization. 5. **I**nformation 6. **C**ognitive Biases. 7. **A**lternatives. 8. **W**ell-Being. 9. **T**olerances and Trade-Offs 10. **F**ormulation. 11. **S**takeholders.

# Chapter 8

# Awareness

*Honesty is such a lonely word.*
*Everyone is so untrue.*
*Honesty is hardly ever heard*
*And mostly what I need from you.*

—"Honesty," a song by Billy Joel

## Ethical Awareness

Awareness of the ethical implications of your decisions is one of the most important elements of ethical decision quality. You cannot expect a person to make an ethical decision toward other stakeholders if they are unaware of the ethical issue or its ethical implications. Ethical issues surround you at work, school, and home, as well as with business affiliates, during your interactions with friends and family, and during most of your daily interactions. The ethical issues you encounter are not all clearly structured like homework problems that you find in textbooks.

> *It is you—yes, you—who needs to recognize when an ethical issue exists, or if it has already occurred. And it is you—yes, you—who needs to decide what you will do about it.*

To build ethical awareness, and to recognize an ethical issue before decision-making, we must first understand what constitutes an unethical act. *Merriam-Webster.com Dictionary* defines "unethical" as "*not conforming to a high moral standard.*"[118]

But there is no global definition or agreement on what comprises a high moral standard. Different views about ethics also disagree on whether an act is considered ethical or unethical based on the act itself or its consequences (such as whether the benefit exceeds the harm). A Kantian

[118] https://www.merriam-webster.com/dictionary/unethical

perspective determines the ethicality of the act by the act itself, while a utilitarian (consequentialist) perspective investigates whether the benefit exceeds the harm. Societal norms and the legal system are not necessarily moral standards either. As we shall see, they can tolerate, enforce, and even encourage unethical acts.

## Acts of deception, harming, or stealing

Our purpose in this chapter is to increase awareness about decisions involving *acts of deception, harming, or stealing from a sentient being* as a first step in ethical decision-making. When you examine the acts associated with ethical collapses in part 1, you will find that they comprise mainly these acts. While predominant in part 1, these acts are also consistent with Howard and Korver (2008) and Howard and Abbas (2015).[119] They also represent a significant number of instances investigated by the Department of Justice.

This focus on acts of deception, harming, or stealing also includes acts that

1. you conduct yourself,
2. you tolerate them when you see them,
3. you coerce someone else into doing them (by using threat, fear, force, social pressure),
4. you manipulate others into doing them by convincing them that it is the right thing to do (or by exploiting their biases or emotions), and
5. you induce others into doing in exchange for benefits, such as receiving a bribe, returning a favor, or becoming members of a social club.

Ethical awareness is a state of proactively recognizing that an ethical issue exists, that a decision needs to be made, and that not making a decision regarding an unethical act is in fact a decision. Training can improve ethical awareness, and individuals can become more aware and sensitive to the

[119] R. A. Howard and C. Korver, *Ethics for the Real World: Creating a Personal Code to Guide Decisions in Work and Life* (Boston, MA: Harvard Business Press, 2008); R. A. Howard and A. E. Abbas, *Foundations of Decision Analysis* (New York, NY: Pearson Publishers, 2015).

ethical issues at hand. Sometimes, domain knowledge and expert assessments may be needed to better understand the ethical implications of an act. A decision involving the ethics of gene mutation or clean energy, for example, might require domain knowledge about the act to better understand its implications on deception, harming, or stealing.

Becoming aware of acts that involve deception, harming, or stealing is an essential element of ethical decision quality. But by itself, awareness is not always sufficient to prevent these acts from occurring. Some people might still engage in various levels of deception, harming, or stealing even when they become aware of them. Examples include telling a "white lie," which some might rationalize by the idea that its benefits exceed the harm. Others might not. Some governments might tolerate fake diesel emission announcements with the rationalization that they do not want to harm their automobile industry. Others might not. Sometimes people engage in these acts subconsciously or under the influence of a particular environment or because of acting on poor information or poor reasoning or rationalizations. Our purpose will be to increase sensitivity toward these acts and their implications on the consequences of the decision even if you will not get caught. We shall also address other aspects that may induce acts of deception, harming, or stealing in future chapters.

## Deception

Deception is knowingly leading someone to believe a statement that is not true. It must be associated with the intent to deceive.

Reuters reported the following about Theranos:

> *Holmes' intent was the "critical issue" in the case.*[120]

If you tell a friend "*My car is in the parking lot, and I will give you a ride home*" when, in fact, your car has just been stolen, and so you cannot give them a ride home, then you have indeed made a false statement. But you have

---

[120] Jodo Codoy, "Elizabeth Holmes' Intent Takes Center Stage as Theranos Fraud Trial Draws to Close," Reuters, December 16, 2021, https://www.reuters.com/legal/government/elizabeth-holmes-fraud-trial-over-theranos-draws-close-2021-12-16/.

not been deceptive because you were not aware that your car had been stolen. Your involvement lies in the fact that you made an assertion without verifying it for that particular situation.

Deception can occur by telling an untrue statement, creating a misleading impression, or simply (and knowingly) leaving a person to believe a false statement without saying anything. This is called "deception"—omitting facts where you do not need to say anything to be deceptive. For example, if your boss bumps into you and then tells you that you did a great job on the project, and you smiled and nodded when, in fact, it was your teammate who did all the work, then this would be an act of deception.

### Is deception common? Yes! "Gaslighting" is *Merriam-Webster*'s 2022 Word of the Year

*Merriam-Webster* chose "gaslighting" as the 2022 word of the year.[121]

> *Gaslighting: the act or practice of grossly misleading someone, especially for one's own advantage.*

In a statement on its website, *Merriam-Webster* noted,

> *In this age of misinformation—of "fake news," conspiracy theories, Twitter trolls, and deep fakes—gaslighting has emerged as a word for our time.*

The site also noted,

> *2022 saw a 1,740% increase in lookups for gaslighting, with high interest throughout the year.*

### Example of deception by omission: Shadow banning on Twitter?

Shadow banning is

> *the practice of blocking or partially blocking a user or the user's content from some areas of an online community in such a way that the ban is not readily apparent to the user.*[122]

---

[121] https://www.merriam-webster.com/words-at-play/word-of-the-year
[122] https://en.wikipedia.org/wiki/Shadow_banning

The deception here affects the user who has been shadow banned yet believes their comments are being posted. They could have done other things with their time spent posting had they known. Deception also extends to other users of the site who believe the user is not posting comments.

Shadow banning became popularized in 2018 as a conspiracy theory when Elon Musk revealed how Twitter shadow banned Republican views. Deception is often given adjectives to portray that it is less of an ethical issue. Elon Musk and journalists Matt Taibbi and Bari Weiss highlighted that the practice was referred to as "visibility filtering" by previous Twitter management.

## Examples of deception at work

Deception is abundant in the workplace. Consider a new product that is not yet functional but already has a planned exhibit. The manager asks the design engineer to pretend that the product is operational during the exhibit or during a funding pitch in the hopes of fixing it later. But then it turns out the new product is built on a fundamentally flawed idea that cannot be fixed. This is a typical example of deception with unanticipated consequences in Theranos's case in part 1.

In terms of human relations, deception can be used to incite people against one another. Consider, for example, a colleague who asks a manager not to renew the contract of a terminal contractor and then goes to the same contractor and tells them that it was the manager's fault that they were not renewed and that he supported them. This deception creates hostility and leads the manipulator to escalate their manipulation until they are eventually discovered.

## Deception is often rationalized

In each of the following examples, identify the acts of deception and the possible rationalizations made by the individuals involved.

## Deception by trying not to hurt people's feelings

Consider the following situation of a classroom discussion:

*Professor: Where is Afghanistan?*

*Student studying politics and world geography: It is in South America.*

*Professor (response 1): Well, you got the planet right. I am so proud of you. You should capitalize on your strengths in world geography and pursue a career in foreign policy and world affairs.*

Would you like to have that professor as your advisor? Can you think of any unintended consequences? What if the professor had responded with the following?

Professor (response 2) in a private discussion: *No, it's not. You might want to read more on world geography and recent world conflicts, especially as you are currently applying for a job at the United Nations.*

As a student, which response would you like to be told? As a professor, which of the two answers would you give?

## Deception rationalized as a prank

Some societal norms encourage deception for fun in what is known worldwide as April Fools' Day. These pranks generally have a mild effect; and after a prank is pulled, the person is told the truth, and it usually ends up in a fun event with no significant harm. But it is still deception. Sometimes these pranks have unexpected consequences. Can you imagine situations where deception on April Fools' Day might escalate? Richard Branson recalls his April Fools' prank:

*Back before the internet, jokes were a little simpler to pull off. My most memorable April Fools' Day joke was back in 1989 when we flew a UFO over London. By the time we'd reached the motorway it was beginning to get light. We could see every single vehicle grinding to a halt and hundreds of people looking up at the UFO flying over them. It was great fun watching their reactions. What we didn't know was three police forces had been mobilised, the army had been alerted and radio and TV stations had all gone on the air about a UFO flying low over London! . . . To begin with, the police didn't see the funny side of it and threatened to arrest us for wasting their time. Thankfully, they soon joined in the fun and left with smiles on their faces.*[123]

## Deception on Instagram's and Apple's block procedures?

If you attempt to block someone from commenting on your Instagram account, you will get the following message:

> *They won't be notified that you blocked them.*

Further, the procedure notes,

> *When you block someone from commenting, they can still view your photos and videos. Any new comments from them won't be visible to anyone else except them.*[124]

Apple posts the following on its web page:

> *When you block a phone number or contact, they can still leave a voice-mail, but you won't get a notification. Messages that are sent or received won't be delivered. Also, the contact won't get a notification that the call or message was blocked.*[125]

## Fraud

Fraud is "intentional deception *to secure unfair or unlawful gain, or to deprive a victim of a legal right.*"[126] Examples of fraud include using a fake passport or driver's license to get into a bar when underage, supplying false documents to obtain a mortgage or a tax relief, and intentionally providing false documents in a court of law.

The SEC cites numerous examples of fraud conducted by individuals in organizations. Other examples abide, including Enron, Elizabeth Holmes, Sunny Balwani, and Volkswagen executives, as well as many others, including ZZZZ Best, Luckin Coffee, Wirecard, and WorldCom.

---

[123] https://www.virgin.com/branson-family/richard-branson-blog/april-fools-day
[124] https://help.instagram.com/234506470408555
[125] https://support.apple.com/en-is/HT201229#:~:text=When%20you%20block%20a%20phone,call%20or%20message%20was%20blocked.
[126] https://en.wikipedia.org/wiki/Fraud

**Reflection**

Can you identify acts of deception or fraud in part 1? Can you identify possible rationalizations?

## Theft

Theft (or stealing) is intentionally taking someone else's rights or property without their knowledge or against their will. It occurs in many forms and has different levels of severity. Theft need not involve any hostility or physical threat. For example, theft can include crypto romance scammers who have fake profiles on dating apps, pretend to be in a remote location, and then ask for your cryptocurrency accounts.[127] Theft can also occur using romantic relationships and actions by a Tinder swindler.

Warren Buffett noted,

> *More money has been stolen with the point of a pen than at the point of a gun.*

## Theft due to a friend's (unverified) recommendation?

Individuals can be subject to theft due to your actions and without your intent. For example, suppose you heard about a new form of cryptocurrency on social media, and you told your friends about it. In the excitement, you got carried away, telling them about how much potential it has without verifying or exercising due diligence on the currency or the exchange dealing with it. Suppose your friends purchased the cryptocurrency and later discovered the exchange was a scam. In that case, your involvement is not in the theft itself, but in allowing yourself to make a recommendation to your friends without verifying it.

Consider statements made by Henry Kissinger, George Shultz, General Mattis, William Perry, and others endorsing Theranos. It is entirely plausible to assume that they were unaware of the details of the fraud at Ther-

[127] Federal Trade Commission, "Reports Show Scammers Cashing in on Crypto Craze," https://www.ftc.gov/news-events/data-visualizations/data-spotlight/2022/06/reports-show-scammers-cashing-crypto-craze.

anos. But their involvement lies in making endorsing statements without verifying the situation. Their statements could have contributed to (or enabled) the defrauding of others.

## Theft need not only be of money: Theft of rights and liberties

Theft need not only be of a monetary amount. It can include depriving someone of something that is theirs, coercing false confessions, or paying bribes or gifts to get college admission while taking a spot from somebody else. Theft can also include theft of unalienable rights or liberties. Restavek Freedom reports about the coercion during the slave voyages from Africa to the Americas:

> *The volume of slaves carried off from Africa reached 30,000 per year in the 1690s and 85,000 per year a century later. More than eight out of ten Africans forced into the slave trade crossed the Atlantic between 1700 and 1850.*[128]

## Theft can be a heist or a small theft of belongings

Theft can range from small amounts to massive amounts of money. Wikipedia reports, *"The largest cash heist in global history took place in March 2003, when approximately US$1 billion was robbed from the Central Bank of Iraq, shortly after the United States began the 2003 invasion of Iraq."* And Ladders reported, *"Almost half of all housekeepers have stolen something from a guest."*[129]

## Theft in the workplace?

Theft can occur in the workplace and can range from large amounts (e.g., embezzlements) to smaller amounts (e.g., reporting sick at work when you are not ill just to get paid sick leave, leaving the office early without anybody noticing when you are on an hourly rate, scrolling social media in the office during your hourly rate, charging personal-use items on an expense account, or practicing wasteful spending when you are managing workplace or government funds).

---

[128] https://restavekfreedom.org/2018/09/11/the-history-of-slavery/

[129] https://www.theladders.com/career-advice/housekeepers-steal-from-guests

## Theft by the government?

Theft need not be initiated by an individual or an organization and need not be conducted in stealth mode. It can also occur openly by society or the government. *Science* magazine reported,

*Indigenous people in the United States have lost nearly 99% of the land they historically occupied, according to an unprecedented new data set.*[130]

PBS noted,

> *From 1877 to 1934, under a range of laws and reneged-upon treaties, the U.S. government appropriated tens of millions of acres of Native American land.*[131]

*Aeon* stated,

> *Between 1776 and the present, the United States seized some 1.5 billion acres from North America's native peoples, an area 25 times the size of the United Kingdom.*[132]

**Reflection**

Can you identify acts of theft in part 1?

## Harming

Harming is intentionally inflicting physical or psychological injury or damage on a sentient being. Harm could cause pain, suffering, changes in health, or loss of life. Inflicting harm need not be physical. Harm can involve using threats of physical violence, tolerating dangers to the safety and well-being of individuals, or inflicting mental harm. Harm can also occur without intention. Suppose you were driving tired after being awake

---

[130] https://www.science.org/content/article/native-tribes-have-lost-99-their-land-united-states

[131] https://www.pbs.org/newshour/show/why-native-americans-are-buying-back-land-that-was-stolen-from-them

[132] https://aeon.co/essays/how-were-1-5-billion-acres-of-land-so-rapidly-stolen

all night, and you had an accident and killed someone. You did not have the intention to kill them. But you did. Your association, in this case, is the extent to which you were aware of the possible consequences and that you tolerated them. Could you have predicted some implications of your action? Did you believe it was more likely (even if still a slight chance) that you could have killed someone by driving tired? If so, then the moral issue is letting yourself (and tolerating the fact) that you could have a higher chance of killing someone while driving tired, and you still did.

## Intentional harming without physical contact

Harming need not be physical. Intentional infliction of emotional distress is a form of deliberate harm that can be pursued in court even if there is no bodily injury. Harming can also occur through defamation or bullying. And with technological advances, many other forms of mental harm are being pursued. The *Independent* published the article "Woman Reveals 'Nightmare' of Being 'Gang Raped' in Virtual Reality."[133]

## Physical harm under duress and coercion

Duress and coercion are deliberate acts that induce deception, harming, or stealing. If a person succumbs to harm under coercion because they have no other choice, it is still an act of harm. As we discussed, one of the drafts of the Declaration of Independence noted the following about the slave trade: *"captivating and carrying them into slavery in another hemisphere or to incur miserable death in their transportation thither."*

Restavek Freedom further reports,

> *The journey from Africa to the Americas was a horror that many did not survive. The ships were tightly packed, low on food, and without proper sanitation. This led to a rapid spread in fatal diseases such as dysentery, fever, and smallpox, killing both the Africans and the ship's crew. Death was commonplace on the slave trade, and when a man or woman passed away, their bodies were simply tossed into the ocean. This was an addi-*

[133] https://www.independent.co.uk/news/uk/home-news/metaverse-gang-rape-virtual-world-b2005959.html

*tional point of shock for the Africans, as they believed that death and burial should be handled with care and honor. Depending on the origin and final destination of the slave ship, this journey could take anywhere from three weeks to several months. Records estimate that between 10 and 20 million Africans were brought to the Americas in this inhumane fashion, although many were cast into the ocean along the way, a tragedy too horrifying to wrap your mind around.*[134]

**Reflection**

Can you identify acts of harm that were either intentional or resulted from the environment in part 1?

## Societal norms and the legal system

### Can I rely on societal norms for setting moral standards? No!

There are several reasons for this: first, societal norms may induce unethical acts; and further, society itself does not agree on the norms.

### 1. Societal norms can induce stealing, harming, and deception

As we discussed, societal norms supported slavery and stealing land from Native Americans. Society did not abolish slavery even with the Declaration of Independence, and these norms are not unique to that situation or that era.

*The Romans believed in physical bravery and its manifestation in combat as a cardinal virtue. And simultaneously they believed that persons of no status, particularly persons who had done something wrong, deserved physical punishment. The Roman arena was used to punish miscreants. Criminals were exposed to the beasts. It catered to an instinct in human nature that is attracted by the suffering and bloodletting of others. And this is certainly an element that is deployed in the modern entertainment media.*[135]

---

[134] https://restavekfreedom.org/2018/09/11/the-history-of-slavery/

[135] https://www.nytimes.com/2001/07/07/arts/q-a-they-too-enjoyed-watching-violence-and-death.html

The Museum of London and the Natural History Museum reported about a joint project examining skulls and human remains that were deposited between AD 120 and AD 160. The skulls show *"evidence of blunt force trauma in the facial area and on the side of their heads around the time of their death."* Further, *"skulls suggest Romans in London enjoyed human blood sports."*[136]

The Colosseum.org also mentions,

> *Contrary to popular belief, gladiator fights didn't cease because of the Empire's move towards Christianity. Rather, cost was the determining factor. The Colosseum was in a state of decay by the 5th century, the Roman Empire was in steep decline, and the resources needed to maintain the building, pay for gladiators, and provide wild animals were hard to come by.*[137]

## 2. Society itself might not agree on the norms

Society is widely split about the appropriate norms on numerous issues. A dramatic exhibition of societal disagreement about norms was exhibited when *Roe v. Wade* was overturned. The Pew Research Center reported,

> *Among the public overall, there is a modest gender divide in views of whether abortion should be legal: 58% of men and 63% of women say it should be legal in at least most cases. Within both parties, the views of men and women are largely aligned. Among Democrats, 80% of both men and women say abortion should be legal in all or most cases. Similarly, 36% of Republican men and 39% of Republican women say the same.*[138]

And on issues of border security and increasing security along the US-Mexico border to reduce illegal crossings, there are also differences in views across political and social parties. Pew reported that *nearly all Republicans and Republican-leaning independents say border security should be an important goal of US immigration policy. In contrast, a smaller majority of Democrats and Democratic leaners say the same.*[139]

---

[136] https://www.nhm.ac.uk/discover/news/2014/january/skulls-suggest-romans-london-enjoyed-human-blood-sports.html
[137] https://www.thecolosseum.org/facts/#were-gladiators-slaves
[138] https://www.pewresearch.org/fact-tank/2022/06/13/about-six-in-ten-americans-say-abortion-should-be-legal-in-all-or-most-cases-2/
[139] https://www.pewresearch.org/fact-tank/2022/09/08/republicans-and-democrats-have-different-top-priorities-for-u-s-immigration-policy/

And society may be divided by race. History revealed the results of polls: *"[A] majority of African Americans believed [O. J.] Simpson to be innocent of the crime, while white America was confident of his guilt."* The jury—composed of *"nine African Americans, two whites, and one Hispanic American"*—*"took just four hours of deliberation to reach the verdict of not guilty."*[140]

## Can we rely on the legal system for setting moral standards? No!

Unfortunately not! There are many reasons why the legal system cannot be the moral standard.

**First, the legal system has limited resources.** The courts and prisons are packed. Therefore, the legal system cannot attend to every incident of deception, harming, or stealing even if it wants to. If the legal system does not attend to an act, it does not mean it is not unethical. It simply means the legal system has no code for it at the current time.

**Second, the legal system is expensive.** The inability to afford an attorney is a deterrent for some individuals to pursue their claims in the legal system, even if there is an established legal violation. And this expense enables wealthy individuals and organizations to engage in unethical acts, relying on the fact that individuals could be deterred from pursuing remedies because of the cost of the legal system.

**Third, most civil pursuits will result in arbitration.** Arbitrators are incentivized to favor large organizations for repeat business, and organizations often befriend the arbitrator to gain a legal advantage. Therefore, a judgment by an arbitrator can be biased in favor of organizations. The *Washington Post* reported, *"Employees were awarded money in just 1.6 percent of arbitration cases in 2020."*[141]

**Fourth, the legal system is subject to lobbying from powerful individuals and corporations.** The International Court of Justice provides immunity for heads of state during their time in power. This includes genocide and crimes against humanity. And even after their time in power, the legal

[140] https://www.history.com/this-day-in-history/o-j-simpson-acquitted
[141] https://www.washingtonpost.com/business/2021/10/27/mandatory-arbitration-family-dollar/

system also allows pardoning for those with political connections. History reported about the Watergate scandal:

> *Nixon—the center of the whole scandal—received no punishment at all. He resigned on August 8, 1974 to evade impeachment. One month later, his former vice president, Gerald Ford, pardoned Nixon so that he'd never have to stand trial for his crimes, which were supported by evidence Nixon recorded himself.*[142]

And on an organizational level, Enron, Theranos, VW, and many other powerful organizations lobbied for regulation in their favor.

**Fifth, the legal system has statutes of limitations**, a time frame after which an act can no longer be pursued and has no legal consequences. For example, criminal violations of antibribery provisions must be enforced within five years (18 U.S.C. § 3282). While such actions may no longer be deemed unlawful after the statutes of limitations expire, they remain unethical. This incentivizes organizations to delay the processing or acknowledgment of errors until statutes expire. In contrast, the ethical system does not have such statutes.

**Sixth, the legal system has different standards, and it can get it wrong:** Civil cases are determined by the concept of "preponderance of evidence," which implies that it is more likely than not that one thing occurred over another, while criminal cases require a more stringent threshold of "beyond a reasonable doubt." This means a less-rigorous assertion of facts would determine civil cases than criminal ones. And even with the "beyond reasonable doubt" threshold, there are numerous cases of individuals who have been victims of criminal codes within the legal system and have spent years in jail before a DNA test, other evidence, or technology proves their innocence. The *New York Times* reported on November 17, 2021, "2 Men Convicted of Killing Malcolm X Will Be Exonerated after Decades."[143]

The article further noted, *"Their exoneration represents a remarkable acknowledgment of grave errors made in a case of towering importance."*

---

[142] https://www.history.com/news/watergate-nixon-john-dean-tapes
[143] https://www.nytimes.com/2021/11/17/nyregion/malcolm-x-killing-exonerated.html

And cases where the legal system failed continue. The Equal Justice Initiative reported the following on December 7, 2021:

> *2,500+ Exonerations since 1989 in the National Registry of Exonerations, 367 People exonerated through DNA evidence since 1989. Each exonerated person spent on average more than 8 years 10 months in prison for crimes they did not commit. Only 1.5% of prosecutor's offices in the U.S. have conviction integrity units.*[144]

**Seventh, the legal system is asymmetric toward stakeholders.** For example, the legal system allows the entrapment and deception of citizens by a federal agency, such as the FBI, but does not allow the same toward the FBI. The Innocence Project reported the following about police interrogations:

1. *It is almost always legal for police to lie during interrogations.*
2. *False confessions are a leading cause of wrongful conviction in the U.S.*
3. *Minors are particularly vulnerable to deceptive police tactics.*
4. *Police deception is currently allowed in every state.*[145]

In contrast, it is illegal to lie to an FBI agent "knowingly and willingly" (18 U.S.C. § 1001), but it is okay by the legal system if an FBI agent "knowingly and willingly" lies to you. On November 4, 2021, the *Washington Post* published the article "Igor Danchenko Arrested, Charged with Lying to FBI about Information in Steele Dossier."[146] Politico reported, "Fortenberry Indictment Raises Questions about the FBI's Tactics."[147]

**Eighth, the legal system changes with time and location.** Ethics does not. Deception, harming, and stealing do not change with time. Wikipedia reports about Claudette Colvin, an American pioneer of the 1950s civil

---

[144] https://eji.org/issues/wrongful-convictions/
[145] https://innocenceproject.org/police-deception-lying-interrogations-youth-teenagers/
[146] https://www.washingtonpost.com/national-security/steele-dossier-arrest-danchenko-trump-durham/2021/11/04/7e76b9ae-3d77-11ec-8ee9-4f14a26749d1_story.html
[147] https://www.politico.com/news/2021/12/12/fortenberry-indictment-524107

rights movement who was arrested at the age of fifteen for refusing to give up her seat to a white woman in a crowded bus.[148] And while this incident occurred nine months before the more widely known incident involving Rosa Parks, Colvin's case was not picked up or accredited by civil rights campaigners at the time because she was an unmarried pregnant woman. Rosa Parks stated, *"If the white press got ahold of that information, they would have [had] a field day. They'd call her a bad girl, and her case wouldn't have a chance."* These arguments for dropping her case would not apply today.

Possessing small amounts of marijuana for personal use was once deemed illegal in all states. Now this activity is legal in many states, and marijuana is sold in dispensaries around the nation. Licensed dispensaries were deemed essential businesses that did not shut down during the Covid-19 pandemic. Yet many individuals have already spent time in jail for possession of marijuana.

**Ninth, even judges within the legal system have different views on the legality of an act.** The statistics of US Supreme Court nominations by US presidents illustrate that political parties attempt to gain a legal advantage by nominating Supreme Court judges of their party. Further, the overturning of *Roe v. Wade* has shown us that not only was the country split about the views of the Supreme Court, but so was the Supreme Court itself with a 5–4 vote on the issue.

Further, numerous individuals have since called for a US Supreme Court code of ethics, asking the highest legal authority to abide by an ethical code. The *Washington Post* reported,

> *Reggie Walton calls for a Supreme Court code of ethics.*[149]

And Reuters reported an article titled "Federal Judge Takes Rare Step of Backing U.S. Supreme Court Ethics Code."[150]

And besides the split on the *Roe v. Wade* issue, another split Supreme Court

148 https://en.wikipedia.org/wiki/Claudette_Colvin
149 https://www.washingtonpost.com/dc-md-va/2022/05/28/reggie-walton-supreme-court-ethics/
150 https://www.reuters.com/legal/legalindustry/federal-judge-takes-rare-step-backing-us-supreme-court-ethics-code-2022-05-26/

decision occurred with lifting Title 42, which would allow the government to take emergency action and return asylum seekers if they posed a health threat of spreading Covid. The *LA Times* wrote,

> *Court refuses to lift Title 42. By a 5–4 vote.*[151]

Even with cases below the Supreme Court level, the legal system continues to be perceived as favoring the political party that appointed the judge. CNN reported, *"A federal judge has struck down President Joe Biden's student loan forgiveness program, declaring it illegal."*[152] The article highlighted that then President Donald Trump nominated the judge.

**Tenth, the legal system takes time to catch up, and it may struggle to anticipate and comprehend the effects of technology**. *Roll Call* reported, *"The U.S. is woefully behind the rest of the world in enacting universal, comprehensive data privacy laws that protect consumers. A messy patchwork of disjointed and woefully outdated laws leaves Americans vulnerable to attacks on their private data."*[153] *USA Today* released the article "A Woman Said She Was 'Raped' in the Metaverse. When Will It Matter?"[154]

## The need to create legal and ethical distinctions for decision-making

How can we reason about ethical issues if we cannot rely on the legal system or societal norms? Regarding ethical awareness, it will be important to identify four regions based on legal-ethical distinctions. As you read through this section, identify instances in part 1 that belong to each region.

---

151 https://www.latimes.com/politics/story/2022-12-27/supreme-court-refuses-to-lift-trump-era-rule-at-the-southern-border

152 https://www.cnn.com/2022/11/10/politics/biden-student-loan-forgiveness-struck-down

153 https://www.rollcall.com/2021/10/14/us-must-catch-up-with-rest-of-the-world-on-data-privacy/

154 https://www.usatoday.com/story/life/health-wellness/2022/02/22/raped-online-womans-metaverse-abuse-controversy-debate/6815695001/?gnt-cfr=1

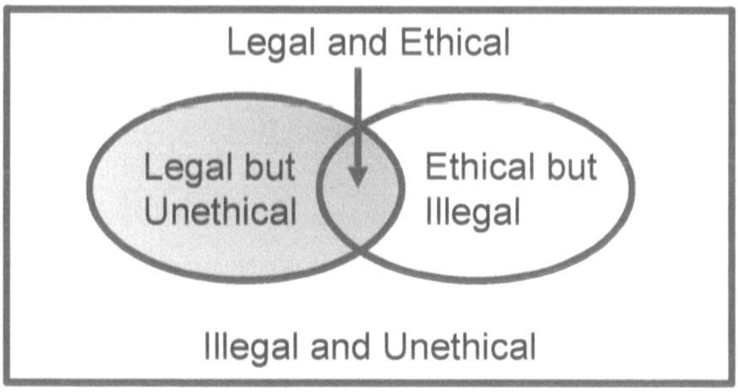


## Region 1: "Illegal, but ethical"
## Illegal acts that do not involve deception, harming, or stealing

Are there things that are illegal even if they do not involve deception, harming, or stealing? Yes. The *LA Times* reported, *"In 1938, L.A. woman went to jail for wearing slacks in courtroom."*[155] The article explained how Hulick arrived at the courthouse in downtown Los Angeles to testify against burglary suspects. Instead, she was faced with a courtroom conversation about her wearing slacks. The judge rescheduled her testimony so she could come back in a dress. She returned to court five days later in slacks.

The infuriated judge said, *"The court has to maintain what it considers orderly conduct,"* and ordered her to return the next day in "accepted dress." The judge warned her that if she insisted on wearing slacks, she had to be prepared to be punished for contempt of court. The next day, Hulick arrived in slacks, was held in contempt, and given a five-day sentence to jail. Her act was regarded as a violation of the legal system represented by the court. This action led to hundreds of letters and protests until the judge's contempt was overturned. She was free to come back to court wearing slacks. The *Times* reported, *"A couple of months later, Hulick returned to court. Her point made, this time she wore a dress."*

## Region 2: "Legally unethical"
## Legal actions involving deception, harming, or stealing

People are more willing to engage in unethical acts if perceived as legal than illegal. Legally unethical actions are therefore abundant and also vary

[155] https://www.latimes.com/local/california/la-me-california-retrospective-20141023-story.html

in severity. Some of them include deceptive self-promotion, schmoozing with leadership to get benefits at the expense of others, and exploiting peoples' vulnerability and cognitive biases to your advantage.

Some legally unethical instances can cause mental harm and anguish. Cheating on your wife, husband, boyfriend, girlfriend, or partner is a legally unethical act. Having a secret child without telling your partner is also a legally unethical act. Other examples of legally unethical actions involving deception abide. Frank Sinatra's publicist, George Evans, auditioned girls in Sinatra's early performances to find those who could sing the loudest. He then paid them $5 each to sit at strategic locations in the audience to scream, pretend to faint, and whip up excitement upon the appearance of Sinatra.[156]

How about deception when a person pretending to be a sign language interpreter crashes a press conference about recent killings in Seminole Heights, Florida, and shows up on national television when she does not even know sign language and was certainly not an interpreter in the first place?

> *It's a bizarre situation: Derlyn Roberts is the woman who pretended to interpret the news conference. Police say she can't be charged with anything because what happened is not a crime—it's an ethical violation.*[157]

## Region 3: "Legally ethical" Legal and ethical acts

The legal and ethical domain is a coveted spot that includes donating to a charity or a good cause, philanthropy, and deducting the donation you made from your income while filing your taxes. Examples of individual and organizational legally ethical acts with different levels abide. CNN published the article "A Pennsylvania Waitress Was Shocked When She Received a $3,000 Tip."[158] The tip was added to a $13.25 bill. In another case, the *Washington Post* wrote that *a McDonald's franchise owner paid his employees for months while*

[156] https://www.pbs.org/newshour/nation/8-things-you-didnt-know-about-frank-sinatra
[157] https://www.wcpo.com/news/national/fake-sign-language-interpreter-behavior
[158] https://www.cnn.com/2022/07/24/us/scranton-pennsylvania-waitress-huge-tip-trnd/index.html

*the store was shut down due to renovations.*[159] CNBC reported that *Bill Gates was donating $20 billion to the Bill & Melinda Gates Foundation and was reiterating his pledge to give away virtually all his wealth to the foundation.*[160]

## Region 4: Illegal and unethical acts

Illegal and unethical acts are abundant on individual, organizational, and government levels. These acts include criminal offenses like fraud or murder, giving a bribe for college admissions, a gynecologist assaulting women, laundering campaign funds, etc. It is easier to oppose illegal and unethical acts within an organization than it is to oppose legally unethical acts. The moment the organizational structure learns it is unlawful, there will be less backing for the act out of fear of the legal repercussions regardless of their view of the ethical component.

**Reflection**

- Should the outcome of litigation about whether an act was legal or illegal necessarily determine whether the act was ethical or unethical?
- Refer back to part 1 and identify actions that are legally unethical and illegally unethical.
- Think of jobs that may tolerate/encourage deception, harming, or stealing. If you were to work for one of these jobs, would you be comfortable with the ethical conduct?

## Can we rely on compliance with corporate policies for setting the moral standard? No!

## Corporate ethics vs. compliance

If we cannot rely on the legal system or societal norms for ethical standards, can we rely on compliance with corporate policies within an organization

159 https://www.washingtonpost.com/lifestyle/2022/07/11/tony-philiou-mcdonalds-renovation-payroll/
160 https://www.cnbc.com/2022/07/15/bill-gates-plans-to-give-away-virtually-all-his-113-billion-fortune.html

for setting the moral standard? Unfortunately, there is a big difference between ethics and compliance. The two concepts are widely misused and need to be clarified. Compliance is a set of policies scribed by the organization that may contain unethical clauses or is silent about clauses to give the organization a legal advantage in case of a dispute.

## Unethically compliant? Compliance with a coercive mindset to enable deception, harming, or stealing

Compliance policies might even be set deliberately to coerce individuals into doing acts that enable unethical actions from leadership.

> *Mr. Weinstein enforced a code of silence; employees of the Weinstein Company have contracts saying they will not criticize it or its leaders in a way that could harm its "business reputation" or "any employee's personal reputation."*[161]

Once you sign a contract like this, you are compliant with company regulations, and the likelihood that you will oppose an unethical act when you see it becomes much smaller. We shall refer to such instances as being "*unethically compliant.*" The following is the script between Ian Gibbons, Theranos scientist, and Theranos's internal legal team from *The Dropout* when he received notice of a deposition:

> *Ian: I can't sleep. I can't think. I need to know what to do. I'm going to have to testify at some point. And then when I do, if I violate the nondisclosure agreement, then Theranos will sue me.*
>
> *Legal: That's not necessarily true.*
>
> *Ian: Oh, you will. You'll sue me, and you'll win.*[162]

Gibbons ultimately committed suicide. Many organizations have what they refer to as "ethics officers," who are, in effect, compliance officers that enforce company policies. But if the policies themselves are unethical, so too are the policies that are enforced. Quite often, compliance officers are

---

[161] Jody Kantor, "Harvey Weinstein Paid Off Sexual Harassment Accusers for Decades," *New York Times*, October 5, 2017, https://www.nytimes.com/2017/10/05/us/harvey-weinstein-harassment-allegations.html.

[162] https://tvshowtranscripts.ourboard.org/viewtopic.php?f=1262&t=51828

under the influence of the legal department and do not have much power to change policies even if they deemed them unethical.

**Reflection**

- How would you describe the level of awareness about acts of deception, harming, or stealing in your organization?
- How would you describe the level of awareness about what is ethical versus legal in your organization?
- How would you describe the level of awareness about what is ethics versus compliance in your organization?

# Chapter 9

# Motives

*Everyone here is running a game.*
*Everyone here is hustling.*
*Everyone here wants something.*
*Money, power, image, love.*

—Neff (Anna's hotel concierge friend), from the Netflix series *Inventing Anna*[163]

## We all have motives

The word "motive" comes from the Latin word *motivus*, meaning "moving." *Merriam-Webster* defines "motive" as "*something (such as an intention, need, or desire) that causes a person to act*." We all have motives about some aspects of our lives. Some motives are well-intentioned. Others are not. When making a decision that impacts other stakeholders, understanding the motives driving your decision is an essential aspect of ethical decision quality.

An individual might have personal motives, such as getting an education, losing weight, getting a job, having an income, managing sleep, engaging in sports, acquiring wealth or property, and working in public or social service. We also have motives related to the workplace. *Forbes* magazine cited these five common motives at work: **achievement**, **power, affiliation, security,** and **adventure.**[164] **Figure 2.1 shows a** tag cloud (courtesy of Ahoona Corp) compiled from a list of objectives that motivate individuals ages twenty to twenty-four when pursuing a new job.

---

[163] https://thescriptlab.com/wp-content/uploads/scripts/8932-Inventing-Anna-101.pdf

[164] https://www.forbes.com/sites/markmurphy/2018/07/29/what-motivates-you-at-work/?sh=6a218a35c1f9

**Figure 2.1.** *Tag cloud of objectives of individuals ages twenty to twenty-four when pursuing a new job*

Individuals also have **social motives** like the need for self-esteem and the desire to gain social status, social approval, and self-actualization. And individuals might also have motives for community and societal service. Four common motives for community involvement are (1) **egoism**, the ultimate goal of which is to benefit oneself; (2) **altruism**, to benefit other(s); (3) **collectivism**, to increase the benefits for a group; and (4) **principlism/moralism**, to sustain moral principles (Batson et al. 2002).[165]

## Being motivated by money is not unethical!

Being motivated by money is not unethical. It is the actions that some people do in pursuit of money that may cause them to act unethically. You can be motivated by money to become the world's largest philanthropist. Examples include Bill Gates and Warren Buffett. Even Mother Teresa would have preferred more money to less. Suppose that some philanthropist would have approached Mother Teresa and asked her to choose between a donation of $10 million or $100 million. Which deal do you think she would have chosen? Most likely, she would have picked the $100 million. Why? Is it because she was obsessed with worldly possessions? Probably not.

[165] https://www.researchgate.net/publication/227541135_Four_Motives_for_Community_Involvement

But she would have still preferred the $100 million because she could have helped more people with that amount.

### Not having motives is not a good thing!

If we did not have motives, then we would be less inclined to act on things that could benefit humanity. You might have the motive to cure cancer or Alzheimer's disease, so you dedicate your life to finding the cure. You might have the motive to eliminate poverty and take actions that include acquiring significant wealth to become the world's largest philanthropist. And even if you have a motive, such as acquiring another person's property, there could be many ethical ways to achieve that motive. One action might be to openly discuss the sale of the property and agree on a price and then "*give him an offer he can't refuse*."

## What is the issue with motives in relation to ethical decision-making?

### 1. Getting caught up in achieving your motives can cloud judgment

Focusing solely on achieving some motives or incentives can cloud judgment. For example, you might have the motive to show improvement, increase your company's stock price, meet specific sales numbers of diesel vehicles or bank accounts, or make money trading on electricity markets. These motives do not need to include acts of deception, harming, or stealing. But in pursuit of these motives, individuals may "do whatever it takes" to get the job done. In so doing, their judgment can be clouded, and this situation is often referred to as being "*blinded by their own ambition*."

The *WSJ* released the article "When Meeting Targets Becomes the Strategy, the CEO Is on the Wrong Path."[166] This statement is true from not only a prudential standpoint but also an ethical standpoint. What amounts of deception, harming, or stealing are you willing to tolerate to meet the targets?

---

[166] https://www.wsj.com/articles/SB111024383366673014

Think of the incentives of a real estate agent who receives a 3 percent commission on a sales transaction or nothing if they do not sell your house. This incentive can lead the agents to try to convince you to lower the selling price so that they get some return on their effort, even if it means you lose a significant amount of funds by selling at a lower price.

The legal team can also get caught up in achieving their motives and "doing whatever it takes" to win a lawsuit. The *New York Times* reported,

> *The Times publicly fired Mr. Boies' firm, which had been representing the newspaper, after learning that he had been personally involved in an undercover operation to smear Mr. Weinstein's victims and deceive Times reporters.*[167]

And when you are motivated by being elected or reelected for a political position, you might offer special favors to heavy donors or push for regulation to favor their interests and harm other stakeholders along the way. In thinking about achieving your motives, it is helpful to ask what harm to other stakeholders (if any) you are willing to tolerate. By itself, this question might provide room for some reflection on the actions you take to achieve your motives.

### Reflection

- Identify situations in part 1 where individuals engaged in deception, harming, or stealing to pursue their motives. Identify situations where politicians may have influenced regulation in favor of some stakeholders for personal motives.
- Think of actions resulting from the incentives of a project manager contracted to supervise a project and who receives a payment based on an agreed-upon percentage of the project cost: the "cost-plus" principle. The higher the cost of the raw materials purchased, the higher their commission.

---

[167] https://www.nytimes.com/2018/09/21/business/david-boies-pleads-not-guilty.html

### 2. Motives can amplify certain biases that impact decision-making

A motivational bias demonstrates the tendency of individuals to conduct certain acts to favor desirable outcomes or to achieve certain motives. The desire to see a family member placed in a job can lead to actions like bribing a government official or giving kickbacks or favors to an agency that hires the family member.

Funding bias, also known as "sponsorship bias," is an example of a motivational bias that shows the tendency of a research study to favor the interests and desires of the study's financial sponsor. With this bias, there becomes an uncertainty about whether researchers reported the truth or the whole story. Wikipedia reports the following:

> *A 1996 study on the effects of nicotine on cognitive performance revealed that findings of nicotine or smoking improving performance were more likely to be published by scientists who acknowledged tobacco industry support.*

### 3. Negative motives can lead directly to unethical acts

Sometimes the motives themselves lead directly to unethical acts. Examples include the motive to harm someone, smear them, manipulate them, or rise above another person at any cost. We refer to these motives as "negative motives." Retaliation and revenge are negative motives that may result in unethical acts like murder and may even be misguided for falsely believing an individual caused damage.

A motive to retaliate may result in harm.

> *A female student has been stabbed to death outside her university for allegedly refusing a marriage proposal from a fellow student. Naira Ashraf was attacked by a man as she stepped off a bus outside Mansoura University in Mansoura, central Egypt, on Monday morning. The attack took place in front of horrified onlookers who attempted to pull the man off of Naira and in full view of security cameras. Naira was pronounced dead at the scene after suffering several wounds to the neck, local media has reported.*[168]

---

[168] https://metro.co.uk/2022/06/22/egypt-student-stabbed-to-death-after-refusing-marriage-proposal-16875466/

It is prudent to avoid negative motives because they can lead to negative actions. Mahatma Gandhi once said,

> *A man is but the product of his thoughts; what he thinks, he becomes.*

In pursuing negative motives, an individual might even believe they are doing the right thing under manipulation by others or by their rationalization. Humans can rationalize unethical acts. But Proverbs 16:2 (New American Standard Bible) says,

> *All the ways of a person are clean in his own sight, But the LORD examines the motives.*

## 4. Other people's motives can cloud your judgment

Even if you are clear about your motives, other individuals you interact with, such as manipulators, can influence your decisions. Leadership in an organization or a political entity might hint at what decisions they would like and influence/coerce your decision-making. Understanding the motives of others helps you become aware of (and more sensitive to) the acts and their influences. An individual you interact with might dislike another individual and want to hurt them because he feels job insecurity or that is the only way to get a promotion. That individual might continually fabricate allegations and explain how bad the other individual is so you can team up with them or support their motives. As a consequence, you might even engage in unethical acts and rationalize them to yourself by the fact that you are doing a just cause. Understanding the motives of that individual can help you become more sensitive to the situation at hand.

Network for Business Sustainability reported about the motives of manipulators:

> *Overwhelmingly, these employees are driven by self interest. For example, they manipulate others for their own personal gain, fail to see the connection between their actions and outcomes, and believe that ethical choices are driven by circumstance. They obey authority figures' unethical directives and act merely to avoid punishment.*[169]

---

[169] https://www.nbs.net/articles/3-reasons-employees-act-unethically

## 5. Conflicting motives impact decision-making

When your motives conflict with the interest of other stakeholders and you are making decisions on their behalf, there is potential for acts of deception, harming, or stealing. This issue has existed for centuries.

In September 1787, Dr. Benjamin Franklin said about the Constitution,

> *I doubt whether any other convention we can obtain may be able to make a better Constitution . . . for when you assemble a number of men to have the advantage of their joint wisdom, you inevitably assemble with those men all their prejudices, their passions, their errors of opinion, their local interests, and their selfish views. From such an assembly can a perfect production be expected?*

Many times, individuals involved might have special interests that impact the quality of decisions. And sometimes organizations themselves place incentives that lead to conflicting objectives. Enron's Andrew Fastow and the trades made provided an example of conflicting motives and interests—interests that need not have been in the interest of other stakeholders.

## 6. Hidden (ulterior) motives impede ethical decision quality

Knowing individuals' motives (or their hidden agendas or interests) will make their actions more predictable and can alert you to unethical acts before they occur. In some cases, individuals hide their motives for intentional deception or fraud. One way of doing this is to pretend that they have no interest in something by giving a false image that they already have it. The *Daily Mail* reported about Anna Delvey, who tried to get a $20 million loan without credentials: "It's Easier to Ask for $20 Million When People Assume You Have It."[170]

In other cases, some individuals hide their motives, believing that revealing motives or intentions obstructs their chances of achieving their goals: it "jinxes" them. Organizations might also want to hide their motives to gain a competitive advantage. It is not unethical to hide your motives unless there is deception about the contract being signed or if there is harming or stealing.

---

[170] https://www.dailymail.co.uk/news/article-10617817/Fake-heiress-Anna-Sorokin-reveals-effortlessly-conned-New-Yorks-high-society.html

## Understanding your motives and the motives of others: *Mais c'est difficile*

When you face a decision, you should ask yourself, "What are my motives?" Take the time to be clear about your motives. By itself, understanding your motives can help improve the ethical quality of your decisions. If you are making a decision involving others or if others are involved in the decision-making, you should also be clear about the motives of others influencing your decision. Are the motives of other individuals driving the decision-making in a direction that suits their purpose at the expense of others? Are they pushing you in a direction you would otherwise not have done? Does a member of the decision-making team have hidden motives? Hidden biases? Hidden agendas? Understanding the motives of the different stakeholders will improve ethical decision quality.

Unfortunately, it is not always simple to determine other people's hidden motives. For one, people might not be aware of their motives or the implications of their actions in pursuit of. In other cases, people intentionally hide their motives. Nevertheless, observing peoples' actions might help you infer their motives, but this is not straightforward. Actions could be attributed to different motives.

Knowing motives helps predict actions and increase awareness of unethical acts. But knowing actions is not necessarily an indicator of motives. By observing a sequence of actions over some time, however, inferring motives becomes more feasible.

## Examples of hidden motives?

Sometimes identifying incentives or benefits can help reveal hidden motives. In the following examples, think about possible hidden motives that may have contributed to the acts. Think about who benefited from this and the level of trust once this information is revealed.

### Previous recommendations about alcohol consumption are false!

Recent studies have contradicted the widely held notion that a glass of wine a day is good for your heart. WebMD reported,

*The widely held notion that consuming small to moderate amounts of alcohol is good for cardiovascular health is not supported by the data, the World Heart Federation (WHF) says in a new policy brief. In fact, the evidence is clear that any level of drinking can contribute to loss of a healthy life, the organization says.*[171]

## Should your credit score decrease if you pay off your mortgage?

A year ago, my credit score was 850. I had a monthly mortgage payment that I was making. One day, I decided to pay off the mortgage to save on the interest I was paying. I thought that paying off my mortgage would no doubt increase my credit score (or at the least keep it the same) because I could now afford more things. About two months later, my credit score dropped to 815 and then to 795, and then it jumped back to 815 without anything else happening in my financial situation. I was puzzled. I ran a score report through a company, which gave the following two explanations:

1. *Lack of recent installment loan information: Your credit report shows no recent non-mortgage loans or sufficient recent information about your loans. Having a loan along other types of credit demonstrates that you are able to manage a variety of credit types.*

2. Two few accounts currently paid as agreed: Your score considers the number of accounts where you are paying your bill as agreed. *In your case, this number is too low because you have very few accounts* or because you've missed payments recently on some of your accounts.

The report allows you to click on each point to get advice on what to do about it to increase the score. Here are the recommendations.

- To remedy point 1, the algorithm suggests you take out a loan. It also notes that "while that may lower credit score on the short term for the credit check, it will increase it in the long term."

- To remedy point 2, the algorithm recommends taking out a few more credit cards.

---

[171] https://www.webmd.com/heart-disease/news/20220125/no-amount-alcohol-safe-heart-whf

Can you think of any hidden motives or stakeholders benefiting from this credit score algorithm?

## Hidden motives influencing decisions?

Examples of hidden motives or motivational biases impacting decisions are prevalent. The *LA Times* reported that a surgery conducted on a patient in Los Angeles was unnecessary and that the physician who ordered the surgery was on the payroll of the device manufacturer.[172]

## Hidden motives of managers?

Some managers at work can also have motives, such as keeping their jobs, winning a popularity contest, or making their bosses happy. In achieving these motives, managers might "do whatever it takes" or "follow the strongest wind direction" while harming others. In so doing, they might engage in (or tolerate) acts of deception, harming, or stealing toward others. New managers might have a hidden motive to show improvement at any cost and blame others.

The following dialogue from the Netflix documentary *Inventing Anna* between a journalist and her manager exemplifies a manager's motives to keep his job and blame someone else:

> *Vivian Kent: You wanna set the record straight, you explain how you f— —ed up and threw me under the bus, and left my reputation with this stink on it so you could save yourself.*
>
> *Paul: I never meant to ever . . .*
>
> *Vivian Kent: You did mean to. We were friends, Paul. I believed in you. You made a choice to hurt me for your own personal gain. You are not innocent.*[173]

---

[172] https://www.latimes.com/business/story/2023-03-07/harbor-medical-surgery-medtronic

[173] https://tvshowtranscripts.ourboard.org/viewtopic.php?f=1240&t=51155

**Reflection**

- Identify hidden possible motives of various individuals in part 1 that were not revealed to stakeholders.
- Take a moment to consider the motives (and possible hidden motives) of the following:
  - o Internal legal counsel
  - o Outside legal counsel
  - o Engineering department
  - o Marketing department
  - o Employees close to retirement
  - o Management consultants
  - o Arbitrators

## Actions inconsistent with stated motives

While observing a few actions might not necessarily reveal hidden motives, it is easier to spot actions inconsistent with stated motives. And this can draw your attention to inconsistencies in their statements and to other acts. For example, Enron stated they value integrity; yet judging by their actions, it is easy to assert that management did not really value integrity.

## Can Freudian slips reveal hidden thoughts or motives?

A Freudian slip is an unintentional error that may reveal subconscious feelings or desires and can therefore reveal hidden past, present, or future motives. The error may result from unconscious desires or thoughts and can be expressed while speaking (a slip of the tongue) or by misreading or mishearing things that may support an internal desire or train of thought.

The UK's Great Britain (GB) News published the article "George W Bush Makes 'Freudian Slip of Century' after Mixing Up Ukraine and Iraq in

'Brutal Invasion' Speech":

> *It came as he referred to the "wholly unjustified and brutal" invasion of Iraq, when he intended to be talking about Putin's invasion of Ukraine. Discussing the military assault, he said: "The result is an absence of checks and balances in Russia, and the decision of one man to launch a wholly unjustified and brutal invasion of Iraq."*[174]

The article revealed these reactions online:

> *"GeorgeWBush didn't do a Freudian slip. He did a Freudian Confession," tweeted US actor John Fugelsang.*
>
> *Another user wrote: "Holy smokes GeorgeWBush with an all-time Freudian slip."*
>
> *Andrew Stroehlein from Human Rights Watch tweeted: "Freudian slip of the century . . ."*

**Reflection**

How would you rate the effects of motives and motivational biases on your organization's ethical decision-making?

---

[174] https://www.gbnews.uk/news/george-w-bush-makes-freudian-slip-of-century-after-mixing-up-ukraine-and-iraq-in-brutal-invasion-speech/298403

# Chapter 10

# Environment

*[W]hen you assemble a number of men*
*to have the advantage of their joint wisdom,*
*you inevitably assemble with those men*
*all their prejudices, their passions, their errors of opinion,*
*their local interests, and their selfish views.*

—Dr. Benjamin Franklin

## Effects of the environment on ethical decision-making

The surrounding environment you operate in can significantly impact the quality of decisions you make. Have you ever seen people act differently in a social setting than when they operate on an individual level? Yes, of course! If the surrounding environment encourages, allows, or induces unethical acts, then it is highly likely that your actions or the actions of others will be influenced by it. A well-known human bias known as the "conformity bias" revolves around the tendency of individuals to modify their behavior in a way that makes them better fit into the environment surrounding them. The environment can involve high-ranking politicians or celebrities or individuals with personal interests and can induce attempts to cover-up unethical acts due to possible embarrassment, exchange of favors, and reliance on the strength of the environmental support. The surrounding environment might also entail coercion, threats, and deception and can encourage rationalizations that impede ethical decision quality. It takes more than ethics training, compliance, or value statements to maintain ethical decision quality in the workplace if the surrounding environment impedes ethical decision-making.

## The environment influences people's actions. Ask John Travolta

The following script from the classic movie *Grease* illustrates the effects of the environment on behavior even in high school. Danny Zuko (John Travolta) and Sandy (Olivia Newton-John) met during the summer and fell in love, as described by the song "Summer Nights." Sandy was heading back to Australia. Danny and his "guy" friends, a gang of boys who call themselves the T-Birds, are back in school when one of the Pink Ladies (a group of female students in the same school) named Rizzo approaches Danny:

*Rizzo: Hey, Zuko, I got a surprise for you.*

*Danny: Oh yeah?*

*Rizzo: Yeah.*

*(Danny sees Sandy and is thrilled and excited to see her.)*

*Danny: Sandy!*

*Sandy: Danny?*

*Danny: What are you doing here? I thought you were going back to Australia.*

*Sandy: We had a change of plan.*

*Danny (very excited and about to say "I can't believe it"): I can't . . .*

One of the T-Birds comes up, astonished, confused, and dismayed that Danny is so excited to see Sandy. Danny suddenly changes his tone when he realizes that his friends (the T-Birds) are watching and have noticed his excitement.

*Danny: That's cool, baby. I mean, you know how it is, rockin' and rollin' and whatnot.*

*Sandy: Danny?*

*Danny: That's my name. Don't wear it out.*

*Sandy: What's the matter with you?*

*Danny: What's the matter with me? Baby, what's the matter with you?*

*(T-Bird boys are laughing and so proud of Danny.)*

*Sandy: What happened to the Danny Zuko I met at the beach?*

*Danny: Well, I do not know. Maybe there's two of us. Why don't you take out a missing person's ad? Or try the yellow pages. I don't know.*

*Sandy: You're a fake and a phony, and I wish I never laid eyes on you.*

*(Sandy leaves while Danny appears troubled and upset by what he has just done.)*

## Environments offering incentives with unintended consequences

Sometimes an individual might operate in a stressful environment that makes them do things they otherwise would not have done due to the stress and insecurity of the work environment. For example, environments demanding impossible sales targets can impact ethical decision-making if there is a sense that the targets will not be achieved. And sometimes incentives can have unintended consequences that affect the ethical quality of decisions. Examples include offering incentives for pharmaceutical companies.

### Reflection

- Think of an environment you surround yourself with that has influenced your decisions. The setting could include friends, family, colleagues in the workplace, or political figures. What decisions would you have done otherwise?

- Identify environments that played a role in the ethical quality of decisions in part 1.

- Recall our definition of unethical acts of deception, harming, or stealing also includes acts you coerce or tolerate. The operating environment created or tolerated by an organization is an element of ethical decision quality.

## "Jumping on the bandwagon" environments

Jumping on the bandwagon is a social phenomenon and a bias. Individuals alter their beliefs and actions to join a popular theme or movement because others are doing it, to gain approval or look good, or have a fear of missing out. It is often referred to as "herd mentality." The direction of the bandwagon (the decision(s) made) is usually not questioned. What is more important to individuals is whether or not they are on the bandwagon.

The bandwagon effect appears in many organizational environments and numerous aspects of our daily lives. It can lead people to rush to purchase items like real estate or a particular stock, leading to a bubble in housing prices or the stock price.

**Reflection**

Can you identify instances of the bandwagon effect in part 1? Could the numerous people who endorsed Holmes and Theranos have been subjected to a bandwagon effect? Could the numerous people who got LASIK surgery instead of buying glasses when Enron's Skilling got LASIK surgery have been subjected to a bandwagon effect?

## "Obedience to authority" environments

The following two well-known psychology experiments illustrate the effects of obedience to authority on ethical decision-making and on tolerating deception and harm to others.

### 1. Milgram experiments: "Obedience to authority" environments

The Milgram experiment(s) were a series of psychology experiments by Stanley Milgram at Yale University.[175] The experiments aimed to study the level of obedience of individuals to authority if the demands made by authoritative figures included exposing another individual's life to danger.

[175] Stanley Milgram, "Behavioral Study of Obedience," *Journal of Abnormal and Social Psychology* 67, no. 4 (1963): 371–378.

The experiment entailed a subject who was led to believe that they were administering an electric shock to a "learner" if they did not correctly learn a sequence of words. The subject was told to administer an electric voltage shock to the learner each time he gave a wrong answer. The experimenter instructed the subject to start from fifteen volts and to increase the shock level one step each time the learner provided a wrong answer. The "simulated shock generator" had thirty marked levels, ranging from 15 volts to 450 volts. The shock generator had designations *"that range from Slight Shock to Danger: Severe Shock."* The learner who was part of the experiment pretended to suffer from the effects of a severe electric shock as the subject administered the shock. The experiment observed the subjects' reactions as they continued to follow instructions from the experimenter.

**Reflection**

Can you identify instances of deception in this experiment? How many parties engaged in the deception?

## Subjects were told instructors had no clear guidelines

According to the article, subjects were told clearly that the experimenters did not know how much voltage should be administered. They knew *"very little about the effect of punishment on learning because almost no truly scientific studies have been made of it in human beings. For instance, we don't know how much punishment is best for learning."*

## Results of the experiment

The experiment demonstrated that the subjects indeed followed orders from authoritative figures and were willing to administer electric shocks of high magnitude even when knowing the instructors had little idea about the amount of shock needed for learning.

> *Of the 40 subjects, 26 obeyed the orders of the experimenter all the way to the end and proceeded to punish the victim until they reached the most potent shock available on the shock generator (450 volts).*

Further, some subjects did not go all the way, but only after they believed they had administered the shocks.

> *Of the 40 subjects, five refused to obey the experimental commands beyond the 300-volt level, four more subjects administered one further shock at 315 volts and then refused to go on, two broke off at the 330-volt level, and one each at 345, 360, and 375 volts. Thus, a total of 14 subjects eventually defied the experimenter, but after they had conducted a 300-volt punishment level.*

**Reflection**

- Can you identify "obedience to authority" environments in part 1 that led to harming or tolerating harm to individuals?
- Can you identify instances where obedience to authority led to hideous crimes?

### 2. Conforming to social roles: Zimbardo's Stanford prison experiment[176]

Philip Zimbardo's Stanford prison experiment investigated how quickly individuals can change their behavior and conform to social expectations that induce harm to others. The experiments were conducted in the basement of the psychology building at Stanford University in 1971. The experiments investigated the behavioral effects of becoming a prison guard on an individual's ability to inflict harm. The doors of the labs were changed to resemble prison cell doors. Students were recruited to participate in the experiment and were assigned randomly to be either a prisoner or a guard. All students knew that this was an experiment, that the participants were all students, and that they would return to their everyday lives after the experiment.

At the beginning of the experiment, "psychological tactics" were implemented, as noted in Zimbardo's paper:

[176] https://www.prisonexp.org/

*Each prisoner was systematically searched and stripped naked. He was then deloused with a spray to convey our belief that he may have germs or lice.*

## "Do whatever is necessary to get the job done" environments

*The guards were given no specific training on how to be guards. Instead, they were free, within limits, to do whatever they thought was necessary to maintain law and order in the prison and to command the respect of the prisoners.*

At 2:30 a.m. on the first night, the guards entered the prison cells and woke up the prisoners by blasting whistles. Then they asked them to do push-ups.

*At first, the prisoners were not completely into their roles and did not take the counts too seriously. They were still trying to assert their independence. The guards, too, were feeling out their new roles and were not yet sure how to assert authority over their prisoners.*

A rebellion among the prisoners started. So the guards broke into each cell, stripped the prisoners naked, took the beds out, forced the rebellion's ringleaders into solitary confinement, and began to harass and intimidate the prisoners.

## Command and conquer by deceptive tactics

The guards then used deceptive tactics to break up the "resistance." They set up a "privilege cell" and placed the three individuals least involved in the rebellion within it. The three prisoners were given their uniforms and beds back and were allowed to wash and brush their teeth. Shortly after, command and conquer tactics were implemented.

*[T]he guards then took some of these "good" prisoners and put them into the "bad" cells and took some of the "bad" prisoners and put them into the "good" cell, thoroughly confusing all the prisoners.*

This tactic created distrust among the prisoners and solidarity among the guards.

*Some of the prisoners who were the ringleaders now thought that the prisoners from the privileged cell must be informers, and suddenly, the prisoners became distrustful of each other. The prisoners' rebellion also played an important role in producing greater solidarity among the guards.*

**Reflection**

What rationalizations do you believe the guards rationalized to themselves regarding their behavior toward the prisoners and the tactics used?

## Transformation into an "us vs. them" environment

The tactics soon led to an "us vs. them" environment.

*Guards saw the prisoners as troublemakers who were out to get them, who might really cause them some harm. In response to this threat, the guards began stepping up their control, surveillance, and aggression.*

## Escalation of commitment: Deception extends to deceiving parents

When parents and friends of the prisoners came to check in on them, the guards

*manipulated both the situation and the visitors by making the prison environment seem pleasant and benign.*

Prisoners were washed, shaved, and groomed; had their cells cleaned; and fed dinner. Music was played on the intercom, and a former Stanford cheerleader greeted the visitors.

**Reflection**

Can you identify elements of deception and harm in the experiment so far?

## Escalation and getting caught up in motives

One of the prisoners felt sick and had to leave. Rumor spread that there would be a break-in at the prison to free the prisoners. Zimbardo was sitting anxiously, waiting for the intruders to break in, when a colleague who had heard about the experiment came to see what was happening. Zimbardo recalled his colleague asking,

> *Say, what's the independent variable in this study?*

Zimbardo recalled,

> *To my surprise, I got really angry at him. Here I had a prison break on my hands. The security of my men and the stability of my prison was at stake, and now, I had to deal with this bleeding-heart, liberal, academic, effete dingdong who was concerned about the independent variable! It wasn't until much later that I realized how far into my prison role I was at that point—that I was thinking like a prison superintendent rather than a research psychologist.*

The experiment came to an end.

Several articles have since been published about the Stanford prison experiment in media and scientific outlets, discussing its ethical implications and how it escalated into many ethical lapses.[177] For example, the experiment continued even after prisoners expressed their desire to withdraw. Zimbardo acknowledged that he had no idea beforehand that it would escalate to the point that it did.

## Thirty-four years later: Environments that induce/tolerate harm, deception, and theft

When the acts of Abu Ghraib prison in Iraq surfaced, there was a notable similarity with Zimbardo's prison experiment. Zimbardo was quoted as saying,

> *I argue that we all have the capacity for love and evil—to be Mother Theresa,*

---

[177] https://www.nytimes.com/1973/04/08/archives/a-pirandellian-prison-the-mind-is-a-formidable-jailer.html; https://www.newsweek.com/stanford-prison-experiment-age-justice-reform-359247

*to be Hitler or Saddam Hussein. It's the situation that brings that out.*[178]

Zimbardo became involved with the defense team of lawyers representing one of the Abu Ghraib prison guards.

## Coercive environments

Coercive environments pressure individuals to do something using force or threat. In terms of ethical decision-making, coercive environments can pressure outcome-predetermined analysis or pressure individuals to make decisions that support leadership ideas. Coercive environments are also abundant in politics, where donors may pressure political figures to legislate in their favor, or in organizations, where coercion can come from major donors or clients.

## Don Corleone: The godfather "I'm gonna make him an offer he can't refuse"

An example of a coercive environment was portrayed by Don Corleone (Marlon Brando) in the movie *The Godfather*. Don Corleone's Godson Johnny Fontane asked for his help to secure a role in a movie with the executive of a studio. Corleone made the statement "This Hollywood big shot is going to give you what you want,"

> *"I'm gonna make him an offer he can't refuse"*

suggesting that he will give the studio head such a generous offer of cash that he couldn't refuse the request. In fact, Corleone arranged for the severed head of the studio executive's most valuable horse to be in the executive's bed when he woke up. The offer was a threat that if the executive did not give his Godson the role, he would be killed. The executive later gave the role to Johnny Fontane.

Coercive environments are enabled by organizational actions using policies that make individuals afraid to speak up out of fear of losing their job or upsetting powerful stakeholders. Coercive environments usually use tactics that limit free speech.

---

[178] https://en.wikipedia.org/wiki/Stanford_prison_experiment

## "Us vs. them" environments and increased polarization

"Us vs. them" environments within an organization or between internal and external stakeholders of an organization occur when two sides are in effect rivals because of conflicting objectives. For example, a marketing department might want to release a product early to gain market share. In contrast, an engineering department might want to delay the launch to ensure the majority of bugs are fixed. This situation can quickly escalate even though the individuals work for the same company. Once the "us vs. them" environment is established, individuals do not resort to reason but rather to win the "battle." It is no longer about being right—it is about winning.

Many biases, including confirmation bias, contribute to each side not listening to the other side's point of view. Other biases, including escalation, make individuals blindly support their group, ignoring transgressions by their group members.

"Us vs. them" environments also appear frequently in sports. The *Daily Mail* wrote about how MRI scans reveal that football fans use a different part of their brain when watching their team play:

> *Football fans are a passionate bunch and scientists now understand why rival fans can never agree. An ancient region of their brain, which has survived for thousands of years, is activated when fans watch their favourite team play. This tribal reaction then takes control of the brain and often clouds reasonable judgment, with fans being unable to avoid seeing the game in a biased way.*[179]

And of course, "us vs. them" environments also appear in politics, where groups support their political party, highlight other parties' faults, and close an eye on transgressions within their own. Social media provides compelling examples of how individuals do not listen to the faults of their own party.

[179] https://www.dailymail.co.uk/sciencetech/article-6239649/Brain-scans-reveal-football-fans-access-tribal-brain.html

## "Exchange of favors" environments

Exchanging favors is not necessarily unethical, especially if the favors do not impinge on another person's rights. For example, you might mow your neighbor's lawn one week; and in return, the neighbor mows your lawn the week after or brings you apple pie instead. This exchange of favors does not involve actions of harming, stealing, or deception. The issue with an exchange of favors is when one (or both) parties expect some return favors that involve unethical acts.

## Don Corleone: The Godfather (again)

An example of how the exchange of favors can build up was also portrayed by Don Corleone in *The Godfather*. When Amerigo Bonasera pleads with him to take revenge on two men who had assaulted Amerigo's daughter, Don Corleone agrees and says,

> *Someday, and that day may never come, I will call upon you to do a service for me.*
>
> *But until that day, accept this justice as a gift on my daughter's wedding day.*

**Reflection**

Think of the acts Amerigo might be willing to do if the Godfather came to him asking for a favor. While situations like this exist in real life, the exchange of favors we encounter more frequently usually involves quid pro quo, covering up ethical violations or endorsing legislation that may favor significant donors.[180]

## "It's all in the family" environments: Welcome to the social club

"It's all in the family" environment adds a social club aspect to the "exchange of favors" environment, where some stakeholders (members of the social club) gain certain privileges that impinge on the rights of others

---

[180] https://www.latimes.com/entertainment-arts/business/story/2022-11-02/paramount-cbs-moonves-pay-million-ny-ag-settlement

and close their eyes on transgressions within members of the social club. Some people spend much time and effort building relations to become part of the social club. Once you are in, you gain special privileges. The social club can be part of the administration and the leadership team. Social clubs might even extend to socializing with royal figures.

## Environments with high-ranking politicians and celebrities

Environments that include associations with high-ranking political figures or celebrities can add a false sense of security and increased tolerance to unethical acts by individuals who believe they can get away with it or who are embarrassed to acknowledge errors to the esteemed board members. Examples include Theranos and Enron Corporation whose political connections may have enabled the escalation of ethical violations to fraud.

Jeffrey Epstein, who pleaded guilty to soliciting prostitution and procurement of minors in 2007, maintained a large and elite social circle that included presidents, royalty, and Hollywood stars after pleading guilty.

## "Do or say whatever is necessary to get the job done" environments

Some environments coerce (or even expect) you to do whatever is necessary, including deception, harm, stealing, fudging the numbers, or giving a pretense of a culture change to get the job done. These environments induce individuals to achieve a goal (usually short-term) at any cost and to act unethically to keep their job even if they do not necessarily agree with the unethical act. The following classic script from *Miss Congeniality*, where Gracie Hart (Sandra Bullock) is an FBI agent who goes undercover to prevent the bombing of a beauty contest event, sheds a humorous example of contestants in a beauty pageant being asked what they believe society needs most:[181]

> *Stan Fields: What is the one most important thing our society needs?*

> *Contestants reply sequentially:*

---

[181] *Miss Congeniality*, directed by Donald Petrie, performances by Sandra Bullock, Michael Caine, Benjamin Bratt, and Candice Bergen, Chapter Eleven

*World peace!*

*World peace!*

*That's an easy one. World peace!*

*World peace!*

*Stan Fields [to Gracie Hart]: What is the most important thing our society needs?*

*Gracie Hart: That would be harsher punishment for parole violators, Stan.*

*[Crowd is silent. Gracie Hart looks stressed and feels she needs to change her answer.]*

*Gracie Hart: And world peace!*

*[Crowd cheers.]*

*Stan Fields: Thank you, Gracie Lou.*

*Gracie Hart: And thank you, Stan.*

*[Gracie walks offstage.]*

*Victor Melling: That was charming. Are you drunk?*

*Gracie Hart: I'm glad you enjoyed it. Now if you'll excuse me, I have to go unscrew my smile!*

## "Desperate to show improvement" environments

As the saying goes, "Desperate people do desperate things." "Desperate to show improvement" environments relate to individuals operating in despair and doing whatever it takes to show improvement. My colleague Marriane Jennings's book *The Seven Signs of Ethical Collapse* presents the first sign of ethical collapse as "pressure to maintain those numbers," recognizing that individuals under pressure engage in unethical acts that impinge on the rights of others. Maintaining numbers is an important aspect of showing improvement and leads to subsequent escalations and collapses, as was exhibited with Enron. It also occurred with Wells Fargo and the urgent need to show new bank accounts being opened.

Pressure to show improvement can be something other than financial. Individuals may be pressured to show a culture change following an ethical collapse. So they do whatever it takes to achieve that objective, including covering up mistakes at all costs.

**Reflection**

- Identify other environments within an organization that may impact ethical decision-making.

How would you rate the effects of the environment on ethical decision-making in your organization?

# Chapter 11

## Information

*My colleagues, every statement I make today*
*is backed up by sources, solid sources.*
*These are not assertions.*
*What we're giving you are facts*
*and conclusions based on solid intelligence.*

—General Colin Powell,
United Nations address on weapons of mass destruction in Iraq[182]

**Figure 2.2.** *General Colin Powell's address to the United Nations*

[182] https://www.theguardian.com/us-news/2021/oct/18/colin-powell-un-security-council-iraq

## The need to incorporate relevant information and capture uncertainty

Information is an essential element of ethical decision quality. You can be ethically aware and have good motives but still choose unethical acts because of false, inaccurate, or withheld information or a lack of understanding about the implications of a decision. Subject matter experts may provide relevant information, expert assessments and domain knowledge, as well as the relevant uncertainties about the ethical implications and possible outcomes. A common source of error when making ethical decisions is failing to incorporate uncertainty into the analysis.

Observing the information element of ethical decision quality requires knowledge of numerous items, including the following:

1. Incorporating the relevant information, uncertainties, and unintended consequences into the analysis of the decision.

2. The credibility of the information source is appropriately incorporated into the decision, considering the accuracy and repeatability of information sources, motives of individuals, withheld information, contradictory evidence, and any misinformation.

3. New information is incorporated into the analysis using a sound method.

4. Information is gathered without coercion or outcome-predetermined analysis.

5. The effects of cognitive biases that may distort information have been considered.

6. Ethics of handling confidential information have been considered.

7. Recognizing that calculations of common good, benefit, or harm need to include uncertainty, and that decision analysis methods can be used for their calculation.

## Recognizing the need to incorporate uncertainty

Is it essential to incorporate uncertainty into the analysis when making ethical decisions? Most likely there will be aspects of the decision that you are uncertain about. As Dr. Benjamin Franklin said,

> *[I]n this world, nothing is certain except death and taxes.*

Most decisions we face will involve uncertainty. This could be the result of acts of nature such as a meteor, or uncertainty about the amount of harm or benefit that may follow an act, or uncertainty about the truthfulness of the information we have at the time of making a decision.

## False information exists

False information exists and can have drastic effects on ethical decision quality and peoples' livelihoods. Colin Powell's address to the United Nations (UN) about weapons of mass destruction in Iraq (figure 2.2) involved false information that led to decisions with drastic effects. There are many reasons why the information available may be inaccurate or false. This includes blatant lies and intentional deception, memory effects, information obtained by coercion to yield false confessions or predetermined findings, distortion due to cognitive biases, fake news, propaganda and misinformation, accuracy and resolution of detectors or information sources, and untested interventions (such as the performance of new vaccines or medication in the event of a new disease or pandemic).

In part 1, we discussed numerous examples of deception and false information that escalated to fraud. Examples include advocating clean diesel vehicles that did not exist, promoting a blood tester that uses only a few drops of blood and whose technology did not exist, or failing to disclose relations with a company that bears financial risk. Other examples of false information include spreading fake news to win an election or to gain popularity.

This section presents numerous examples of false information and its consequences, as well as the need to assign probability and to assess the credibility of the information source.

## False accusations

Equal Justice Initiative reported on December 7, 2021,

> *More than half of wrongful convictions can be traced to witnesses who lied in court or made false accusations.*[183]

And this can happen on an organizational level as well. NPR noted,

> *Hertz will pay $168 million to customers it falsely accused of stealing its cars. Faulty recordkeeping and failure to rescind police reports led to more than 360 false accusations by the rental car company, resulting in arrests, felony charges, and jail time for some customers.*[184]

## Promoting and coercing predetermined findings and confessions

False information can also arise by coercing others into predetermined findings, particularly if the motivated individuals do not want to make the false allegations themselves. First, we ask the following question: "Can individuals be coerced into saying things that are not true?"

The answer is yes. Absolutely! Not only can they be coerced into saying things that are not true about others to support predetermined findings, but they can also be coerced into saying false and damaging allegations about themselves. Coercing predetermined findings is frequent, and it affects ethical decision quality.

## Coercion in investigation and police department tactics

Numerous articles have been written about physical and psychological coercion in the interrogation methods of US police departments from the late nineteenth century to the present. However, there has been a marked transition from more physical to more psychological and deceptive

---

[183] https://eji.org/issues/wrongful-convictions/

[184] https://www.npr.org/2022/12/06/1140998674/hertz-false-accusation-stealing-cars-settlement#:~:text=Press-,Hertz%20will%20pay%20%24168%20million%20to%20customers%20it%20falsely%20accused,jail%20time%20for%20some%20customers.

methods in recent years.[185] Individuals can also be coerced into making false confessions about themselves. A false confession is a statement of guilt made under duress or coercion.

> *False confessions are the leading cause of wrongful convictions in homicide cases. More than two-thirds of the DNA-cleared homicide cases documented by the Innocence Project were caused by false confessions.*[186]

**Coercion, deception, and predetermined findings in investigations**

The Netflix documentary series *The Confession Tapes* investigates cases where people convicted of murder claim their confessions were coerced.[187] Examples include the following:

- *After his girlfriend is found murdered, a man insists he was coerced into confessing. Years later, DNA evidence tells the truth.*[188]

- *Following a gruesome triple murder, two teens are targeted by undercover police, who use a controversial technique to try to extract a confession.*[189]

- *After the 1994 murder of both his parents and his sister, Atif Rafay and friend Sebastian Burns become suspects. The Royal Canadian Mounted Police use the controversial Mr. Big interrogation technique to extract confessions from the suspected killers. The court refuses to allow the defense to present evidence that the murders may have been conducted by the religious extremist group Jamaat ul-Fuqra, and both are thereafter found guilty and sentenced to life in prison.*[190]

The Mr. Big coercion technique, used by police departments in some countries, is an example of deception in police investigations. Within this technique, the police form a fictitious criminal organization and entice suspects into joining it.[191] They solicit the suspects' help in criminal acts, pay them,

---

[185] https://academic.oup.com/chicago-scholarship-online/book/35805/chapter-abstract/308812976?redirectedFrom=fulltext
[186] https://falseconfessions.org/fact-sheet/#:~:text=False%20confessions%20make%20for%20the,exonerations%20in%20the%20United%20States.
[187] https://www.netflix.com/title/80161702
[188] https://www.netflix.com/title/80161702
[189] https://www.imdb.com/title/tt7351868/
[190] https://www.wikiwand.com/en/The_Confession_Tapes
[191] https://en.wikipedia.org/wiki/Mr._Big_(police_procedure)

and gain their trust. After engaging in criminal acts, the suspect is coerced into revealing their past information. This technique is now prohibited in the United Kingdom, Germany, and the United States.

A recent FBI Whistleblower testimony revealed,

> *"FBI leadership pressured agents to reclassify cases as domestic violent extremism (DVE), and even manufactured DVE cases where they may not otherwise exist, while manipulating its case categorization system to create the perception that DVE is organically rising around the country."*[192]

Allegations about coercion in investigations are not restricted to law enforcement. A whistleblower who is also a licensed attorney and senior investigator within the University of Southern California (USC)'s investigative offices filed a federal lawsuit alleging the following:

> *USC uses corrupt practices in workplace investigations, such as promoting and/or coercing predetermined findings.*

Coercive methods generally include intimidation, having no documented procedures, demanding no recording during the process, demanding no communication with anybody, misquoting suspect statements, ignoring inconsistencies in witness statements, not verifying allegations, and withholding information or documentation that supports the suspect or that contradicts the findings. Ignoring this information often results in wrongful convictions.

## False information due to deliberate distortion of testimony

History reported about Nixon's conversation with John Dean before Dean's testimony in Watergate.[193] Nixon called Dean into his office in the Executive Office Building to try to make sure that Dean didn't implicate him in his testimony.

> *You know when I told you we could get a million dollars [to continue to pay the convicted burglars to remain silent] I was just kidding?" Nixon*

---

[192] https://judiciary.house.gov/sites/evo-subsites/republicans-judiciary.house.gov/files/evo-media-document/2023-05-17-fbi-whistleblower-testimony-highlights-government-abuse-misallocation-of-resources-and-retaliation-sm.pdf

[193] https://www.history.com/news/watergate-nixon-john-dean-tapes

*awkwardly asked at that April 15 meeting. Dean said he hadn't thought that but he'd take his word.*

## Uncertainty due to demand characteristics in psychology experiments

Demand characteristics are subtle clues observed in psychology experiments that enable participants to form interpretations of what the experimenter would like to find or how they should behave. Participants then change their behavior and responses to fit that interpretation. Demand characteristics can influence the outcome of an experiment, research findings, or the results of an investigation.

## Uncertainty due to the misinformation effect

The misinformation effect occurs when a person's recollection of past events is altered because of post-event information or misinformation that is provided to them. Some studies have attributed the misinformation effect to the idea that the original information and misleading information have been blended after the fact.[194] Other studies argue that misleading information overwrites the initial information,[195] while other studies argue that the misleading information is more recent, so it is more easily retrieved.[196] Quite frequently, individuals forget the actual events, particularly when there are long time lapses or if they hear the misinformation several times. The *Washington Post* reported,

> *[T]he more we see something repeated, the more likely we are to believe it to be true. This "illusory truth effect" arises because we use familiarity and ease of understanding as a shorthand for truth: the more something is repeated, the more familiar and fluent it feels whether it is misinformation or fact.*[197]

---

[194] Dana Challies, "Whatever Gave You That Idea? False Memories Following Equivalence Training: A Behavioral Account of the Misinformation Effect," *Journal of the Experimental Analysis of Behavior* 96, no. 3 (2011): 343–362, doi:10.1901/jeab.2011.96-343. PMC 3213001. PMID 22084495.

[195] Ben Davis, "What Is an Example of the Misinformation Effect?"

[196] Han Yuhwa, "The Misinformation Effect and the Type of Misinformation: Objects and the Temporal Structure of an Episode," *American Journal of Psychology* 130, no. 4 (2017): 467–476.

[197] https://www.washingtonpost.com/wellness/2022/11/03/misinformation-brain-beliefs/

The Association of Workplace Investigators noted,

> *Whether or not misinformation exposure permanently impairs the original memory, it is evident that witnesses can report misinformation that is suggested to them.*[198]

## Uncertainty due to reflecting self-image in testimony

Sometimes individuals' testimonies may reflect their personal and motivational biases. A case study of John Dean's testimony to Congress against Nixon in the Watergate scandal compared his testimony with the actual transcripts of the tapes that were later revealed.[199] The study found that his recollections boosted his self-image within the testimony.

> *Comparison of his [John Dean's] testimony with the actual transcripts shows systemic distortion at one level of analysis combined with basic accuracy at another. Many of the distortions reflected Dean's own self-image; he tended to recall his role as more central than it really was. Moreover, his memory for even the "gist" of conversations was quite poor except where that gist had been rehearsed in advance or frequently repeated.*

## Uncertainty due to errors in judgment

CNN reported that after twenty-five years of wrongful imprisonment, two Georgia men were set free after newly uncovered evidence exonerated them of murder charges.

> *"Despite the circumstances, which strongly indicated that Bowling accidentally shot himself in the head, at the urging of Bowling's family members, police later began investigating the death as a homicide," according to a motion filed by Clark's attorneys, requesting a new trial. The two teenagers were sentenced to life in prison after being convicted of murder and conspiracy to commit murder following a weeklong trial in 1998.*[200]

---

[198] "The Memory Conundrum: How Social Conditions and Misinformation Affect Eyewitness Memory," *AWI Journal* 10, no. 1 (May 2019).

[199] Ulric Neisser, "John Dean's Memory: A Case Study," *Cognition* 9, no. 1 (1981).

[200] https://www.cnn.com/2022/12/10/us/georgia-men-exonerated-wrongful-imprisonment/index.html

## Uncertainty due to accuracy of information sources or testers

Sometimes there is uncertainty about the accuracy of information because a detector might have low resolution (e.g., you might have X-ray results that are not as clear as an MRI). Alternatively, you might have information regarding a new situation that has not previously been encountered (such as the efficacy of a drug or a vaccine in light of a new pandemic), but sufficient test results are not yet available. Information might also have been gleaned from scientific research that is not reproducible, or there was misrepresentation about the accuracy of a test, as was the case of syphilis tests with Theranos testers. All these factors are examples of why there is a need to incorporate uncertainty into reasoning about information from detectors when making ethical decisions.

## Accuracy of information due to cognitive biases

Humans are subject to numerous cognitive biases that distort information. Examples of such biases include anchoring, confirmation bias, cognitive dissonance, and representativeness biases, which will be discussed in the next chapter. Many debiasing techniques have been proposed in the literature, and it is the ethical responsibility of the analyst to work on minimizing the effects of these biases during testimony or elicitation.

## Prior belief about the uncertainties

Having recognized that information may be false or inaccurate or that there are elements of a decision that are out of our control, the next step is to assign a probability to the occurrence of a particular outcome or to the credibility of the information. This is known as assigning a prior probability to the uncertainties. The elicitation of probability from individuals is well studied and applied in practice. See, for example, Abbas et al. (2008), Howard and Abbas (2015), and Spetzler and von Holstein (1975).[201]

[201] A. E. Abbas et al., "A Comparison of Two Probability Encoding Methods: Fixed Probability vs. Fixed Variable Values," *Decision Analysis* 5, no. 4 (2008): 190–202; Howard and Abbas, *Foundations of Decision Analysis*; C. Spetzler and C. Von Holstein, "Probability Encoding in Decision Analysis," *Management Science* 22, no. 3 (1975): 261–389.

## Ethics of gathering information before making a decision

Gathering information can help improve the quality of information and the corresponding decisions. If you have a decision involving uncertainty, such as the impact of a virus or the spread of fake news, you must verify the information before taking it as is. Further, the process used to gather information should be ethical, without misquoting individuals or subjecting them to harm. Clinical trials, a form of information gathering, need to observe specific ethical guidelines, such as the privacy of patients, identifying whether any harm might occur as a result of the trials, and not exposing patients to unnecessary risk. Theranos conducted clinical trials on cancer patients despite knowing the devices were not operational.

Unethical information gathering by the government was manifested in the Tuskegee experiments, which studied the effects of untreated syphilis from 1932 to 1972.[202] The experiment was conducted by the US Public Health Service (USPHS) and the Centers for Disease Control and Prevention (CDC). The Tuskegee experiment was conducted on six hundred participants (399 African Americans with syphilis and 201 who did not have the disease).[203] Participants were not told of the true nature of the experiment and were enticed by free meals and health-care coverage. Syphilis treatments with penicillin were widely available by 1947. Yet the men were not given the treatment and instead left to suffer with the disease so that the center could study its effects on the body when left untreated. The experiment continued for almost four decades. In 1972, a whistleblower leaked it to the press, after which the study was terminated. The direct impacts of this deception were that twenty-eight patients died directly from syphilis, and one hundred others died from complications related to untreated syphilis. In addition, forty of the patients' wives were infected with syphilis, and nineteen children were born with congenital syphilis.

There is also a need to make sure that no information is intentionally unrevealed. "Willful blindness" is a term used to describe a situation in which a person seeks to avoid civil or criminal liability for a wrongful act by deliberately keeping themselves unaware of facts that would render them liable

[202] https://www.cdc.gov/tuskegee/timeline.htm
[203] https://en.wikipedia.org/wiki/Tuskegee_Syphilis_Study

or implicated if they knew them.[204] Examples of willful blindness include intentionally failing to make reasonable inquiries of wrongdoing despite suspicion or awareness of the high probability of its existence.[205] Suppose, for example, you had a tenant in a property you owned; and you suspected that the tenant was growing and dealing with illegal drugs inside your property. You had this suspicion because of what you smelled as you stopped by the property. Failing to make a reasonable inquiry is a tendency to avoid potential problems, but you may still be liable for it.

And sometimes you need to search for hidden information. History reported when Butterfield was asked about tapes in Nixon's office:

> *"I'm sorry you asked," Butterfield responded. "But, yes, there was a taping system that taped all presidential conversations."*
>
> *The tapes were what brought the whole thing down.*[206]

As part of information gathering, scientists are now calling for replicating published results in all forms of scientific research, including biology, physics, and social sciences. This replication will require applying scientific reasoning and math tools to verify research results. Neuroscientist Malcolm Macleod is quoted by the BBC as saying,

> *The issue of replication goes to the heart of the scientific process. . . . Without efforts to reproduce the findings of others, we don't know if the facts out there actually represent what's happening in biology or not.*[207]

## Ethics of updating information: Use appropriate mathematical tools

*Dr. Teddy Oglethorpe (Rob Morgan):*
*"You're just telling a story. Keep it simple. No math."*
*Dr. Randall Mindy (Leonardo DiCaprio): "But it's all math!"*

—*Don't Look Up*, a movie directed by Adam McKay

---

[204] https://en.wikipedia.org/wiki/Willful_blindness
[205] https://www.merriam-webster.com/legal/willful%20blindness
[206] https://www.history.com/news/watergate-nixon-john-dean-tapes
[207] https://www.bbc.com/news/science-environment-39054778

After you have gathered new information, the next step is to incorporate the new information into the decision appropriately. Incorporating new information by relying on intuition alone is not sufficient.

## Why do we need to rely on math tools when updating information?

First, our mental abilities are limited when there is uncertainty. The well-known scenario of *Let's Make a Deal* and the backlash against Marilyn vos Savant's response (even from academics within the field who relied on intuition) is a simple indicator that we need to rely on tools when uncertainty is present. The *Let's Make a Deal* scenario goes like this:

> *Suppose you were a contestant on a game show. You have three doors to choose from. Behind one of the doors is a car, and behind each of the other two is a goat. You get to keep what is behind the door that you choose. You pick a door, say A, but do not see what is behind it.*

## New information: Determines different actions

*The host, who knows where the car is, opens another door, say B, and shows you that there is no car behind it. He then offers you the opportunity to switch to door C. Should you switch?*

The answer is yes; you should switch after seeing the new information. Yet many who have not heard of this game would say they are indifferent. Some would even say they would like to stick to their original decision of door A because it shows confidence in their decision-making (cognitive consistency). But a simple analysis of the decision using basic probability tools tells us that we need to switch once we have received new information that there is no car behind door B. Without relying on the tools and with relying on intuition alone, there was much confusion and debate about this problem.

## Can you rely on intuition and experience when dealing with uncertainty?

Relying on intuition may help if the future is like the past. Think of driving while looking in the rearview mirror. If the road ahead is similar to the one behind you and if there are no crossing pedestrians or animals, it is possible to drive looking in the rearview mirror (although it is not advisable). But when you drive on curved mountain roads like in Malibu, driving while looking in the rearview mirror will almost certainly get you into an accident, if not falling off a cliff.

There is no reason to believe that our intuition will be better regarding ethical decisions under uncertainty than with decisions that do not involve an ethical component. Ethical decisions we face are more complex than the *Let's Make a Deal* scenario, and common heuristics are insufficient. Information updates are also more complicated than showing that door B has no car behind it. Think about the decisions associated with shutdowns during the Covid pandemic, where we were dealing with a new situation with a lot of uncertainty that involved new information about the number of deaths and losses to the economy. Recognizing that our mental abilities are limited when uncertainty is present and that we need to rely on machinery is essential in ethical decision reasoning, particularly when uncertainty is present.

Besides our mental limitations, we also have cognitive limitations in the way we update information. A well-known bias (the confirmation bias) shows that we, as humans, tend to digest the information that supports our hypotheses and put less weight on the ones that counter them.

Benjamin Franklin noted the importance of updating information and acknowledging when you are wrong:

> *I have experienced many instances of being obliged . . . to change opinions even on important subjects, which I once thought right but found to be otherwise . . .*

## Example: Updating information "using math" given evidence of false statements

Consider the following question:

> *Suppose an individual (or an information source) made an allegation. In their testimony, they also make other statements. Later, you discover those statements are false. By how much does the credibility of that person (or information source) drop?*

This is an example of updating information. You have received new information that statements were false. Now you need to update your information about the credibility of that individual or the information source. For example, a news agency may report false incidents, so you would like to update your probability about its credibility. There is a whole branch of probability that deals with this situation. It is referred to as "Bayesian analysis." Let us present an application of Bayesian analysis in its simplest form. Three main things would determine the credibility of an individual after making a false statement:

1. Your prior assessment of the person's credibility before making the statement
2. The likelihood that you believe a credible person would make a false statement
3. The likelihood that you believe a person who is not credible would make a false statement

## Prior belief that they are being truthful

The first assessment includes your prior knowledge about that individual or information source. You can think of all motives they would have to make either a false or a true statement. You can think of their ethical fitness, the surrounding environment, their motives (such as retaliation or job insecurity), and any other factors that affect your belief about the person's credibility. You should also think about your own biases that might affect your judgment. If the information is something you desire, ask yourself if this is impacting your assessment of credibility. Suppose you believed a priori that the person is credible and that there is a 90 percent chance that the information (or allegation) they give will be truthful.

## Second assessment: Accuracy if credible

The second assessment is the probability that if the person were credible, they would make a true or a false statement. There are several reasons why they might report a false statement, even if they are credible (e.g., human error, miscommunication, fatigue, poor recollection of events, impaired memory by misinformation, human biases, or fitness). There are also the effects of the nature of the situation through which they provided the statements. Were they subject to demand characteristics or given cues? Were they in a coercive environment? Suppose you also believe that if a person filing a complaint is credible, there is a 95 percent chance they will give a false statement.

## Third assessment: Accuracy if not credible

The third assessment is the probability that if the person were not credible, they would make a false statement. Again, they might make a true statement because of environmental or human errors. Suppose you also believe that if a person filing a complaint is not credible, there is a 95 percent chance they will give a false allegation.

The left-hand side of figure 2.3 shows the assessments obtained so far.

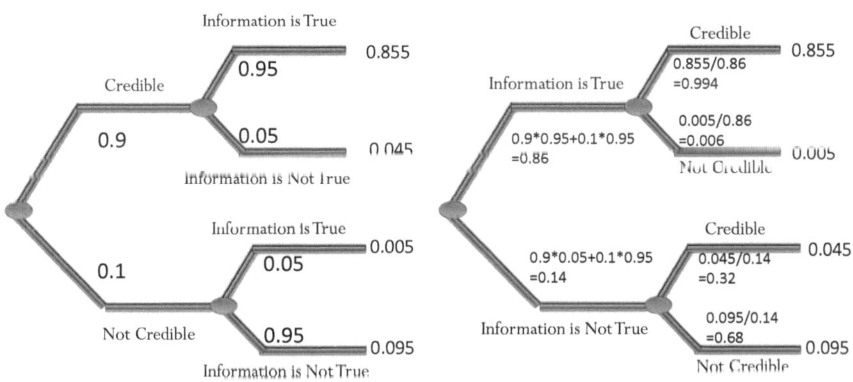


**Figure 2.3.** *Credibility assessments and updating information*

## Credibility after verifying allegation

Now we want to determine the credibility of future statements, given that we have observed that they made either a true or a false allegation.

**Example:**

Suppose you believe a priori that there is a 90 percent chance that a person coming in to file a complaint is *credible* and will give truthful statements.

That means you assign a 10 percent chance that they are *not credible* and will provide false statements. Note that this is actually a high number because you should try to give both sides the benefit of the doubt, but let us use this number for now.

Suppose you also believe that if a person filing a complaint is *credible*, then there is a 95 percent chance they will give a truthful allegation. You allow a 5 percent chance that an allegation is false. You also believe that if the person filing the complaint is *not credible*, there is a 95 percent chance they will give a false allegation.

Now suppose you discover that this person complaining, who you initially believed was 90 percent *credible*, gave one allegation you can prove false. Now what chance should you believe they are *credible*?

> *The answer drops from 0.9 to 0.32. That is, it is more than likely that statements they make will be false (i.e., on average, for every three statements they make, two will be false).*

If the allegation was proven true, what chance should you believe they are *credible*?

> *The answer increases from 0.9 to 0.994. Their credibility has increased but is less than the decrease in the case where their allegation was false.*

**Reflection: Preponderance of evidence**

The concept of "preponderance of evidence" in the legal system suggests that we make a decision based on the determination that the information is more likely to be true than false: if we believe that the information is true with a chance that is higher than 50 percent, then should we assume that it is credible, and we act accordingly. Most individuals who work on the preponderance of evidence, however, do not use probabilistic methods to incorporate or update information; nor do they include the effects of biases in calculating the likelihood.

- How often are mathematical models of updating belief used in court systems to determine "preponderance of evidence" or "beyond reasonable doubt" standards?

- How accurate is human intuition regarding the credibility of information after observing new evidence?
- Can failing to incorporate new information properly result in wrongful convictions?

## Updating information from multiple statements

What if the individual made two statements that you can prove are false? Assume that the chance of each false statement is independently 0.95. The chance that they are *credible* after giving two false statements now drops to 2.3 percent. And if they make three false statements, the probability drops to 1 in 1,000. Figure 2.4 shows the updated credibility after making several false statements. Without relying on mathematical tools, it would be difficult to determine these updated probabilities with this level of precision.

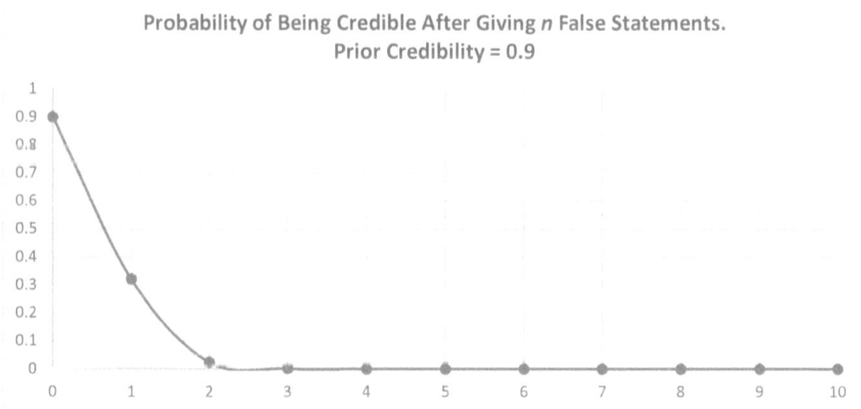


**Figure 2.4.** *Credibility after multiple false statements*

On the other hand, if they make true statements, the credibility does not increase much. If they make one statement that turns out to be true, the probability that they are *credible* increases to 0.994. If they make two correct statements, it becomes 0.9996; for three correct statements, it becomes 0.99998. Figure 2.5 compares the credibility after making multiple true or false statements.

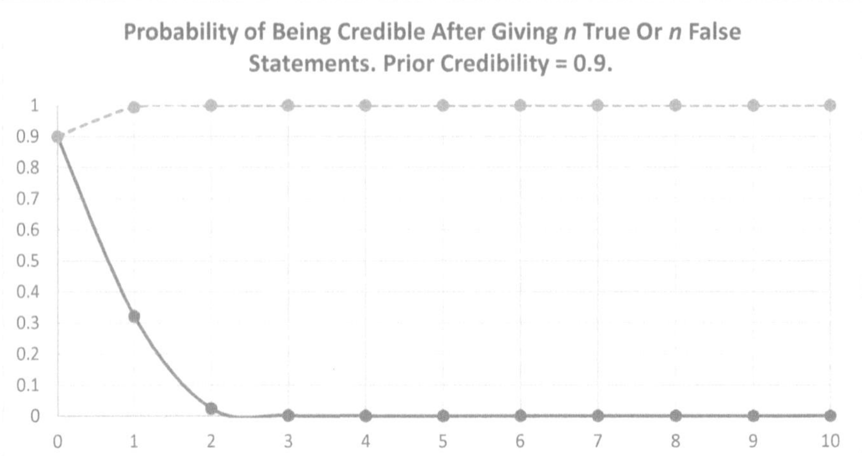


**Figure 2.5.** *Comparing the credibility after multiple true or false statements*

Suppose you had instead started with a 50/50 chance that the person is *credible* (your rationale is that you know nothing about either of them, so you are giving each the benefit of the doubt). Then the curve would be even lower. Figure 2.6 shows credibility after making false statements in this case. After one false statement, the probability of being *credible* would drop to 5 percent; and after three false statements, approximately 1 in 10,000.

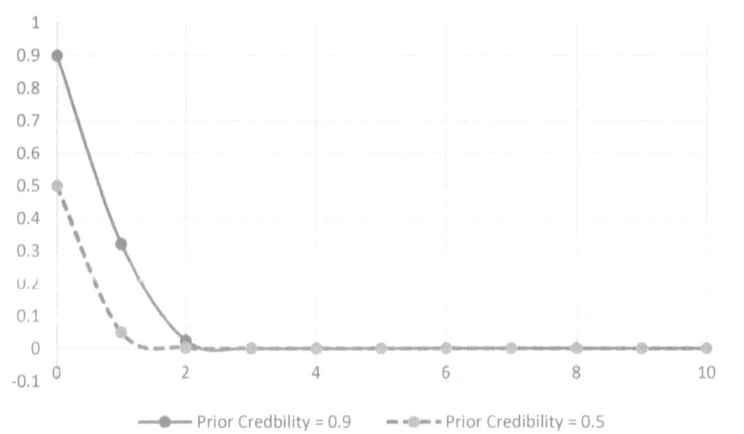


**Figure 2.6.** *Probability of being credible with different prior credibility levels*

**Reflection**

- When you make false allegations, your credibility drops, and it drops very fast. No matter how credible the prior assessment is (0.9 or 0.5), the credibility drops quickly after three false statements.
- The "willful blindness" effect can be significant if you do not validate the statements because it keeps the credibility at 90 percent.
- If you want to frame someone or conduct an outcome-predetermined investigation, you make the information source be perceived of high credibility, and you do not verify any allegations they make. Because if you verify and they are wrong, their credibility drops significantly. However, if you verify that they are correct, their credibility increases only slightly.

## Ethics of incorporating dependence due to witness-collusion

The previous example related to statements from a single decision-maker. What if there are multiple witnesses? How does credibility change? This depends on whether the statements made were from independent witnesses or witnesses who colluded about a narrative. If you ask pedestrians who observed a car accident and had not colluded or had any motivation to fabricate allegations, their testimony can be considered independent. However, even multiple testimonies can be discarded if they have discussed and planned a narrative. The misinformation effects play a role with various witnesses as well. For example, suppose a person bringing an allegation had communicated with and shared a narrative with multiple individuals, and those individuals went on to tell others. You might often hear statements like "I did not see anything but heard it from *x*." Multiple witnesses can also be coerced or manipulated into saying things. All these effects lead to another level of modeling dependence vs. independent statements. Once again, our minds cannot perform these analyses without relying on mathematical tools. Fortunately, we also have the tools to help with these narratives.

# Chapter 12

# Cognitive Biases

*You only see what your eyes want to see*
*How can life be what you want it to be?*
*You're frozen when your heart's not open.*

—"Frozen," a song by Madonna
explaining the confirmation and desirability biases

## What are cognitive (and motivational) biases? And why should we care about them?

Are humans wired in a certain way that makes us engage in systemic acts that may have ethical implications without even realizing it? Can these inherent features distort our information and perception of the world? And can these features be exploited for our manipulation? Can these features, referred to as "biases," affect decision-making? The answer to all of these questions is yes, absolutely!

Cognitive biases (also called "unconscious biases") are systemic errors in reasoning that we make unknowingly and relate to our perception of a situation, the distortion of information, and our updating of belief. For example, one of the cognitive biases known as "confirmation bias" explains the tendency of individuals to focus only on the information that supports their view when presented with various pieces of information giving opposing views. This bias describes how individuals deviate from methods of belief updating discussed in the previous chapter.

Not all biases are cognitive. Some are motivational, and some are a mix of both. For example, confirmation bias can also result from a conscious focus on information that supports a particular view. This is frequently exhibited by politicians or partisan politics that focus on specific aspects of the presented data that relate to the other party's performance. Desirability, or optimism, bias is an example of a bias that leads people to believe that the likelihood of the occurrence of an event they desire is a lot higher. The desirability bias is also referred to as "wishful thinking."

Biases can also make us prone to being manipulated by individuals who exploit the biases within us. We can never eliminate biases, but we can work to minimize their effects. By recognizing and identifying our biases, we can improve our understanding of ethical behaviors and become less prone to being manipulated by them.

There are many human biases, some of which we have already discussed, including the bandwagon effect, obedience to authority, and conformity. This chapter presents some more biases that affect ethical decision quality. It also highlights some debiasing techniques.

**Reflection**

As we go through these biases, consider how they could be misused in ethical decision-making. Think about how these biases may have played a role in part 1.

## Examples of systemic (and predictable) errors in judgment

What does it mean when there is an error we do systematically and are unaware of it? Let us take a simple example from Howard and Abbas (2015). In Figure 2.7, which stick is longer?

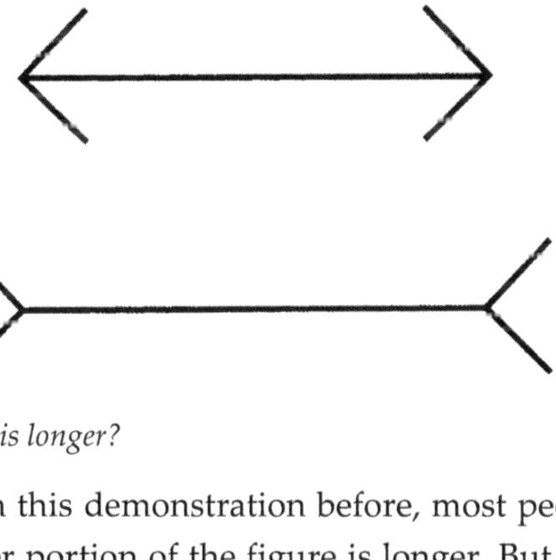

**Figure 2.7.** *Which stick is longer?*

If you have not seen this demonstration before, most people will say that the stick in the lower portion of the figure is longer. But in fact, they both have the same length. The way the arrows are pointed at the end of the stick gives the illusion that one stick is longer than the other. If you have seen this demonstration earlier and end up in a situation where you must bet on the length of one of the sticks, you would be more careful when making rush judgments. Also, if you knew that people are more likely to say that the stick in the bottom part of the figure is longer, you might design a gambling situation and bet that they are both of equal length, where you might end up making a fortune. This is an example of how a systemic error within us can be exploited.

## Confirmation bias

When Madonna sang, *"You only see what your eyes want to see,"* she could not have done a better job explaining to a broad audience what confirmation bias means. The confirmation bias relates to your selective digestion of information to your benefit.

### Head-head-head (HHH) or head-tail-head (HTH)? Confirmation bias: It's bad data

In class, we conduct the following demonstration with graduate students. We ask students which sequence is more likely to occur first in a series of coin tosses and whether the probability of getting any sequence is higher or lower than the other. That is, if you tossed a coin until you got either a

> *heads-tails-heads (HTH) or a heads-heads-heads (HHH)*

For the first time, is it more likely that you will get *heads-tails-heads* or a *heads-heads-heads* first?

Most students initially say (incorrectly) that it is equally likely to get either sequence first. So the probability of getting any sequence first is the "same" as the other sequence. Only a few say the heads-tails-heads sequence is more likely to occur first. So the probability of getting one sequence first is "different" from the other. But the real purpose of the demonstration is not to do probability calculations. It is to explore the effects of the confirmation bias.

We then ask a representative from each group to explain why they believe the chances of getting each sequence are the "same" or "different." The representatives describe their views, and after hearing the explanation, we then ask the class for their vote: "same" or "different." The vote seldom changes after each representative has spoken—students in each group do not listen to the arguments made by the representative of the other group.

Sometimes representatives make compelling arguments: They say that if you tossed the coin only three times, you are equally likely to get either sequence. But if you tossed it four or more times, you are more likely to get HTH over HHH. Students draw the permutations of possible outcomes of tossing four times to demonstrate their rationale, which is true. But the vote rarely changes. The majority of those who voted for "same" continue to vote "same," and those that voted "different" continue to vote "different."

In one executive seminar, everybody voted "same." There was no representative to explain why the probabilities were "different." Then we asked the twenty participants to take a coin out of their pocket and toss it till they got either a HHH or an HTH and see how many participants obtained each sequence first. The results were that sixteen out of twenty got the HTH sequence first, and four out of twenty got the HHH sequence first. Then we asked them again which sequence they believe is more likely. Again, they all said "same," that the sequences are equally likely to occur first. When asked how to interpret the results of their coin tossing, they said, "This must have been bad data." People did not internalize any data that would contradict their views.

## Debiasing the confirmation bias

Besides making people aware of the confirmation bias, another technique is to ask individuals who see opposing data and do not incorporate it,

> *If we told you what you are saying is false, how would you explain it?*

This question quickly gets people thinking about the confirmation bias and digesting opposing views.

## Did not get a job: Which story would you believe?

Suppose you were not selected for a job or your contract was not renewed due to performance or lack of funds. As you are about to leave, an individual tells you that you are an asset and that a single person is responsible for your nonrenewal. You know that you were not renewed for lack of funds, but nevertheless, which scenario are you more likely to believe? Convenient lies or unpleasant truths? How would your relations be toward the manager and the person who told you a story you prefer to hear develop? Would you be more willing to conduct unethical behavior toward that manager? And would you establish an affinity toward the individual who told you? This is an example of being exploited by biases.

## Are you being exploited by your confirmation bias? Why do schmoozing and flattery work (at first)?

Suppose that every time you meet someone, they tell you things that support your view of the world or something you would like to hear. Under the effect of biases, you will develop a likeness for those individuals and a desire to keep them in your company.

But that by itself is not unethical from your side. As you go up the organizational ladder, however, you will hear more and more of what you want to hear from people. You might promote those individuals instead of others who are more worthy and listen to those individuals more than others. This is where the actions can become unethical.

## If your preferred candidate was not reelected: Which story would you believe?

Suppose your preferred political candidate lost the election. Are you more or less likely to believe information that the election was rigged? The *Hill* reported the article "Why Do So Many Still Believe the 2020 Election Was Stolen?"

> *Undeniably, Trump's words continue to have a powerful influence among his supporters. Many psychologists believe "people filter ambiguous*

*information through an ideological lens, preferring interpretations that favor their political affiliations." When Trump tells his supporters the election was stolen, what else are they to believe?*[208]

**Reflection**

- Can you envision how the confirmation bias can obstruct organizational decision-making?
- Can you envision how the confirmation bias can be used for your manipulation?
- Could the confirmation bias have played a role in Elizabeth Holmes's case or any other cases in part 1?
- How do you believe confirmation bias may be exploited in politics? Or in the workplace?

## Anchoring

Anchoring is a cognitive bias in which individuals fixate on a number or word, usually in their salient memory, and modify their responses starting from that anchor.

### Anchoring demonstration: Attila the Hun

A group of MBA students participated in an exercise that asked,

*What are the last three digits of your home phone number?*

Participants answered, "XYZ."

Next, participants were told,

*I'm going to add 400 to your answer.*

[208] https://thehill.com/opinion/campaign/3263802-why-do-so-many-still-believe-the-2020-election-was-stolen/

Participants calculated XYZ + 400.

Participants were then asked,

*In what year would you guess Attila the Hun was defeated in Europe?*

The answer to this question, which they were not told, is AD 451. Participants' responses were higher if the number XYZ + 400 in their salient memory was higher. Table 2.1 summarizes the responses.

| *Range of the Initial Anchor (Last 3 digits of phone number plus 400)* | *Average Estimate of the Year of Attila's Defeat* |
|---|---|
| 400 to 599 | 629 |
| 600 to 799 | 680 |
| 800 to 999 | 789 |
| 1000 to 1199 | 885 |
| 1200 to 1399 | 988 |

**Table 2.1.** *Summary of responses exhibiting anchoring*

## Strength of anchoring: The population of Turkey—before or after Thanksgiving?

In one executive seminar, we discussed anchoring through a well-known demonstration wherein participants were divided into two groups.

Group A was given two questions:

1. *Is the population of Turkey greater than or less than 40 million?*
2. *What is the population of Turkey?*

Group B was given only one question:

*What is the population of Turkey?*

Participants observed the trend that group A gave responses closer to 40 million with much less variance than group B. This was attributed to group A having 40 million in their salient memory. This demonstration was conducted shortly after Thanksgiving. Before we collected the results, one of the participants in group B raised their hand and asked genuinely,

> *Are you referring to the population of Turkey before or after Thanksgiving?*

The participant was not joking but soon realized that he had anchored on the word "Turkey" from Thanksgiving and laughed. It was an unanticipated real-time demonstration of anchoring. CNN reported soon after that Turkey is changing its name: "*'The main reason why Turkey is changing its name is to eliminate the association with the bird,'* said Sinan Ulgen, Chairman of Istanbul-based think-tank EDAM."[209]

## Minimizing the effects of anchoring

When you become aware of this bias, ensure you do not subject yourself (or individuals) to an anchor when providing (or eliciting) information. This is particularly important in probability elicitation (see Howard and Abbas 2015).

**Reflection**

Can you think of ways in which the anchoring bias can be used in manipulation?

## Reference dependence

Reference dependence is a cognitive bias where humans set a reference (or aspiration) level based on their expectations of a situation. They are more willing to act if the situation exceeds their expectation and less inclined if it does not. Once humans set an aspiration level for themselves about a situation they regard as satisfactory, they would be willing to accept anything above the aspiration level and reject anything below it.

Herbert Simon won the Nobel Prize for work on aspirational levels. Daniel Kahneman, who also won the Nobel Prize for his work with Amos Tversky, described reference dependence as a fundamental principle in prospect

[209] https://www.cnn.com/2022/06/03/middleeast/turkey-name-change-mime-intl/index.html

theory. People evaluate outcomes relative to an existing reference point or status quo.

### Reference points are used to influence your purchase decisions

Infomercials always attempt to influence your purchase of an advertised item by setting a reference point. Consider, for example, the following two situations:

**Situation A:** An infomercial sets your reference point for an item at a high value at first and says,

> *You will not pay $1,000 or even $900.*

Then they tell you,

> *If you call now, you will pay only $200.*

**Situation B:** Imagine if, instead, the infomercial sets your reference point at a low value and says,

> *You will not pay $20 or even $30.*

And then they say,

> *If you call now, you will pay only $200.*

In which situation are you more likely to make a call? Most people will say the first. Yet it is the same item, offered at the same price, and, in fact, with the same second statement in both cases. This is an example of many human biases that affect judgment and decision-making and make us prone to manipulation.

## Availability bias

Availability is a cognitive heuristic that relies on information easily brought to mind to make decisions and predictions. The more accessible the information to recall, the higher the likelihood our minds assign to the events recurring.

One day, following the crash of EgyptAir flight 804, which vanished from the radar on its way from Paris to Cairo, I was asked to write an article for CNN about the risks of flying.[210] The data showed that the chance of dying in an airplane accident is *less than 1 in 14 million globally, while the chances of dying in a car accident are about one hundred per million*. In fact, the chances of dying in an airplane accident are considerably less than the odds of being killed by a coworker (nine in 1 million).

> *These numbers will clearly vary depending on how much you fly. But even if you were a member of the million-mile club, the fact remains that flying is a very safe activity. So why are so many people nervous when it comes time to flying? And why is the perception of the risk of flying so different from the statistical reality?*

One explanation arises from the availability bias, which is the tendency to overestimate the likelihood of an event with greater "availability" or "detail" in our memory. Why does this happen with airplane accidents? Because airplane incidents are often far more catastrophic than car accidents in terms of lost lives, they get more media attention. We learn a lot about airplane incidents, such as the time the incident occurred, the route, the passengers, and the type of airplane; and we sympathize with the families and loved ones. This is only human. And we hear less about car accidents on the highway.

## Follow-up: Different perspectives from different stakeholders who saw the same data

Over the next few days, I received emails from safety officers of airline companies thanking me for highlighting the issue. I told them it was just the data and the science. About three days later, I received emails from truck companies and drivers asking why I wrote that article and that this could impact their business. I told them it was just the data and the science.

---

[210] https://www.cnn.com/2016/05/19/opinions/fear-of-flying-misplaced-abbas

## Overconfidence bias

Overconfidence bias is a tendency of individuals to overestimate their abilities. This is manifested when underestimating the time it takes to achieve a task (such as writing a book) or in overprecise estimates. Most people overestimate their driving capabilities, and CBS News reported about a study where "*32 percent of the employees of a software company said they performed better than 19 out of 20 of their colleagues.*"[211]

Overconfidence bias is manifested when obtaining precision estimates or when eliciting probability distributions from experts. The probability distributions elicited are narrow, which means that the quantity of interest will most likely fall outside the midrange (the range characterizing the 0.25 to 0.75 quantile of the distribution).

Overconfidence is also manifested when individuals overestimate the chance of a high-probability event and underestimate the chance of a low-probability event.

### Debiasing techniques

Some studies have suggested modifying expert distributions by a probability weighting function, a reverse S-shaped function that leads to a broader midrange and more calibrated low-probability and high-probability events.

**Reflection**

Can the overconfidence bias be used for manipulation?

## Cognitive Dissonance

The American Psychological Association (APA) defines "cognitive dissonance" as "*an unpleasant psychological state resulting from inconsistency between two or more elements in a cognitive system.*" When we encounter this unpleasant state, our minds have the motive to look for alternate theories that might reduce the unpleasantness.

---

[211] https://www.cbsnews.com/news/everyone-thinks-they-are-above-average/

The term "cognitive dissonance" was coined in 1957 by Leon Festinger. Festinger conducted an experiment wherein subjects were provided with boring tasks and paid either $20 or $1. Examples of the tasks included having the participants turn forty-eight pegs in a board in a clockwise direction.

Subjects were then asked to perform a favor for the experimenter: to tell the next participant (who was a member of the experimenter's team) that the task was enjoyable.

> *Of the participants who received $1 or $20, who do you believe reported most that the experiment was fun?*

Most participants who were paid $1 reported that the experiment was more enjoyable than those who were paid $20.

The explanation for this observed effect was that those who were paid $1 were not paid enough to convince them to participate in the experiment in the first place or to lie for the experimenter. And so they experienced dissonance and had an alternate theory for why they were doing the task: the whole situation was a favor, or it must have been fun if they did it for $1. Those paid $20 believed they were paid adequately for the task. And so they did not experience the same dissonance effect of why they participated in the experiment in the first place.

## The Benjamin Franklin effect is a form of cognitive dissonance

Benjamin Franklin understood the effects of cognitive dissonance long before its discovery. The dissonance resulting from a person doing a favor to you, even if they do not like you, results in their explanation to themselves that they must like you and become more willing to do more favors.

### Reflection: Exploiting cognitive dissonance and confirmation bias with new managers?

Suppose you had a change in leadership, and you went to the new leadership and complained about how the previous leadership was not kind to you. You worked on their confirmation bias and told them how great of a job they were doing. You then asked them for a small favor, and they did it. And when you saw them again, you continued to tell them how much of a great job they were doing. Can you perceive how their cognitive dissonance and confirmation biases might lead them to do more favors for you in the future?

## Status quo bias

Just like the concept of momentum in physics, where particles tend to remain stationary or in a state of motion unless acted upon by other particles, individuals tend to maintain the status quo and not act unless there is a stimulus. You need extra effort to break the status quo and get them to act. This bias can result in common expressions like "This is how we do things around here, and I cannot change it" or "This is above my pay grade."

## Escalation of commitment bias

The "escalation of commitment" bias describes a tendency to remain committed to past decisions even if new information reveals that they are no longer the best to pursue. The escalation is amplified if the decisions are made publicly or when commitment gradually increases following the sequential revelation of information.

The seriousness of this bias regarding ethical decision-making is that individuals may not want to correct unethical acts because past decisions have already been made. Further, the escalation is also an issue. Individuals might commit a small unethical act at first, believing it is small enough that they will get away with it or that not much harm will be done. But when the situation unexpectedly blows up, individuals engage in more unethical actions and cover up even more. This is where the escalation is manifested.

### Reflection

- In part 1, Theranos presented a prerecorded test sample, after which it was able to raise money from Novartis. Now consider the new situation where they have received money from a customer and must pay salaries and other expenses. Can the commitment bias have led to a gradual escalation of deception?

- If you discovered that what you were doing is ethically wrong upon the revelation of new information, would you change it? Can the commitment bias impede your decision to correct ethical violations?

## Sunk cost bias

The sunk cost bias is a form of commitment bias that represents a tendency to keep doing the same thing—particularly if you have already spent time, effort, money, or other resources on it—even if the decisions were not public. This bias explains why individuals are more willing to throw good money after bad even if the project is no longer a good decision. The familiar words rationalizing the situation are "We have already spent money and resources."

The sunk cost bias can also be used for deception or manipulation. Suppose you wanted a company to continue a particular direction, decision, or project that has already been made even though it was not a good decision. You can say that much effort, time, and money have already been spent on this project. This statement will resonate with many individuals in the room. However, if you know this bias, you will be less prone to falling into this sunk cost trap.

**Reflection**

- Can the sunk cost bias impede ethical decision quality?
- Could the escalation and sunk cost biases have led to some of the issues in part 1?

## Decision vs. outcome, regret, and hindsight

### "Decision vs. outcome" trap

The main idea of decision quality is to judge the quality of a decision at the time it is made rather than when you have already received new information about the outcome of an uncertainty following your decision. Fear of a bad outcome or knowing that people judge your decisions by an outcome that is out of your control makes individuals less amenable to acting. This "decision vs. outcome" trap can lead individuals to make suboptimal decisions that minimize the chance of a negative outcome, ignoring the upside.

Suppose you were a project manager, and for simplicity of demonstration, suppose that you had only two alternatives:

**Alternative A:** Make some minor improvements to last year's vehicle. That would get you an 80 percent of a $2 million increase in profit and a 20 percent chance of a $100,000 loss.

**Alternative B:** Introduce an innovative new vehicle. That would get you a 6 percent of $500 million or a 4 percent chance of losing $200,000.

Now consider the following:

- Which alternative would you choose for your company if you cared about minimizing the chance of a loss (a bad outcome)?
- Which alternative would you choose if you were judged by the quality of the decision?

By recognizing the difference between a decision and an outcome, people would be more willing to make decisions and rectify that bias. Further, this bias can be reduced if organizations reward based on the decision-making, not the outcome. If a decision were judged by the outcome alone, no project manager would engage in developing new drugs or cures for cancer and Alzheimer's disease because the probability of getting a loss in the short term is relatively high.

But how can that bias be used for deception or manipulation? Suppose you observed in the workplace that an individual had a bad outcome. Then you can tell the managers that the person made bad decisions. Managers who do not know the difference will fall into that trap even though it might have been a good decision. Further, suppose an individual is about to decide, and you bring up that they will be judged by the outcome. In that case, they may make a different decision that avoids loss instead of also looking at the upside potential of decisions.

### Reflection: Impacts of being judged by the outcome

Imagine if we moved from a situation where we judge politicians by the outcome and instead judge them based on the rationale or the decision-making method they used when making the decision. Imagine if we asked them for the information they had, the trade-offs and tolerances used, the risk tolerance, the frame, the alternatives, and the stakeholders, among other elements of ethical decision quality. What a dramatic difference this method of judgment could induce!

## Regret of action and inaction

Some psychological studies have shown that people regret negative outcomes more when they are a result of action than of inaction (e.g., Kahneman and Tversky 1982).[212] For example, consider these two scenarios:

**Scenario 1:** Suppose you owned stock in company A and then sold it to buy stock in company B. Later, you realize that by switching, you lost $5,000.

**Scenario 2:** Suppose you owned stock in company A. A friend told you to sell the stock and switch to company B. You did not. Later, you realize that if you had switched to company B, you would have gained $5,000.

Individuals express more regret in scenario 1 than in scenario 2 because of the action they took. It is this regret that often makes individuals reluctant to make decisions. Other studies have shown that regrets of action are more substantial in the short term, but regrets of inaction (such as not pursuing your passions or not getting the education you desired) are more significant in the long term.[213]

### Reflection

Can you envision how regrets of action and inaction can be exploited to manipulate individuals?

---

[212] D. Kahneman and A. Tversky, "The Psychology of Preferences," *Scientific American* 246, no. 1 (1982): 160–173.

[213] https://news.cornell.edu/stories/2018/05/woulda-coulda-shoulda-haunting-regret-failing-our-ideal-selves

## Hindsight bias

Along the lines of judging after observing an outcome, hindsight bias is the tendency of individuals to believe the outcome was more predictable once it has been revealed. If you try to predict stock market prices versus if you look back, you will find reasons why it was easy to predict it would have ended the way it did.

How can this bias be used in manipulation? Once an outcome is determined and suppose it was good, an individual might undermine the effort by saying it was predictable given the circumstance. And if the outcome was bad, an individual might question the decision-making with the idea that the particular outcome was easily predictable to be negative in this situation.

## Group biases and ethical decision-making

The previous biases apply to individuals and groups. For example, a group can be subject to confirmation bias in selecting the information that suits its purpose. Escalation of commitment can also be exhibited by groups where the group amplifies previous decisions made by the group (and those decisions need not have been good decisions) by following the same path even if new information deems it more appropriate to take a different course of action. But other biases that are specific to groups also exist. Just like having social motives when people operate in a group, there are also biases that make them more prone to doing things in a group that they would not have done on an individual level.

### Conformity bias

Humans tend to act in a way that makes them fit within groups and conform to the group's norms. This bias strengthens the effect of the environment on ethical decision quality. The conformity bias makes it difficult to oppose unethical acts if the organization is doing it, and as a result, individuals tend to go with the flow. You could be regarded as not playing with the team or as a troublemaker if you oppose an act, even if it is unethical. For example, Theranos CFO Henry Mosley was fired and accused of not being a team player when he expressed concerns about the Novartis demonstration and using prerecorded results.

**Reflection**

Could the conformity bias have played a role in the endorsements made by the board members of Theranos?

## False consensus and groupthink

Groupthink is a situation that arises when members of a group focus on (and strive to reach) a consensus on a decision due to pressure or conformity instead of analyzing and challenging the proposed alternatives or expressing an opposing view. The results are often disastrous, and people often wonder how such decisions could have been made. Groupthink played a role in the *Challenger* space shuttle disaster,[214] where concerns about the sealing abilities of an O-ring at a particular temperature were ignored. This was cited as the main issue that led to the explosion.

There was pressure on NASA to launch after surveys showing that the popularity of the Space Shuttle Program was fading. President Ronald Reagan also had plans to refer to the launch in his 1986 State of the Union address. A teleconference where concerns were made was put on hold for a private discussion, after which management ignored concerns about the O-ring. Instead of mentioning the success of the mission in his State of the Union address, President Ronald Reagan announced,

> *Ladies and gentlemen, I'd planned to speak to you tonight to report on the state of the Union, but the events of earlier today have led me to change those plans. Today is a day for mourning and remembering. Nancy and I are pained to the core by the tragedy of the shuttle Challenger. We know we share this pain with all of the people of our country. This is truly a national loss. Nineteen years ago, almost to the day, we lost three astronauts in a terrible accident on the ground. But we've never lost an astronaut in flight; we've never had a tragedy like this.*[215]

Another incident of groupthink was displayed in John F. Kennedy's Bay of Pigs invasion decision, where he was surrounded by individuals who did

---

[214] https://en.wikipedia.org/wiki/Space_Shuttle_Challenger_disaster#Decision_to_launch

[215] https://history.nasa.gov/reagan12886.html

not express any opposing views. The incident later led Kennedy to change his decision-making process. A committee called ExComm was formed, wherein the members would be free to express opposing views and meet without the president to minimize "obedience to authority" bias.

## Group polarization

Group polarization is the "*tendency of the group to make decisions that are more extreme than the initial inclination of its members. These more extreme decisions are towards greater risk if individuals' initial tendencies are to be risky and towards greater caution if individuals' initial tendencies are to be cautious.*"[216]

The polarization effect is closely associated with group polarization, in which "*a disagreement becomes more extreme as the different parties consider evidence on the issue.*" The disagreement is amplified by various biases, such as the confirmation and "us vs. them" biases. Group polarization and polarization effects are often observed in social media comments, particularly in political discussions where the conversation shifts into hostility and "us vs. them" comments regardless of the evidence presented.

### Does leadership exploit the "us vs. them" and group polarization biases?

There are numerous instances where the leadership of a corporation or government enterprise engages in "us vs. them" tactics to manipulate others or to create bonds among the team. An example was presented in Theranos's Sunny Balwani, who rallied the employees after a government investigation into Theranos was launched.

> *Remember, these are the guys who are after us, and they are attacking the work that you guys are doing. Are you ready? One, two, three, f— — you!*

[216] https://en.wikipedia.org/wiki/Group_polarization

**Reflection**

- Could the "us vs. them" bias have contributed to the January 6, 2022, attack on the US Capitol?[217]
- Can you think of other instances where leaders used "us vs. them" biases to gain support?

**Reflection: Have you been polarized or manipulated by your biases?**

Think of how individual and group biases may be exploited for manipulation. What can you do to minimize the effects of these biases in ethical decision-making?

[217] https://www.justice.gov/usao-dc/one-year-jan-6-attack-capitol#:~:text=Approximately%20140%20police%20officers%20were,from%20the%20Metropolitan%20Police%20Department.

# Chapter 13

# Alternatives

*Dr. Teddy Oglethorpe: A man's always got choices, Randall! Sometimes you just gotta choose the good one!*

From the movie—*Don't Look Up*

## What is a decision alternative?

A decision alternative is one of the possible actions that you can take in a given situation. An alternative must be feasible. You can include an alternative of donating a billion dollars to charity or ending malaria only if you have the means or the scientific knowledge to do so.

Because uncertainty is present, an alternative can result in several possible consequences, each having different effects on stakeholders. For example, the purchase of stock results in numerous consequences relating to the future stock price, increasing the price of drugs can have various consequences, the pursuit of a technological alternative that is not yet feasible can have different consequences, and a mitigation strategy for a pandemic can result in multiple values of lives saved (or lost). While you do not know which consequence you will get when you choose an alternative, you still need to decide because not making a decision is itself an alternative that impacts stakeholders.

Studies have shown that individuals need to spend more time developing good alternatives for themselves.[218] Individuals usually limit themselves to one or two alternatives, and the decision revolves around "Should we do this or that?" In organizations, people often anchor on alternatives proposed by others and are influenced by the effects of conformity and the surrounding environment or the alternatives mandated by the legal department or influential individuals without putting enough effort into generating additional alternatives.

---

[218] R. Keeney, *Give Yourself a Nudge* (Cambridge, UK: Cambridge University Press, 2020).

Selecting ethical alternatives also requires you to take action once new information is revealed. If you consider an alternative of a blood tester that uses only a single drop of blood and discover that the alternative is not feasible, then there is a need for follow-up alternatives once this new information is revealed.

Our purpose in this chapter is to create distinctions to characterize decision alternatives and to provide guidance on creating ethical alternatives in decision situations.

Several aspects need to be considered:

1. Distinctions about the ethicality and feasibility of an alternative, including the ethicality of the alternative itself versus its consequences
2. The need to explore alternatives that might score higher on the ethical front or are feasible
3. The need to incorporate uncertainty and to think about the possible consequences of the alternatives before making a decision
4. The need to create alternatives to help gather more information ethically
5. The need to act upon the revelation of new information
6. The recognition that not making a decision is a decision

## Ethical distinctions for alternatives

A Kantian perspective determines the morality of the act (or the chosen alternative) by the act itself, not by the situation, the consequences, or the benefits. Kant's doctrine is as follows;

> *Act only according to that maxim by which you can at the same time will that it should become a universal law.*

If you deem an act unethical through a Kantian lens, you remove that decision alternative from consideration. But even with the removal of unethical alternatives, you still need to determine the best decision alternative out of the remaining alternatives. Simply removing an act from consideration is only one part of ethical decision-making.

Utilitarianism determines the morality of the act by the consequences, among other things. When uncertainty is present, a decision alternative has multiple consequences with different probabilities. The ethical characterization of an alternative requires identifying the possible consequences that may follow and using a sound method to determine each alternative's benefit and harm and then decide on the best course of action.

The Rights approach considers whether an alternative respects or violates the basic rights of each individual involved. Examples of rights include the UN's Universal Declaration of Human Rights, which comprises thirty articles, including the following:

- *Article 1: All human beings are born free and equal in dignity and rights. They are endowed with reason and conscience and should act towards one another in a spirit of brotherhood.*

- *Article 2: Everyone is entitled to all the rights and freedoms set forth in this Declaration, without distinction of any kind, such as race, colour, sex, language, religion, political or other opinion, national or social origin, property, birth or other status.*

- *Article 4: No one shall be held in slavery or servitude; slavery and the slave trade shall be prohibited in all their forms.*

- *Article 11: Everyone charged with a penal offence has the right to be presumed innocent until proved guilty according to law in a public trial at which he has had all the guarantees necessary for his defence.*[219]

The Rights approach would require removing an alternative from the set of feasible alternatives if it violated fundamental human rights.

The "common good" approach pursues alternatives that seek the benefit of all people. Dictionary.com defines the "common good" as *"the advantage or benefit of all people in society or a group."*[220] The "common good" approach has

---

[219] https://www.un.org/en/about-us/universal-declaration-of-human-rights
[220] https://www.dictionary.com/browse/common-good

also been a subject of appeal.[221] In particular, researchers have highlighted that different people might have different notions, values, and trade-offs about the attributes that comprise the common good—making it difficult to reach a consensus about which alternatives achieve higher on the "common good" aspect. In addition, the "common good" approach might entail different burdens on different stakeholders and the possibility of free riders.

The fairness approach strives to give each person their due. This could entail the exchange of payments or other methods to compensate affected stakeholders.

The virtue approach pursues alternatives that reflect virtues and values in our actions, including honesty, fairness, and compassion. The actions we choose should reflect these virtue values.

**Reflection**

- Of the chosen alternatives in part 1, identify those that belong to the different ethical distinctions about alternatives. Identify those that violate some of the ethical distinctions about alternatives.
- Identify arguments and situations (if any) for when you would not follow any of the ethical approaches mentioned above.

## What is a "legal, ethical, and prudential" alternative?

We can classify decision alternatives according to what is legal (does not violate a current legal system) and what is ethical (as determined by your ethical code and the ethical distinctions about alternatives). But even if the actions are legal and ethical, they need not be smart or prudential. For example, you might not have captured the expertise or domain knowledge of various individuals involved, so you might provide less value to stakeholders. Or you may be investing at rates above the organization's risk tolerance, jeopardizing its wealth and value to its shareholders. Or you might be investing with a low risk tolerance and missing out on opportu-

---

[221] Originally appeared in *Issues in Ethics* 5, no. 1 (Spring 1992), https://www.scu.edu/ethics/ethics-resources/ethical-decision-making/the-common-good/

nities that can significantly provide value to the organization. We want the alternatives to be legal, ethical, and prudential.

The best decision that comes out of an analysis is one of the alternatives already selected for the analysis. Therefore, it is important to put extra effort into brainstorming good alternatives. Ethical reasoning is about not just avoiding unethical alternatives but also exploring new alternatives in a given situation that may resolve ethical dilemmas. Exploring a feasible set of legal, ethical, and prudential alternatives might help avoid the ethical issue. Therefore, it is essential to make sure we have considered good alternatives in the analysis to start with.

## What you can do to improve your ethical alternatives

### Step 1: Brainstorm good alternatives

Some tips for brainstorming good alternatives:

1. Come up with good alternatives for consideration. You should identify many, not just two. Avoid "It's either this or that" situations. Sometimes you might even hire a consulting firm that rushes to implement an idea because it is in their comfort zone, and they are anchored on it. Make sure you have explored a broad range of alternatives before any analysis.

2. Brainstorm alternatives that help achieve your motives and objectives.

3. Brainstorm alternatives that account for different stakeholders' interests.

4. Brainstorm alternatives that manage the harm that has occurred possibly by exchanging payments to resolve the issue for affected stakeholders.

5. Identify the alternatives that involve deception, stealing, and harming. Identify other alternatives that can achieve the same objectives and avoid deception, such as conveying information to stakeholders.

6. Ask yourself what motives (if any) drive specific alternatives that might harm others.

7. Brainstorm alternatives by which you can gather more information before making the decision.

8. Brainstorm alternatives that enable you to pursue other actions in the light of new information or unintended consequences.

9. Brainstorm methods to help you minimize the effects of biases, groupthink, the environment, and the escalation of commitments in your selection of alternatives.

### Step 2: Give your alternatives an ethics boost!

Brainstorm alternatives corresponding to the following:

1. Utilitarian approach that would yield more benefit than harm.

2. Rights approach: Can you identify or modify any alternatives to preserve the basic rights of individuals?

3. Fairness approach: Can you modify your alternatives to give each person what they are due?

4. Virtue approach and Kantian perspective: Identify alternatives you would not do based on Kantianism and virtue ethics and cross them out of your list.

5. Identify some "common good" alternatives.

6. Can you come up with a hybrid of the above? Do not anchor any one of the above. A mix of the above alternatives could be useful.

### Step 3: Create distinctions to facilitate thinking about different scenarios

It is also essential to think about the consequences that will materialize following your decision. Think about possible unanticipated or unintended consequences. It is helpful to create distinctions to facilitate the inclusion of possible scenarios. Figure 2.8 shows examples of creating a distinction in the decision about whether or not the information is accurate or whether or not a person committed a crime.

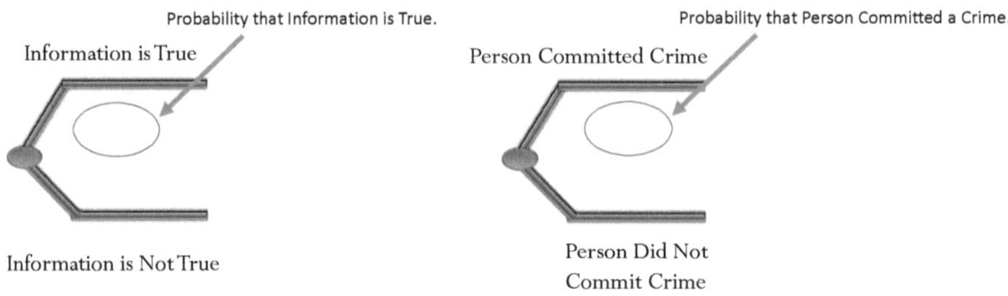


**Figure 2.8.** *Creating distinctions within an alternative*

Thinking about unintended consequences helps minimize deception, harm, and stealing, even if unintentional. Further, brainstorming unintended consequences can also improve decision-making and can act as a deterrent against unethical actions. What if a whistleblower reports this act? What if the act lands on the front page of the *New York Times*, the *WSJ*, or the *LA Times*?

**Reflection: Identify distinctions that could have been created for the situations below**

CBS News reported,

> *A man who spent more than 38 years behind bars for a 1983 murder and two attempted murders has been released from a California prison after long-untested DNA evidence pointed to a different person, the Los Angeles County district attorney said Friday.*[222]

Business Insider said,

> *At Theranos, tension was mounting. Ian Gibbons, the chief scientist at Theranos, was growing uncomfortable with some of the issues the blood-testing technology had. In May 2013, Holmes scheduled a meeting with Gibbons, in which he expected Holmes would fire him. The night before, he attempted to take his own life. He died a week later.*[223]

---

[222] https://www.cbsnews.com/news/maurice-hastings-freed-1983-murder-conviction-dna-evidence-points-to-different-person/

[223] https://www.insider.com/the-history-of-silicon-valley-unicorn-theranos-and-ceo-elizabeth-holmes-2018-5

Business Insider also wrote,

> *Lottery winners have to be prepared for mooching friends who want to benefit from their newfound wealth. . . . Your winning might also bring out the worst in family members, too. . . . When people know you have that much money, you're also in greater danger of being robbed. Whittaker, the 2002 West Virginia lottery winner, said he was robbed of [$545,000] he'd left sitting in his car. . . . Winners also face an increased risk of bankruptcy.*[224]

*Time* reported,

> *Examples of the "curse of the lottery" abound—from the West Virginia man whose daughter and granddaughter died of overdoses after he won $315 million in 2002, to the Kentucky man who claimed a $21 million prize in 2001 and lost it all by 2006.*[225]

US News & World Report stated,

> *Eminent domain allows governments to acquire private property from unwilling sellers for public use. In many cases, however, "public use" has been ignored or twisted beyond recognition, as local governments use it to take people's homes and businesses for different private uses, as long as these provide more of a "public benefit." The subtle switch from use to benefit spells trouble for many. Now a carpet store in Glendale, Colorado, can be seized and handed over to a developer so that an entertainment complex can be constructed, as this provides jobs and a bigger tax base for the city. As for the proprietor's livelihood, who cares?*[226]

CNN reported some unanticipated consequences of a border security plan:

> *The Department of Homeland Security put together a plan months ago to deal with thousands of migrants arriving at the border: flying some of them to cities deeper inside the US for processing. But the*

---

[224] https://www.businessinsider.com/winning-lottery-downsides-2018-12
[225] https://time.com/5427275/lottery-winning-happiness-debunked/
[226] https://www.usnews.com/opinion/economic-intelligence/2015/11/17/the-injustice-of-eminent-domain

*plan is dead for now, officials tell CNN, in part after the White House grew hesitant over the complicated logistics. Agency officials dream up a plan but then struggle to get White House approval, even as the problem compounds and Republicans step up their criticism.*[227]

COVID relief funds NPR wrote,

*California is slowly clawing back some of the estimated $20 billion in unemployment money stolen by domestic and international criminals, money earmarked for jobless relief during the height of the pandemic.*[228]

The Department of Justice reported,

*Three people were arrested today on criminal charges in three separate indictments filed in the District of Idaho. These charges relate to the defendants' alleged roles in fraudulently obtaining and misusing Paycheck Protection Program (PPP) loans. . . . The defendants, along with others, allegedly falsified information and submitted fraudulent documents to collectively obtain over $2.4 million in relief funding guaranteed by the Small Business Administration (SBA) under the Coronavirus Relief, Aid, and Economic Security (CARES) Act for small businesses struggling with the economic impact of COVID-19.*[229]

## Reflection

- Consider some actions made by an organization in part 1 and their unanticipated consequences.
- Consider some of the unanticipated consequences (and their magnitude) of announcing that Iraq had weapons of mass destruction.

---

[227] https://edition.cnn.com/2022/10/20/politics/immigration-migrants-biden-border-policy/index.html
[228] https://www.npr.org/2022/10/18/1128561539/pandemic-fraud-billions-california
[229] https://www.justice.gov/opa/pr/three-charged-covid-19-relief-fraud-scheme

## Step 4: Create options and think about the downstream alternatives for different scenarios

Many people think that ethical decision-making involves a onetime decision. This is certainly not the case! There may be a need to act upon the revelation of new information. Thinking about the uncertainties that are most relevant to your situation can help you consider the various scenarios that might follow before making the decision. In addition, you also need to consider the alternatives you would pursue in each scenario following the revelation of new information, such as the technical infeasibility of a blood tester.

And finally, it might be important to create options in advance to enable you to make decisions that you otherwise could not have made upon the revelation of new information. For example, if you are making an investment decision on behalf of a real estate firm, consider alternatives of buying insurance if the value of insurance is less than its cost.

Some people argue that you do not need to consider unanticipated consequences or downstream decisions in advance and that you can make decisions as the situation arises:

> *Well, can't we just start and modify step-by-step as we go along?*

There are many issues with this statement. First, if you wait till that revelation of new information or unanticipated consequences, it might be too late to choose some alternatives because you have yet to take steps toward creating them. For example, you cannot purchase insurance after an earthquake has already hit. Think of a situation where you are "building the plane while flying it."

In addition, by waiting, your commitment biases and saving face might impede your willingness to modify a course of action. Further, you might have already hurt stakeholders along the way.

And finally, it is essential to realize that sometimes you can make good decisions at each stage separately, but they were bad decisions when viewed holistically. If you maximize step-by-step, you might make worse decisions than if you had incorporated all the scenarios and made a decision based accordingly. This relates to the appropriate structuring of decisions.

It is essential to structure decision alternatives with downstream decisions and uncertainties. For example, suppose you had a choice of two alternatives and uncertainty about whether your information is true or false, as shown in figure 2.9.

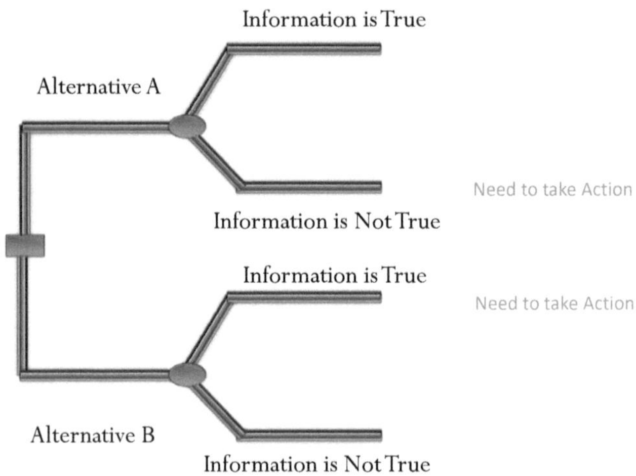


**Figure 2.9.** *Characterization of two decision alternatives and an uncertainty*

The next step would be to brainstorm downstream decisions following each scenario. Figure 2.10 presents a decision tree with downstream decisions following the revelation of information.

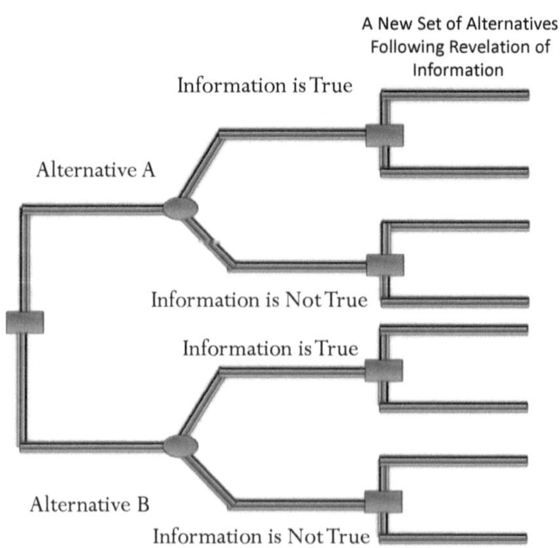


**Figure 2.10.** *Decision tree with downstream decisions following the revelation of information*

By doing that, we can create options or consider other courses of action that we otherwise would not have considered. People need to spend more time creating alternatives for themselves or options (which are sequential alternatives that can be pursued upon the revelation of information) or hybrid alternatives that may help reach a resolution among stakeholders.

## Step 5: Brainstorm alternatives to help you gather more information

Sometimes the best decision alternative is to gather more information. Gathering more information is essential if it could avoid harm to stakeholders. Consider, for example, uncertainty about whether the information is accurate:

- If we knew that *information is true*, you might choose alternative A.

- If we knew that *information was false*, you might choose alternative B.

If you could gather more information, it could help avoid harm to stakeholders. Note that if you choose alternative A when the information is *true* and alternative A when the information is *not true*, you should choose alternative A. You would not need to assign probabilities, and you would not need to gather information about this uncertainty.

In most cases, however, (1) our decision will change if we know the outcome of an uncertainty in advance. Further, (2) we will only know the outcome after making a decision. But we can gather more information and update our probabilities with the new information.

Examples of decisions where information was later revealed after the decision was made abide. And it generally comes with drastic consequences for stakeholders. Fox News reported the following about *Making a Murderer*:

> *This new evidence creates a reasonable probability that, had the jury heard the new evidence, it would have had a reasonable doubt as to the defendant's guilt. Therefore Mr. Avery should be granted a new trial.*[230]

---

[230] https://www.foxnews.com/us/steven-avery-attorney-claims-new-compelling-evidence-emerged-making-murderer-case

## Step 6: Act in the light of new information

Finally, it is essential to note that ethical decision-making does not end once a decision is made. If new information that reveals ethical violations is revealed, you have a new decision and a need to act in the light of this new information. In some cases, the legal system has mandated the need for action following new information. Examples abide:

NPR released an article titled "The Men Exonerated in the Malcolm X Killing Will Receive $36 Million."[231]

CBS News reported,

> *Two men who served nearly 17 years in prison after being wrongly convicted of attempted murder after a 2004 shooting were declared innocent Thursday by a California judge. Under a new law, the state is required to pay them each $140 for every day they spent behind bars, or about $900,000.*[232]

---

[231] https://www.npr.org/2022/10/31/1132757141/the-men-exonerated-in-the-malcolm-x-killing-will-receive-36-million#:~:text=Press-,Men%20exonerated%20in%20Malcolm%20X%20killing%20to%20receive%20%2436%20million,men%20spending%20decades%20behind%20bars.

[232] https://www.cbsnews.com/news/dupree-glass-juan-rayford-wrongly-convicted-declared-innocent-california/

# Chapter 14

# Well-Being

*Neither a man nor a crowd nor a nation can be trusted*
*to act humanely or to think sanely under*
*the influence of a great fear.*

—Bertrand Russell

## Decisions under the influence and decisions under impairment (DUIs)

The well-being element of ethical decision quality considers whether the individuals involved are ethically fit and whether they can recognize and make ethical decisions. Mental health, an example of well-being considerations, can impair a person's decision-making and make them subject to manipulation. In addition to impairment, the ethical well-being element identifies factors where an individual's ability to make ethical decisions is compromised. Examples include fear, fatigue, stress, addiction, and coercion.

This chapter will identify several factors affecting an individual's well-being and ability to make ethical decisions. We shall refer to these factors as "SSSSFFDDAAMCC," which stands for

> *Survival/Security/Safety/Stress/Fatigue/Fear/Despair/Depression/ Addiction/Anxiety/Mental Health/Coercion/Compromise*

## Operating in SSSSFFDDAAMCC mode

There are several reasons why identifying individuals in this state is essential. First, if an individual is not ethically fit, their judgment might be clouded; so they could make unethical decisions that would impact others. Second, individuals in this state may be exploited by others. Even CEOs of organizations may find themselves operating in this mode. Third, recognizing the existence of this environment provides perspective on how to improve the ethical decision culture within an organization. For example, if the operating environment is causing excessive fatigue that impacts individuals' ethical fitness, ethical collapses may be a recurring theme. Simply providing training and ethics courses to individuals in that environment will not be sufficient to solve the ethical issues that arise. Instead, it would be more effective to change the operation and well-being of individuals. Fourth, recognizing this environment also provides perspectives on organizational actions that can induce this state and impediments that can be addressed to improve ethical decision quality.

**Reflection**

- As you read this chapter, refer to part 1 and identify situations where individuals were operating in SSSSFFDDAAMCC mode.
- Identify situations in part 1 where organizations played a role in increasing employee stress levels.

## Survival mode: I will survive!

According to Wikipedia, *"Survival, or the act of surviving, is the propensity of something to continue existing, particularly when this is done despite conditions that might kill or destroy it."*[233] Operating in survival mode can impede an individual's fitness to make decisions. Survival mode can be triggered by biological motives, such as hunger, thirst, regulation of body temperature, and need for oxygen, sleep, and avoidance of pain,[234] as well as other factors like insecurities in a job and the feeling of a need to lie, harm, or steal to survive.

### Operating in survival mode: The Squid Game

*Squid Game* is a Netflix series that depicts examples of individuals operating in survival mode. Individuals who fail to meet tasks of a game are "eliminated," which is the term used for being killed. One of the players, Sang-woo, was known to be a person of high integrity before engaging in the squid game. During one of the games, the players were given a bag of

[233] https://en.wikipedia.org/wiki/Survival
[234] https://www.psychologydiscussion.net/motive/types-of-motives-biological-social-and-personal-motives-psychology/694

marbles and were asked to get the marbles from the other players. They were not given instructions or guidelines on how to take the marbles. All they knew was that if a player lost their marbles or failed to get another player's marbles, they would be eliminated. Sang-woo knowingly tricked his friend Ali by taking Ali's marbles and giving him an empty bag. Sang-woo knew that this act would lead to Ali's elimination, which it did, but it would also lead to Sang-woo's survival. Sang-woo was operating in survival mode in an environment that threatened his existence. Had this environment not existed, Sang-woo would most likely not have engaged in this act, knowing that it would eliminate another individual.

**Reflection**

Think about that extreme environment of being in the squid game. More effective strategies than ethics training are needed to address ethical issues for individuals facing this game. Fortunately, we do not face the squid game often in our daily lives.

### Fear/safety

Fear about one's safety or well-being can also cloud judgment, impede ethical decision-making, and make people (individuals, groups, organizations) do things they otherwise would not have done.

## Operating under fear: The wolf's flying head

A famous ancient eastern fable called "The Wolf's Flying Head" explains the influence of fear on decision-making. The legend talks about a lion, a wolf, and a fox who went hunting together one day and caught a deer. After catching the deer, the lion asked the wolf and the fox how they should divide it. The wolf was quick to reply,

> *It is clear that we should divide it into three equal parts: you [the lion] take the head and shoulders, the wolf [myself] takes the abdomen, and the fox takes the thighs.*

The lion did not like the division suggested by the wolf, so he immediately knocked the wolf's head off and beheaded him with one punch. The fox watched in shock as the wolf's head went flying off his body and hit a nearby tree. The lion then turned to the fox and asked,

> *Fox, how do you think we should divide the deer?*

The fox replied,

> *Dear king of the jungle, we should divide the deer into three parts: The head and shoulders are for your breakfast, Your Highness. The abdomen is for your lunch, Your Majesty. And the thighs are for your dinner. I am not hungry and do not want any part of it.*

The lion replied very happily,

> *What an excellent idea, fox! Who taught you this fair way of dividing the deer amongst us?*

The fox replied,

> *The wolf's flying head.*

This ancient fable demonstrates how our ancestors knew early on that fear can affect decision-making.

Building on individuals' actions in fear, many tactics have been introduced. According to Wikipedia,

> *Fearmongering, or scaremongering, is a form of manipulation that causes fear by using exaggerated rumors of impending danger. . . . Fearmongering can produce a rally around the flag effect, increasing support for the incumbent political leaders. For example, official warnings about the risk of terrorist attacks have led to increased support for the president of the US. . . . Fearmongering is routinely used in psychological warfare to influence a target population.*[235]

Fear affects ethical decision-making in many ways, even if it is not about

---

[235] https://en.wikipedia.org/wiki/Fearmongering#:~:text=Fearmongering%20or%20scaremongering%20is%20a,exaggerated%20rumors%20of%20impending%20danger.

safety or warfare. The fear of getting a bad outcome is a well-known trap in decision-making under uncertainty, resulting from confusing the quality of the decision with the quality of the outcome. This trap renders people unable or unwilling to decide.

Fear can also be about losing a job and can lead individuals to avoid being on one side of an ethical issue they believe is proper if the other side has influential individuals (e.g., current and former politicians, billionaires, and celebrities) and others they do not want to confront. Organizations also use fear tactics to impede moral courage and to curtail ethical complaints against the leadership. Some organizations also use associations with politicians and celebrities for that purpose. Examples of such tactics are presented in part 1.

Mike Coates, a former HSBC employee who worked on financial crime compliance and left the bank in 2018, said the industry's profit-focused incentive structures can still override the fight against financial crime. "*You can't get a man to believe in something when a salary depends on him not believing it,*" said Coates.[236]

**Reflection**

Some organizations install a sense of fear in employees by having vague or undocumented procedures or firing individuals who speak up against the organization. Reflecting on the "Wolf's Flying Head" story, consider the implications of these strategies on enabling further ethical violations within the organization. Identify instances in Part 1 where these strategies were implemented and their consequences in enabling ethical violations.

## Stress/insecurity

Stress is an important factor affecting an individual's performance and decision-making ability.

[236] https://www.icij.org/investigations/fincen-files/hsbc-moved-vast-sums-of-dirty-money-after-paying-record-laundering-fine/

CNN reported,

> *People with elevated stress levels are more likely to experience a decline in cognitive function, a new study found, affecting their capacity to remember, concentrate and learn new things.*[237]

The APA stated,

> *Americans are struggling with multiple external stressors that are out of their personal control, with 27% reporting that most days they are so stressed they cannot function.*[238]

In the workplace, while a nonzero chance of being killed by a coworker exists (approximately nine in a million),[239] most insecurities and stress at work arise from job insecurity. Insecure individuals make decisions focusing on short-term prospects to alleviate their emotional state.

Several studies have investigated the impact of job insecurity on employees' unethical behavior.

> *Results from data collected from 107 professionals at two points in time and 205 employees from various industries confirm that job insecurity increases emotional exhaustion, which subsequently impairs an employee's ability to activate self-regulating processes to avoid engaging in unethical behavior.*[240]

The relationship between stress and ethical conduct in the workplace has also been explored. For example, 793 Italian researchers on fixed-term contracts participated in an online questionnaire.[241] The study results showed that the stress level and perceived job insecurity were relatively high and that unethical behaviors frequently occur. Another study showed

---

[237] https://edition.cnn.com/2023/03/07/health/high-stress-lower-cognition-study-wellness/index.html

[238] https://www.apa.org/news/press/releases/2022/10/multiple-stressors-no-function

[239] https://www.cnn.com/2016/05/19/opinions/fear-of-flying-misplaced-abbas/index.html

[240] https://www.cambridge.org/core/journals/business-ethics-quarterly/article/abs/exploring-the-impact-of-job-insecurity-on-employees-unethical-behavior/D7C2CD0A7F2074F5F90B9777B6D0E3F6

[241] https://pubmed.ncbi.nlm.nih.gov/30719620/

that stressed individuals developed low-level construal and high materialism values, increasing their tolerance to unethical acts.[242]

Other studies have explicitly measured the perceived chances of losing a job and their relation to mental wellness and stress, further contributing to unethical acts. Insecurities need not be due to the environment at a particular job. They may occur on large-scale levels due to global pandemics and disruption.

The United Nations revealed,

> *Some 1.6 billion people employed in the informal economy—or nearly half the global workforce—could see their livelihoods destroyed due to the continued decline in working hours brought on by lockdowns to curb the spread of COVID-19. . . . More than 430 million enterprises in hard-hit sectors such as retail and manufacturing risk "serious disruption."*[243]

Stress can also result from factors unrelated to the work environment.

The APA reported,

> *A majority of adults cited inflation (83%), violence and crime (75%), the current political climate (66%), and the racial climate (62%) as significant sources of stress.*[244]

## Anxiety

A *Harvard Business Review* article reported,

> *Anxiety can impair our judgment. It can cause us to focus on the wrong things, distort the facts, or rush to conclusions. Ideally, we could postpone critical decisions until we're in a better frame of mind, but that's not always possible.*[245]

---

[242] https://eprints.whiterose.ac.uk/132534/5/PID.R1-Manuscript-stress%20and%20consumer%20ethics.pdf
[243] https://news.un.org/en/story/2020/04/1062792
[244] https://www.apa.org/news/press/releases/2022/10/multiple-stressors-no-function
[245] https://hbr.org/2020/05/leading-through-anxiety

In terms of how prevalent the situation is, the same article said,

> *Anxiety is the most common mental illness in the United States, affecting more than 40 million adults each year. Data from the National Institute of Mental Health has indicated that about 30% of Americans experience clinical anxiety at some point.*

The *Washington Post* shared the results of a survey that 40 percent of college students in the United States struggle with anxiety, 45 percent with depression, and 16 percent with suicidal thoughts. The report further suggested that taking a leave from school might be healthy in some of these situations.[246] Additionally, the Institute for Health Metrics and Evaluation reported that an estimated 284 million people worldwide had an anxiety disorder as of 2017, making it the most prevalent mental illness worldwide.[247]

## Addiction

Addiction is another factor that can impede ethical judgment and can have many forms, such as addiction to gambling, alcohol, drugs, and others. Addiction can lead to unethical acts of deception, stealing, and harm. The *Washington Post* said the following about a Catholic nun:

> *Southern California nun struggled to maintain her promise to the Catholic Church because of a gambling addiction that was out of control for a decade. The Los Angeles native embezzled more than $835,000 from the Catholic school in Torrance, Calif., where she was principal, to pay for 10 years of personal expenses, including her many gambling trips to Las Vegas and Lake Tahoe.*[248]

The Department of Justice reported about crimes against college students, where "*41% of offenders were perceived to be using alcohol or drugs.*"[249] Other studies showed that "*approximately half of all sexual assaults are associated with either the perpetrator's alcohol consumption, the victim's alcohol consumption, or*

---

246 https://www.washingtonpost.com/wellness/2022/11/11/college-mental-health-leave/
247 https://ourworldindata.org/mental-health
248 https://www.washingtonpost.com/religion/2022/02/08/california-nun-gambling-school-prison-kreuper/
249 https://bjs.ojp.gov/content/pub/pdf/vvcs02.pdf

*both."*[250] The CDC revealed that *"more than 140,000 people die from excessive alcohol use in the U.S. each year."*[251]

## Despair

Despair can happen at the individual, group, organizational leadership, or even government level. Despair, or loss of hope, arises from a challenging situation you cannot get out of. A famous saying goes, "Desperate people do desperate things." One typical example of despair in the workplace is "desperate to show improvement." Despair can lead to unethical acts, and it can be amplified at work if a person is under time constraints or pressure, potentially resulting in an announcement of a fake product.

## Duress/coercion/compromise

According to Investopedia, *"Duress describes the act of using force, false imprisonment, coercion, threats, or psychological pressure to compel someone to act contrary to their wishes or interests."*[252] Suppose someone threatens you that they will take your life if you do not give them your wallet or any other belonging, and if you then give them your wallet, it does not mean that you acted voluntarily. It was an act of theft associated with duress. If someone threatens you with the loss of your job unless you remain quiet about unethical actions at work, this is also an act of duress. Individuals may also be compromised in their ability to make ethical decisions if they are exposed to threats of disgrace or if they feel beholden to someone. All these factors impact their ability to make ethical decisions. Part 1 presented several cases where individuals committed suicide when threatened or coerced by the organization or the situation.

## Fatigue

Fatigue is another factor that impairs ethical decision-making as it impairs an individual's ability to function and jeopardizes safety during the job.

[250] https://www.ncbi.nlm.nih.gov/pmc/articles/PMC4616254/

[251] https://www.cdc.gov/alcohol/features/excessive-alcohol-deaths.html#:~:text=Excessive%20alcohol%20use%20is%20responsible,years%20of%20potential%20life%20lost

[252] https://www.investopedia.com/terms/d/duress.asp

Recognizing this state is essential from an organizational perspective because decisions involving fatigue can have ethical implications for the individuals involved. A decision to continue operations during fatigue may cause harm to other individuals and may even get media coverage. CNN wrote, *"József Váradi, CEO of Wizz Air, the European low-cost carrier, told employees at a meeting this week that too many of them were taking time off for fatigue and that 'sometimes it is required to go the extra mile.'"*[253]

## Depression

Depression can affect a range of decision-making domains, including *"attention, response inhibition, executive function during visuospatial navigation, cognitive flexibility, verbal memory, working memory, decision speed, information processing speed, and psychomotor response speed."*[254]

The National Institutes for Health (NIH) posted that approximately 9.5 percent of American adults ages eighteen and over will suffer from a depressive illness each year.[255] Individuals suffering from depression might not be fit to make ethical decisions. Even with antidepressants, a study has shown that individuals may exhibit impairment in five domains: attention, response inhibition, verbal memory, decision speed, and information processing.

## Mental health

It is essential to recognize the potential drastic effects on ethical decision quality that mental health may impose. Studies have shown that the way the brain is activated toward risks and rewards is altered for individuals with mental health disorders.[256] As a result, their decision-making capabilities are impaired, and they are also vulnerable. If you know that a person has a mental health issue that impedes their ability to comprehend a situa-

---

[253] https://www.cnn.com/travel/article/wizz-air-fatigue/index.html

[254] C. Shilyanski et al., "Effect of Antidepressant Treatment on Cognitive Impairments Associated with Depression: A Randomized Longitudinal Study," *Lancet* 3, no. 5 (May 1, 2016): 425–435, https://www.thelancet.com/journals/lanpsy/article/PIIS2215-0366(16)00012-2/fulltext#articleInformation.

[255] https://www.hopkinsmedicine.org/health/wellness-and-prevention/mental-health-disorder-statistics

[256] https://news.stanford.edu/features/2015/decisions/disease-state.html

tion, making them sign an agreement to give up their belongings or rights would be unethical.

Individuals with mental health diagnoses are not rare. An estimated 26 percent of Americans ages eighteen and older—about one in four adults—suffer from a diagnosable mental disorder in a given year.[257] *Fortune* revealed that 60 percent of college kids have mental health disorders, and schools are woefully unprepared.[258]

The *Yale Daily News* wrote, "*The Washington Post published a story on Nov. 11 [2022] that discussed Yale's withdrawal and reinstatement policies in relation to student mental health.*"[259] The *Post* highlighted that Yale is asking students with mental health issues to withdraw and that there is difficulty in being reinstated.

The dean of Yale College and the director of Mental Health and Counseling responded,

> *[The Washington Post story] perpetuated a dangerous belief that college students should stay in school whatever the risk to their mental health and safety. We know firsthand the heartbreaking circumstances that surround mental health crises—including, sometimes, the need for students to take a break from their studies so they can focus on their health.*

## The legal team can suffer from mental health concerns

Two important studies on mental health and well-being among law students and attorneys were featured on the American Bar Association website:[260]

- "Suffering in Silence: The Survey of Law Student Well-Being and the Reluctance of Law Students to Seek Help for Substance Use and Mental Health Concerns"

[257] https://www.hopkinsmedicine.org/health/wellness-and-prevention/mental-health-disorder-statistics

[258] https://fortune.com/well/2022/07/12/mental-health-crisis-college-schools-unprepared/

[259] https://yaledailynews.com/blog/2022/11/17/administrators-defend-mental-health-services-amid-ongoing-criticism/

[260] https://www.americanbar.org/news/abanews/publications/youraba/2017/december-2017/secrecy-and-fear-of-stigma-among-the-barriers-to-lawyer-well-bei/

- "The Prevalence of Substance Use and Other Mental Health Concerns among American Attorneys"

The article highlighted some findings of "Suffering in Silence," in which 3,300 law students from fifteen law schools were surveyed. The survey found the following:

- 25 percent of law students are at risk of alcoholism.
- 17 percent of law students suffer from depression.
- 37 percent of law students report mild to severe anxiety.
- 6 percent of law students report having suicidal thoughts in the last year.

One might argue that this relates only to law students, but not to actual lawyers or practitioners who give legal advice or handle legal cases daily. But the same trends also appear with working lawyers. Another study, with more than thirteen thousand working lawyers who responded to the survey, found the following:

- 28 percent of lawyers suffered from depression.
- 19 percent of lawyers had severe anxiety.
- At some point in their career, 11.4 percent felt that suicide might be a solution to their issues.

**Reflection**

There is value in identifying individuals working in this state.

- Think about the fitness of individuals surveyed in these articles to make ethical decisions.
- Think about the fitness of individuals surveyed in these articles to give ethical recommendations.

The conclusions made recommendations for five central themes:

- Identify stakeholders and the role each of them can play in reducing the level of toxicity.
- Eliminate the stigma associated with help-seeking behaviors.
- Emphasize that well-being is an indispensable part of a lawyer's duty of competence.
- Educate lawyers, judges, and law students on lawyer well-being issues.
- Take small incremental steps to change how the law is practiced and how lawyers are regulated to instill greater well-being in the profession.

## Even law enforcement members can suffer from mental health issues

KQED LA reported,

> *The Alameda County Sheriff's Office in Northern California has stripped 47 deputies of their guns and arrest powers because they failed psychological exams.*[261]

Unfortunately, this audit only occurred after Deputy Devin Williams Jr. was arrested and charged with fatally shooting a couple in their Dublin home. *"Williams' mother, Anitra Williams, told KTVU-TV that her son had been in a romantic relationship with the woman, Maria Tran, and had believed she was unmarried."* KTVU-TV said four sources claimed Williams had failed his psychological exam.

### Reflection

- Identify situations (if any) in part 1 where individuals were operating in situations involving SSSSFFDDAAMCC mode.
- Identify situations where organizational leaders induced or tolerated elements of SSSSFFDDAAMCC mode.

---

[261] https://www.kqed.org/news/11926806/alameda-county-sheriffs-office-finds-47-deputies-hired-despite-failed-psych-tests-strips-officers-of-guns

- Identify situations in your personal or professional life where operating in SSSSFFDDAAMCC mode impeded ethical decision quality.
- Can you identify professions whose individuals regularly operate in SSSSFFDDAAMCC mode?

# Chapter 15

# Trade-Offs and Tolerances

*You can buy measles vaccines and save lives for $1,000 per life saved.*

—Bill Gates, after telling the BBC that he does not think traveling to Mars is a good use of money[262]

## Ethical Tolerance

Ethical tolerance defines the amount of deception, harming, or stealing you are willing to conduct or tolerate in a given situation. For example, would you speak up knowing that your product is defective if the organization might take retaliatory action against you for doing so? What are you willing to do or tolerate in a given situation? And what will you not do in a given situation, no matter what other rationalizations or benefits there are? Behavioral work has shown that people are generally more willing to engage in (or tolerate) small unethical acts than larger ones.[263] Ethical tolerance defines the limit.

Ethical tolerance applies to both action and inaction in a given situation. The tolerance for unethical actions can differ from tolerance to inaction (what you tolerate when you observe unethical stances), in which case both tolerances would be defined.

> *Your ethical tolerance in a given situation defines the acts resulting in deception, harming, or stealing that you are willing to conduct (or tolerate).*

---

[262] https://www.businessinsider.com/bill-gates-elon-musk-rather-fund-vaccines-go-to-mars-2023-2

[263] https://business.time.com/2012/06/18/why-almost-all-of-us-cheat-and-steal/

**Reflection**

Do you believe that people have different ethical tolerances for their own actions versus the actions of others? If so, why is that?

Identify instances in Part 1 where individuals tolerated unethical acts of others.

Suppose you witnessed one of the following situations. What would you do?

- Would you pick the pocket of a passenger standing next to you on the bus if you felt you could get away with it? Are there any conditions that could make you do that?
- You are on a bus and see someone pickpocket another passenger. Would you draw attention to it? Or would you think, "I will mind my own business" or "I could get hurt"?
- You are at a grocery store and see someone take a bottle of wine from a shelf and hide it in their sweater. Would you report them? Or would you ignore the situation and keep shopping?
- You are on your way to work and witness a burglar jump into a nearby house. Would you stop them? Would you call 911? Or would you move on?
- You are on your way to work and witness someone shooting another person in a nearby house. Would you stop them? Would you call 911? Or would you move on?

## Factors affecting ethical tolerance

### 1. Escalation of commitment and "do whatever it takes" environments

Quite often, people look back and wonder how ethical lapses occurred and were tolerated at many stages where people involved could have taken action. The answer is that ethical tolerance increases gradually with our actions. This phenomenon starts with a situation involving something small that is tolerated. But then the situation escalates due to unanticipated consequences, and more unethical acts are conducted amid a desire to cover up.

Knowing your ethical tolerance in advance can help avoid the increase in tolerance to unethical acts that might arise due to escalation. For example, think of the case of Elizabeth Holmes, who started with a fake demonstration in the hopes of later being able to produce an actual product. The escalation increased gradually, and more acts were tolerated along the way. Later, more funding came through; and the escalation continued, as did the increase in ethical tolerance. Soon after, Holmes had high-ranking politicians on her board, and there was a perceived "do whatever it takes to save face" environment that continued to increase ethical tolerance.

### 2. Ethical tolerance under coercive or "obedience to authority" environments

Coercion can affect individuals' ethical tolerance. Suppose you were threatened that you would be terminated if you reported fraud. Your tolerance for fraud in this situation can increase beyond what it normally would have been without the threat.

And similarly, obedience to authority can increase the tolerance for unethical acts and make individuals tolerate or conduct more unethical actions than they would have without the influence of the environment. Recall the Milgram experiments, where individuals were willing to administer an electric shock to others when placed in an "obedience to authority" setting.

### 3. Effects of anger, stress, and parenting on an observer's ethical tolerance

Studies have shown that when you are angry, you perceive things as more under control, and therefore, you take more risks than you otherwise would have.[264] Studies have also revealed an opposite effect on the perception of risk when you are in a state of fear.[265] Another study has shown

[264] https://www.pbs.org/wgbh/nova/body/emotions-decisions.html

[265] J. S. Lerner and D. Keltner, "Fear, Anger, and Risk," *Journal of Personality and Social Psychology* 81, no. 1 (2001): 146.

that stressed individuals develop low-level construal and high materialism values, increasing their tolerance to unethical acts.[266] Yet another study has found that with responsive parenting, girls are more willing to speak up or take action when they witness or experience injustice or harm. In contrast, harsh and restrictive parenting predict both girls' and boys' later reticence in those circumstances.[267]

### 4. Other factors affecting ethical tolerance

Many situation-specific factors affect ethical tolerance. Your ability to rationalize the unethical acts, your not caring about the affected stakeholders, "us vs. them" mentalities, your belief that you can get away with it, your association with high-ranking politicians, your perceptions of the success of a complaint, and your desire to protect members of your social club are all examples of what may contribute to an increase in ethical tolerance. Rationalizations of the form "This is the way things are done here" can also increase your tolerance for unethical acts. Observing an unexpected severe outcome can also change your tolerance upon realizing the extent of the harm caused. For example, observing a suicide, as in the case of Enron or Theranos, could change perspective and ethical tolerance.

**Reflection**

- Which of the following factors either increase or decrease your ethical tolerance? Specify whether they impact ethical tolerance of your actions, observed actions of others, or both.
- Feeling you can get away with it
- Feeling you cannot change the situation
- Bandwagons, where everybody is doing it
- Fear

---

266 https://eprints.whiterose.ac.uk/132534/5/PID.R1-Manuscript-stress%20and%20consumer%20ethics.pdf

267 P. Bronstein et al., "Parenting and Gender as Predictors of Moral Courage in Late Adolescence: A Longitudinal Study," *Sex Roles: A Journal of Research* 56, nos. 9–10 (2007): 661–674.

- Job insecurity
- If a person is compromised or threatened or bribed
- Rationalizations
- Association with politicians, media, and celebrities
- Can you think of other factors that impact one's ethical tolerance?

### Personal vs. organizational ethical tolerance

Thinking about an organization's ethical tolerance before joining it is helpful. When there is a significant difference between your personal ethical tolerance and that of your organization, there is room for conflict and ethical dilemmas down the line. Some actions or previous decisions conducted by the organization can indicate its ethical tolerance.

Suppose that your organization's ethical tolerance is higher than your personal ethical tolerance. This creates a situation where your organization might ask you to do something that you find ethically troubling. Examples include lying, fraud, killing, and entrapment. If you have an issue with shooting someone, then joining a country's armed forces might not be the best job for you.

On the other hand, if your ethical tolerance is larger than that of the organization, you can engage in unethical acts that the organization would find troubling, such as providing fake expense accounts.

**Reflection**

- Can you identify instances in part 1 where individuals had a lower ethical tolerance than that of their organization? What actions did they take?
- Can you identify instances where an individual's ethical tolerance was larger than that of the organization? What actions did they take or did not take?

## Consistency in organizational ethical tolerance?

Suppose that an organization has different ethical tolerances for different individuals. What are the implications and possible consequences of having this structure of different ethical tolerances in an organization?

## When different individuals within an organization have different ethical tolerances

Different people within an organization might have different tolerances for unethical acts. This variability in ethical tolerance creates a situation where some people in an organization might act and others might not when observing ethical issues. This is a typical situation that might result in whistleblowing or in individuals being quiet about unethical acts and exhibiting a feeling of discomfort.

Think of the implications and possible consequences of the following:

Your ethical tolerance is lower than those of members of your group who witnessed an unethical act. Suppose your ethical tolerance is larger than members of your group.

## Ethical trade-offs

Suppose you are facing a decision with two attributes: (1) the number of lives saved and (2) the money spent to achieve that. These two attributes could characterize prospects in a decision about a pandemic or a national security decision. Suppose there are two prospects for a decision: one prospect yields significantly more money than the other but also results in a slightly higher number of lives lost. For example, a decision made by government officials to allow businesses to operate in their normal fashion during a pandemic involves exposure to a prevalent virus, while having businesses cease their operations involves taking an economic loss but increasing the chances of having more lives saved. Which prospect would you prefer? How do you rank the prospects?

Trade-offs define the amount you are willing to give up on one value attribute in exchange for a certain amount of another such that you would be indifferent between the two prospects. If you care about both attributes, then indifference requires you to give up some level of one attribute to get a higher level of another. And this trade-off may vary from one person to another.

Trade-offs need not involve unethical acts. Philanthropy consists of an individual (or individuals) willing to pay from their personal money to benefit others. The benefit may include the cure for a disease, providing clean water or scholarships, or other forms of philanthropy. But even in philanthropy, trade-offs can be discussed. How much benefit to others does one need to observe to incur a certain amount of loss from their wealth? This would be the individual's trade-off for this situation. Even philanthropists care about the trade-offs and the benefit that would be materialized. If the benefit did not warrant their expenditure, they might stop payment and find another venue for their philanthropic activities. The *Washington Post* published the article "Amazon Is Closing Its Charity, Which Donated Millions, Citing Limited Impact."[268]

The trade-offs often relate to acts of deception, harming, or stealing; and we refer to those as "ethical trade-offs." A family member might call to ask how you are feeling, and you feel pretty ill. You know that if you tell them the truth, they will worry. You believe that relieving them from the worry justifies the act of lying and telling them you are okay, and so you tell them a lie.

But the acts relating to ethical trade-offs can also be of higher magnitudes. In achieving your personal or organizational motives, for example, some actions might involve deception, stealing, or harming with various magnitudes. Ethical trade-offs define the amount of deception, harming, or stealing you are willing to conduct or tolerate in exchange for specific amounts of benefits on other value attributes.

## Incurring a benefit from loss or harm to others

Suppose that an individual (or a group of stakeholders) would gain some benefit in exchange for unethical acts you conduct or tolerate. For example,

268 https://www.washingtonpost.com/business/2023/01/19/amazonsmile-charity-closing/

in the workplace, the benefit could be job security, a promotion, a bonus, a better image, winning a popularity contest, or any other possible workplace benefit. The harm could be acts of deceiving employees or customers by using a blood tester that is not functioning, increasing drug prices that make them out of reach to individuals who do not have health insurance, or having power outages to increase the cost of electricity. The ethical trade-off is determined by the amount of harm and the given benefit. If the harm exceeds the required benefit, then you would not do it or tolerate it; and if the harm is less than the benefit, then you would do it. Different people will have different ethical trade-offs.

Bethany McLean notes in a Vanity Fair[269] article,

> *Valeant was the pure expression of the view that companies are there to make money for shareholders, every other consideration be damned.*

## Trade-offs between present and future

Trade-offs need not be related to benefits you realize at the present. Ethical decision-making can involve trade-offs between certain actions you take today in exchange for a benefit in the future that may not even be realized in your lifetime. Examples include actions you take or forgo today to provide more protection against climate change, reducing carbon emissions, or relying on other sources of energy for heating or transportation. And alternate sources of energy might also require making trade-offs that would be realized in the future.

BBC reported, on "*Finland's plan to bury spent nuclear fuel for 100,000 years*", a project that would cost $1.07 bn,

> *Finland is on the verge of becoming the first nation to bury spent nuclear fuel rods deep underground for the long term... It's our generation of scientists' and engineers' responsibility to undertake the challenge to dispose of the waste, instead of leaving it to future generations.*[270]

[269] https://www.vanityfair.com/news/2016/06/the-valeant-meltdown-and-wall-streets-major-drug-problem

[270] https://www.bbc.com/future/article/20230613-onkalo-has-finland-found-the-answer-to-spent-nuclear-fuel-waste-by-burying-it

## Inferring bounds on ethical trade-offs by observing decisions: Foodie calls

It is insightful to observe situations in part 1 and see how much harm an individual conducted or tolerated for the given benefit. This can place a lower bound on the benefit that was needed to engage in acts of deception, harming, or stealing that occurred. Observing peoples' decisions can provide bounds on their ethical tolerance in a given situation. For example, if a person was willing to engage in an unethical act and receive a $1 million bribe, it is reasonable to assume they would have done the same act for $2 million.

The *New York Post* reported the results of a study on a "foodie call,"[271] which occurs when a person chooses to go on a date to receive a free meal despite a lack of romantic attraction to a suitor.[272].

The study showed,

> *A quarter to a third of heterosexual women have gone on a date with a guy they weren't interested in—just for a free meal.*

Researchers found that any gender could perform foodie calls. Observing this decision tells us that the individuals were willing to engage in a foodie call act of deception for the amount equal to the dinner they received. It is more than likely that they would do it for a higher amount. But we do not know the lowest amount they would accept to engage in this activity. Therefore, we have an upper bound on their ethical trade-off.

## Personal philanthropic trade-offs need not be the same as an organization's trade-offs

It is okay to have personal philanthropic trade-offs that differ from those of your organization. Bill Gates, Warren Buffett, and Jeff Bezos have all donated or promised significant amounts of personal funds for charity.[273] This does not mean that if they were making decisions on behalf of their

---

271 https://nypost.com/2019/06/21/a-third-of-women-only-date-men-because-of-the-free-food-study/
272 https://journals.sagepub.com/doi/abs/10.1177/1948550619856308
273 https://www.cnn.com/2022/11/14/business/jeff-bezos-charity/

organization, they would give these amounts of money to society from the organizational coffers. In fact, they have a fiduciary responsibility to the stakeholders. But they can make these trade-offs when it comes to their personal wealth.

## Ranking prospects based on your ethical trade-offs

If you spend $10 billion of your personal funds and if that expenditure can contribute to the cure for Alzheimer's or cancer or it can be spent wastefully, you would prefer a situation where more benefit comes from the money you spent. Individuals can have different ethical trade-offs from that of an organization or other individuals, and this does not mean they are more or less ethical. It simply means they have different preferences and rank prospects differently.

Bill Gates told the BBC that he thought there were better uses for money than traveling to Mars:

> *You can buy measles vaccines and save lives for $1,000 per life saved.*

This statement tells us about the personal ethical trade-offs Bill Gates has toward the impact he would personally like to see for money at a given cost. From Bill Gates's perspective, the increase in knowledge and gains gained by going to Mars is not worth the trade-off of spending that money on saving lives in the current state. But this need not be the ethical trade-off of SpaceX or the Tesla organization and its employees and structure, and this does not mean that SpaceX or Tesla is acting unethically. Gates further said that he believes Elon Musk has had a positive impact (presumably on climate change and clean energy) through Tesla even though it's not philanthropic.[274]

## Ranking consequences based on ethical tolerance and trade-offs

You should be able to rank the consequences, even if some are unethical and even if it means placing those unethical consequences at the bottom of the list. For example, consider the following acts:

[274] https://www.businessinsider.com/bill-gates-elon-musk-rather-fund-vaccines-go-to-mars-2023-2

**Action A:** An act of deception that would result in a loss of twenty lives and a $1 million personal benefit to you

**Action B:** The same act of deception but would result in a loss of only fifteen lives and the same $1 million personal benefit to you

Both acts are unethical, but you can still prefer the action that leads to a lower loss of lives than the one with a higher loss. Even Al Capone might have favored the act with lower loss of lives.

The point is that for any set of consequences, you should be able to rank them in a list, from the most preferred to the least desired (ties are allowed). You cannot be indifferent to all consequences. We shall refer back to this ordering in "Reasoning and Rationalization."

### What happens when you do not specify your trade-offs?

One standard mistake organizations and governments make is setting values and objectives without specifying trade-offs. What trade-offs are you willing to incur to achieve one objective over another? How much money is the US government willing to spend to save a life? And while this question might seem hypothetical initially, its implications exist in many decisions made about shutting down the economy, going to war, border security, and others. Organizations set their core values but do not state the level of trade-offs. This makes it difficult to choose between alternatives when there is more of one value attribute and less of another. And just like there is a need for consistency with ethical tolerance, there is also a need for consistency with ethical trade-offs.

## Risk tolerance

Some might wonder why risk tolerance is related to ethical decision quality, but it is quite relevant if you are making decisions under uncertainty. Recall that chosen alternatives need to be ethical, legal, and prudential. Risk tolerance determines your taste for risk: what deals you would accept and what deals you would not accept. And from a utilitarian perspective, risk tolerance determines the amount of benefit and harm (or net benefit) that might occur when an ethical situation involves uncertainty.

You do not need to consider risk tolerance if there is no uncertainty, but having no uncertainty is rarely the case. If you make decisions on behalf of an organization or other stakeholders, you will almost surely encounter uncertainty. What level of risk is acceptable? For example, recall the case of Enron traders who were engaged in high-risk deals for the corporation. Risk tolerance also helps you determine if you are operating with a consistent approach toward risk. The concept of risk tolerance was introduced by Nobel laureate Kenneth Arrow and John Pratt.[275]

If you use a risk tolerance that is too low, you will leave good deals on the table. You are said to be "risk-averse." When your risk tolerance is very low, you value deals close to their worst outcome and effectively ignore the upside potential. You will never embark on the cure for cancer or Alzheimer's or start a company called Tesla with a low risk tolerance. When your risk tolerance is very high, you value deals close to their mean value. This is called being "risk-neutral." Most large organizations could operate at a risk-neutral range within their day-to-day operations. If your risk tolerance is negative, you are said to be "risk-seeking," and you value deals higher than their mean. When your risk tolerance is extremely negative, you value deals by their highest outcome, ignoring any downside. Somewhere between a low and a very high-risk tolerance is the approximate amount of risk suitable for you and the stakeholders you represent.

And just like "personal vs. organizational" ethical trade-offs and tolerances, "personal vs. corporate" risk tolerances exist. When making decisions on the organization's behalf, you should use the organizational risk tolerance. Again, think of Enron traders, the Wall Street collapse, and many banks that collapsed for carrying significantly high risk.

## Assessing risk tolerance

An approximate method to determine the risk tolerance you should operate with is the monetary value of $x$ that makes you indifferent between a 50/50 chance of receiving $x$ or losing $x/2$. This assessment should be made

---

[275] K. J. Arrow, "The Theory of Risk Aversion: Aspects of the Theory of Risk-Bearing" (lecture 2, Yrjö Jansson Foundation, Helsinki, Finland, 1965); J. W. Pratt, "Risk Aversion in the Small and in the Large," *Econometrica* 32, nos. 1/2 (1964): 122–136.

on behalf of the organization and not your personal risk tolerance. For example, if you were making decisions on behalf of stakeholders, would you accept a decision that gives you \$1,000, or would you pay −\$500 with equal chances? You keep increasing the value of $x$ until you reach an indifference point. How about \$1 million if you win and −\$0.5 million if you lose? The indifference point is approximately equal to your risk tolerance.

Different people or groups will have different risk tolerances. Bill Gates, Jeff Bezos, Elon Musk, and Warren Buffett would happily engage in this deal for values of $x$ that may approach \$10 billion. Others might stop at a few thousand dollars even though it is better than any deal you would get in Las Vegas.

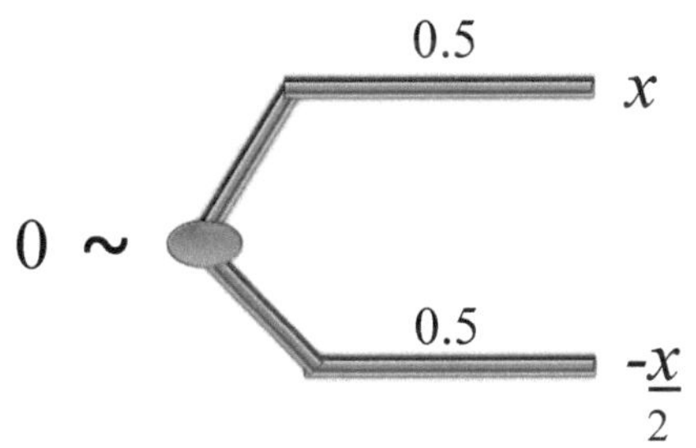


**Figure 2.11.** *Risk tolerance assessment*

## Certain equivalent using the risk tolerance

Once the risk tolerance is determined, we can evaluate the certain equivalent for an uncertain amount. The approximate formula for the certain equivalent is as follows:

certain equivalent = mean of the deal − (variance of the deal) / (2 x risk tolerance)

Note that if the risk tolerance is high, the certain equivalent is effectively the mean of the deal. This would mean that the mean of the net benefit is the certain equivalent when there is uncertainty about the benefit (or harm) amount. However, if the risk tolerance is lower (i.e., you are risk-averse), the value of the certain equivalent of the net benefit decreases and is less than the mean.

## Combining risk tolerance and ethical trade-offs

When making a decision under uncertainty that may involve harm (such as loss of lives) and another attribute (such as money), you first need to determine your trade-offs. This helps you rank the prospects of the decision. This can also help you convert the prospects into monetary prospects. The next step is to use the specified risk tolerance to decide. These types of decisions abide, such as pandemic or national security decisions.

# Chapter 16

# Formulation

*I like friends who have independent minds because they tend to make you see problems from all angles.*

—Nelson Mandela[276]

Ethical formulation inspects how you view and perceive the ethical situation at hand. Ethical formulation requires you to understand that how you formulate a situation significantly affects the chosen alternative, that frames can change with time, and that how you present the situation (such as reporting lives lost versus saved) impacts the decision. Ethical formulation requires you to think about the situation from the perspectives of different stakeholders and understand that the scope of the frame also has ethical implications.

## Ethical purpose: What are you doing?

Every frame for analyzing a decision has a purpose with possible ethical implications. When defining the purpose of the frame, it is important to ask, "What are we doing?" and "Why are we doing this?" The next step is to identify the motives behind "what we are doing" and the ethical implications involved. Different people (with different motives) associated with the decision might have different purposes for the decision being made.

## Ethical perspectives

Different stakeholders might have different perspectives about the situation based on many factors, such as their information, prior experiences, motives, and fears. Ethical formulation requires listening to the different

[276] https://www.nelsonmandela.org/content/page/selected-quotes#:~:text=I%20like%20friends%20who%20have,see%20problems%20from%20all%20angles.&text=I%20have%20never%20regarded%20any,life%20outside%20or%20inside%20prison.&text=I%20never%20think%20of%20the%20time%20I%20have%20lost.

perspectives even if, at first, they seem strikingly different. Ethical formulation also involves identifying the aspects of deception, harming, or stealing in the different perspectives as well as the impacts of the different perspectives on the various stakeholders. Some perspectives might minimize or even omit the ethical implications of a decision, while others might favor only a group of stakeholders.

## The perspective of an Australian senator toward Queen Elizabeth II's acts

Before her passing in 2022, Queen Elizabeth II and the rest of the world saw the jubilee celebrations marking the seventy-fifth anniversary of her reign. Viewers around the world were touched by the moments. Meanwhile, in Australia, an indigenous Australian senator initially refused to say an oath of allegiance to the queen without mentioning that the queen was a colonizer. The transcript from the Australian Senate below shows her comments:

> *Senate president: Miss Thorpe, please recite the affirmation on the card handed to you.*
>
> *Miss Thorpe: I, sovereign Lidia Thorpe, do solemnly and sincerely affirm and declare that I will be faithful and I bear true allegiance to the colonizing, Her Majesty Queen Elizabeth II . . .*
>
> *Senate president: Senator Thorpe.*
>
> *Audience: You're not a senator if you don't do it properly.*
>
> *Senate president: Senator Thorpe, you are required to recite the oath as printed on the card.*

And even following the queen's death, the *Washington Post* reported,

> *While many in the West have expressed sorrow and nostalgia over the loss of Queen Elizabeth II, her death has also sparked painful memories among former British colonies.*[277]

[277] https://www.washingtonpost.com/world/2022/09/12/queen-elizabeth-death-africa-colonialism/

## Different perspectives toward Edward Snowden

Edward Snowden is an American and is now also a naturalized Russian citizen. In 2013, he leaked classified information about global surveillance programs run by the National Security Agency (NSA) in cooperation with telecommunication companies and European governments. His actions prompted a discussion about national security and privacy.

Snowden has been viewed from different perspectives, including being a traitor, a hero, a whistleblower, a coward, and a patriot.[278] Amnesty International UK stated,

> *Edward Snowden took the brave decision to blow the whistle on human rights abuses by the National Security Agency (NSA). . . . Snowden revealed human rights abuses on a mass, global scale—yet he continues to be punished for blowing the whistle, and telling the world about the abuses. Snowden's decision changed the face of digital communications around the world. Thanks to him, we now know that governments—including the UK, USA, Canada, New Zealand and Australia—are capturing and storing our private information without our consent.*[279]

On September 2, 2020, a US federal court ruled in *United States v. Moalin* that the US intelligence's mass surveillance program exposed by Snowden was illegal and possibly unconstitutional.[280]

Thanks to Elon Musk, we have a survey of over 3.3. million respondents who voted on two perspectives of whether or not Snowden should be pardoned.

> *Elon Musk @elonmusk*

---

[278] https://www.theguardian.com/world/2013/nov/25/edward-snowden-nsa-wikipedia-founder; https://www.newyorker.com/news/john-cassidy/why-edward-snowden-is-a-hero; https://www.nytimes.com/2014/01/02/opinion/edward-snowden-whistle-blower.html; https://www.washingtonpost.com/news/post-politics/wp/2013/06/11/dnc-chair-debbie-wasserman-schultz-snowden-is-a-coward/; https://www.washingtonpost.com/news/wonk/wp/2013/08/09/edward-snowden-patriot/

[279] https://www.amnesty.org.uk/edward-snowden-nsa-whistleblower-pardon

[280] https://en.wikipedia.org/wiki/Edward_Snowden

*I am not expressing an opinion but did promise to conduct this poll.*

*Should Assange and Snowden be pardoned?*

*Yes 80.5%, No 19.5%*

*3,316,014 votes*[281]

## Mikhail Gorbachev: Hero or traitor?

Mikhail Gorbachev was the last leader of the Soviet Union before it collapsed in 1991. He was loved and celebrated by the West, but not so much by Russia, and there are different perspectives for why this is so.

Reuters said,

> *While Gorbachev, who died aged 91 in Moscow on Tuesday, is revered by many in the West for helping end the Cold War, many Russians regard him as a bumbling politician who accidentally destroyed a great country, triggering years of economic hardship, humiliation and a loss of geopolitical clout.*[282]

History News Network reported how Gorbachev became a hero to the West:

> *Despite what Americans want to believe about the man whom they credit with doing much to end the Cold War, Mikhail Gorbachev is probably best described as the greatest failure of a leader in Russian history.*[283]

The *Moscow Times* wrote the following in an article titled "Gorbachev the Traitor":

> *The Soviet Union did not disappear because of a great flood or a major earthquake. Somebody was at the helm, making decisions and setting a political course. Politicians should be responsible for their actions.*[284]

---

[281] https://twitter.com/elonmusk/status/1599224347121500160
[282] https://www.reuters.com/world/europe/kremlin-gorbachevs-romanticism-about-west-was-not-justified-2022-08-31/
[283] https://historynewsnetwork.org/article/183846
[284] https://www.themoscowtimes.com/2011/03/16/gorbachev-the-traitor-a5661

Elon Musk has yet to conduct a Twitter poll on this one, so we will not be able to determine the percentage of respondents for the different perspectives—at least not in the near future.

## Benefits of exploring different perspectives

After identifying the different perspectives, you might end up with a new perspective that is a combination of different perspectives. Besides the ethical implications and a better understanding of the situation, there may be prudential benefits to exploring different perspectives. As an example, you might highlight a need for both long-term and short-term investments in your portfolio, or you might want to explore a different angle. In 1998, Bill Gates mentioned,

> *It is not clear that anybody would have even worked with us if they had known that would be the eventual impact of running standards like our operating system on those machines.*

### Reflection

- Refer back to part 1 and reflect on the perspectives the decision-makers chose and those not considered. Identify a perspective you would take in each of the decisions made in part 1.
- Reflect on the different perspectives of individuals toward the following societal issues:
  - Affirmative action
  - *Roe v. Wade* reversal
  - Gun control
  - Climate change
  - Border security
  - Homelessness

## Ethical scope of the frame

Sometimes you might not be able to simultaneously address all decisions relating to a situation. Therefore, the scope of the decision will be limited. Decision quality provides guidance on identifying the appropriate scope of the frame. It is helpful to identify three layers: (1) what is "taken as given," (2) what is "to be decided now," and (3) what is "to be decided later."

When purchasing a fixer-upper real estate investment, some decisions are taken as given (e.g., you will invest in real estate and not crypto). Other decisions might be decided now (e.g., which property to purchase). And some decisions will be decided later (e.g., the type of finishing, the floor type, the contractor, and the colors of the walls). You do not need to decide all the details of the follow-up decisions at the time of purchase unless they affect the current decision.

When thinking about the scope of the frame from an ethical perspective, however, it is also essential to identify the stakeholders impacted by what you will take as given, what you will decide now, and what you will decide later.

### Ethical scope?

Are organizations willing to take a challenge to include the following in their scope?

- Taken as given: The elements of ethical decision quality will be included in our decision-making.
- To be decided now: The ethical quality of decisions will be assessed and addressed when making decisions.
- To decide later: We will not defer to ethical issues till later.

**Figure 2.12.** *Three layers of ethical scope*

## Ethical scope for VW emissions: What was taken as given?

When news spread about the disparity between announced and measured emissions, VW executive Oliver Schmidt mentioned to the board,

> *It should first be decided whether we are honest. If we are not honest, everything stays as it is.*

Do we need to decide if we are honest? This statement demonstrates that their frame did include ethical decision quality as "taken as given." It was something that would be decided at that moment.

Let us edit Oliver Schmidt's statement using an ethical scope:

> *It should not be decided whether we are honest. This is of course taken as given.*

And instead of the observation that if they are not honest, everything stays as it is, it would state,

> *If indeed it turns out we are honest, everything stays as it is.*

In the sense that if there is no need to change, then things can stay as they are. On the other hand, it would say,

> *If weak elements or mindsets impede ethical decision quality, we must rectify them.*

## Ethical scope of the Declaration of Independence?

As we discussed, a draft of the Declaration of Independence had a clause about slavery:

> *He has waged cruel war against human nature itself, violating its most sacred rights of life and liberty in the persons of a distant people who never offended him, captivating and carrying them into slavery in another hemisphere or to incur miserable death in their transportation thither.*[285]

With this clause, the scope would have "taken as given" that captivating and carrying people into slavery would violate the "most sacred rights of life." When they did not get support from the delegates who were profiting from the slave trade, the paragraph was dropped. And while Jefferson and others opposed slavery, the chosen scope at the time did not abolish it. This topic was placed in the "to be decided later" category.

## Frames change with time and have ethical implications

Frames can change with time, and when they do, there might be ethical implications. Nelson Mandela was once viewed as a terrorist and served twenty-seven years in prison for his opposition to the apartheid in South Africa. He was released from jail, was engaged in the negotiations that ended the apartheid, and became the country's president.

Muhammad Ali was viewed as a traitor for refusing to fight in Vietnam. His perspective at the time is as follows:

> *My conscience won't let me go shoot my brother, or some darker people, or some poor hungry people in the mud for big powerful America. And shoot them for what? They never called me nigger, they never lynched me, they didn't put no dogs on me, they didn't rob me of my nationality, rape and kill my mother and father. . . . Shoot them for what? How can I shoot them poor people? Just take me to jail.*[286]

---

[285] https://www.npr.org/2015/07/03/419824340/scrapped-declaration-of-independence-passage-denounced-slavery

[286] https://www.theatlantic.com/news/archive/2016/06/muhammad-ali-vietnam/485717/

This frame led the boxing commission to stop granting Ali a boxing license, and he almost went to jail. His trainer would say about Ali, "He was robbed of his best years, his prime years."

But the perspectives changed as the antiwar movement in America grew. In 2005, former president Bush presented Ali with the Presidential Medal of Freedom. And upon Ali's death, then President Obama noted Ali's perspective:

> *It would earn him enemies on the left and the right, make him reviled, and nearly send him to jail. But Ali stood his ground. And his victory helped us get used to the America we recognize today.*

## The presentation or relabeling of outcomes affects the decision

Different ways by which you present the same situation or even label its outcomes can impact the decision, change the frame, and have significant ethical implications. As the saying goes, "One man's terrorist is another man's freedom fighter."

In 1981, Tversky and Kahneman (1981) introduced this phenomenon through what they referred to as the "Asian disease problem," where they provided a compelling example of how choices change by a simple relabeling or by thinking in terms of a "loss vs. gain" frame.[287] In their experiment, participants were asked two sets of questions related to how they would respond if the United States were preparing for the outbreak of an unusual Asian disease.

In the first set of questions, participants were asked to choose between the following two alternatives (programs):

**A:** If program A is adopted, two hundred people will be saved.

**B:** If program B is adopted, there is a one-third probability that six hundred people will be saved and a two-thirds probability that no one will be saved.

*Approximately 72 percent of the respondents chose program A over B.*

---

[287] A. Tversky and D. Kahneman, "The Framing of Decisions and the Psychology of Choice," Science 211, no. 4481 (January 1981): 453–458.

In the second set of questions, there was a relabeling of the outcomes that inspired thinking about loss versus gain. Participants were asked to choose between programs C and D:

**C:** If program C is adopted, four hundred people will die.

**D:** If program D is adopted, there is a one-third probability that nobody will die and a two-thirds probability that six hundred people will die.

*Approximately 78 percent of the same respondents chose program D over C.*

The results showed a reversal of preferences by simply changing the frame from a gain frame to a loss frame or that relabeling of the outcomes led to a preference reversal. The ethical implications of this observation are that by changing the presentation (and the frame), you can impact the decisions and responses obtained, even those related to decisions about life and death.

**Reflection**

- Do you spend enough time considering different perspectives of the frame in your decisions?
- Do you spend enough time considering the ethical implications of the scope of the frame?
- Do you spend enough time considering the effects of the presentation on ethical decision-making?

# Chapter 17

# Stakeholders

*All I care about is our shareholders.*

—Mike Pearson, Valeant

(US insurance premiums have gone up by 43 percent since 2008.
Valeant lost more than 90 percent of its value, or more than $80 billion.)

## Identifying the stakeholders

Stakeholders are individuals that can affect or are affected by the decision. They comprise one of the most important elements of ethical decision quality. As we discussed, there is no point in discussing ethical decision-making if there are no stakeholders. You cannot be unethical if there are no stakeholders or sentient beings. You can talk about how prudent your decisions are. But you cannot deceive, harm, or steal if there is nobody to deceive, harm, or steal from. In most ethical collapses, there are stakeholders whose rights have been impinged upon.

It is important to identify stakeholders for several reasons:

1. If you have not identified the affected stakeholders, you can act unethically toward a group of stakeholders without knowing it.

2. Knowing the extent of stakeholders affected by your decision might act as a deterrent if the harm involves many stakeholders, bringing the act above your ethical tolerance.

3. Third, to determine the amount of benefit or harm from a decision (such as in a utilitarian approach), you need to consider the stakeholders for whom there is a common good and those for whom there is harm.

4. Fourth, some stakeholders might have hidden motives that impact your decision. When stakeholders have different motives or inter-

ests, there is a potential for conflict that is escalated with different biases, beliefs, perspectives, environments, feasible alternatives, and different levels of well-being. Identifying their relation with the decision helps reveal potential hidden motives and some common grounds.

5. And if these reasons are not enough, a fifth reason is that stakeholders affected by your decision might end up being whistleblowers about actions in your organization.

**Reflection**

For decisions made in part 1, identify the stakeholders affected by the decision. Identify the impacts of the actions on the stakeholders in terms of money (including lost pensions), well-being, and others.

### Awareness about stakeholders vs. shareholders

Shareholders are individuals who own a share in an organization. Stakeholders cast a much larger net, comprising shareholders, employees, customers, society, and other individuals affected or can affect organizational decisions. Examples of stakeholders include major donors, lenders, and borrowers.

An organization need not make all decisions to favor all stakeholders equally. In fact, the organization has a fiduciary responsibility toward its stakeholders. But when it comes to decisions involving deception, stealing, or harm, the ethical standard applies to any stakeholder. The ethicality of the act itself should not depend on who did it, and the organization should not have a double standard in tolerance to unethical actions based on whether it was a shareholder or a stakeholder. This includes acknowledging ethical violations if a faulty product could lead to loss of lives, an act of deception that results in a Ponzi scheme, or intentionally increasing electricity prices by shutting off power plants.

## Elon Musk offers stakeholders a say in Twitter, but not necessarily the lead

Different organizations offer different stakeholders more of a say in organizational affairs. Elon Musk, who paid $44 billion to buy Twitter, gave stakeholders a say in whether he should continue running the social network or step down.

> *Elon Musk @elonmusk*
>
> *Should I step down as head of Twitter? I will abide by the results of this poll.*
>
> *The results of the poll were as follows:*
>
> *Yes 57.5%, No 42.5%,*
>
> *17,502,391 votes*

The Associated Press (AP) reported,

> *More than half of the 17.5 million respondents voted "yes" in answer to Musk's Twitter poll asking whether he should step down as head of the company.*[288]

Following the poll, he did step down. Note that Musk can be ethical and still not have to offer that poll to the stakeholders. There would be no element of deception, harming, or stealing by not giving stakeholders of a social network this opportunity. In this case, it was a decision to engage stakeholders who use the social network.

When it came to a stakeholder offering to run Twitter for free, though, there was a catch:

> *Lex Fridman @lexfridman*
>
> *Fun suggestion @elonmusk: Let me run Twitter for a bit. No salary. All in. Focus on great engineering and increasing the amount of love in the world. Just offering my help in the unlikely case it's useful.*[289]

---

[288] https://apnews.com/article/elon-musk-twitter-inc-technology-business-8dac8ae023444ef9c37ca1d8fe1c14df

[289] https://twitter.com/lexfridman/status/1604624131626090497?lang=en

(Friedman is an MIT researcher and podcast host.)

Shortly after, Musk responded,

> *You must like a lot of pain. One catch: you have to invest your life savings in Twitter, and it has been in the fast lane to bankruptcy since May. Still want the job?*

**Reflection**

Why do you believe Elon Musk offered that condition of investing the stakeholder's life savings (i.e., making the stakeholder a shareholder before running Twitter)?

Would a stakeholder who is not a shareholder have the same interests as shareholders within the organization?

## Implications of decisions to stakeholders

Identifying the stakeholders is an important step in understanding the ethical nature of the decisions. The next step is to identify the impact of the decisions on the stakeholders you have identified.

## Example: Stakeholders impacted by Mexico drug cartels

- People harmed: Since 2002, over one hundred thousand people have been killed in Mexico due to drug cartel violence affecting individuals and their families. Other stakeholders include the families of those individuals, some of whom may be relying on them for support, as well as friends of those individuals.

- Examples of cartels include Beltran Leyva Organization (BLO), Cartel Jalisco New Generation (CJNG), Guerreros Unidos (GU), Gulf Cartel, Juarez Cartel and La Linea, La Familia Michoacana, Los Zetas Cartel, Sinaloa Cartel, and Tijuana/Arellano Felix Cartel.[290]

---

[290] https://www.cnn.com/2013/09/02/world/americas/mexico-drug-war-fast-facts/index.html

- Examples of crime include the following: *"In March 2014, three men kidnapped Reynaldo Pacheco and bludgeoned his head with rocks, leaving the 44-year-old father of a young daughter dead in a creek bed in California's Napa County. Local authorities determined that his murder was a consequence of an investment fraud that targeted low-income Latino and Asian immigrants around the world."*[291]

- Examples of troops to fight cartels include this *LA Times* article: "Mexico's President Vowed to End the Drug War. Instead, He's Doubled the Number of Troops in the Streets."[292]

- From 2002 to 2014, heroin-overdose-related deaths in the United States quadrupled.

- Examples of bank involvement include the following: *"HSBC was profiting from an international criminal scheme even while on probation for having served murderous drug cartels and other criminals. HSBC had admitted to U.S. prosecutors in 2012 that it had helped dirty money flow through its branches around the world, including at least $881 million controlled by the notorious Sinaloa cartel and other Mexican drug gangs."*[293]

- Politicians in the United States and Mexico use the issue for political campaigns.

- Can you think of others?

- **Example: Stakeholders impacted by shoplifting**

Identify the various stakeholders affected by shoplifting. One immediate response might be the shareholders in the shop itself. Another set of stakeholders could be the security personnel. But shoplifting also affects other customers in many aspects. Customers who are affected by missing supplied. Or customers who may be affected by consequences of shop-

[291] https://www.icij.org/investigations/fincen-files/hsbc-moved-vast-sums-of-dirty-money-after-paying-record-laundering-fine/
[292] https://www.latimes.com/world-nation/story/2022-08-19/mexicos-president-vowed-to-end-the-drug-war-instead-hes-deployed-twice-as-many-troops-as-his-predecessors
[293] https://www.icij.org/investigations/fincen-files/hsbc-moved-vast-sums-of-dirty-money-after-paying-record-laundering-fine/

lifting. Walmart CEO announced that rising thefts at Walmart could lead to price jumps and store closures.[294]

## Which stakeholders would be harmed, and which stakeholders would benefit?

Once you have identified the stakeholders, the next step is to identify (if any) the stakeholders benefiting and those subject to deception, harming, or stealing. If so, what are you going to do about it? This step helps identify the issues that might arise. It can also act as a deterrence or can help with the calculation of harm and benefit. Further, it also helps generate hybrid alternatives that may resolve the issue. For example, are there middle grounds that can be pursued? It is therefore important to understand the extent of stakeholders affected by your decision.

It is important to note here the focus on deception, harming, or stealing. For example, suppose there is a contract where stakeholders were told beforehand that prices might increase at any time. The stakeholders agreed and signed this contract under no pressure. In this case, raising the price does not entail deception. The stakeholders knew the deal they were getting before signing. On the other hand, suppose they were led to sign, and this information was not made clear or even disclosed; then there would be an element of whether the absence of disclosure was made with the intent to deceive.

### Reflection

- Who are the stakeholders in the following decisions? Think about the implications of these decisions to the stakeholders.

- **Feds increasing interest rates.** Hint, think about banks, stock market investors, housing price effects, renters, homeowners, foreclosures, layoffs (Wells Fargo laid off home-lending employees in at least five major markets in April as the Federal Reserve started ticking interest rates higher),[295] and others.

---

[294] https://www.cnbc.com/2022/12/06/walmart-ceo-says-shoplifting-could-lead-to-price-jumps-store-closures.html

[295] https://www.businessinsider.com/latest-wells-fargo-news-hirings-layoffs

- o *Roe v. Wade* reversal by the Supreme Court
- o President Joe Biden's **student loan forgiveness program**
- o **Tenant eviction** moratorium in Los Angeles (due to Covid, if you do not pay rent or if you bring in others not in the lease, you cannot be evicted)
- o **Eminent domain.** The right of the government to seize private property with compensation, but without necessarily the owner's consent. Three conditions must be satisfied: (1) the property must be taken for "public use," (2) "the state must pay just compensation," and (3) there must be a due process of law.
- o **Elon Musk's** purchase of Twitter

- Can you identify situations in part 1 where some stakeholders benefited and where others were harmed?

## The "do not care" (DNC) and "easy target" (ET) stakeholder syndromes

When you think of some of the significant ethical lapses, many of them involved two categories of stakeholders:

1. **Do not care (DNC):** Actors were aware of the acts but did not care about those stakeholders. Examples include actions favoring shareholders versus stakeholders

2. **Easy target (ET):** Actors were aware but felt that the stakeholders were easy targets, and therefore, they would get away with it. Examples include Enron tapes revealing conversations about power outages; they involved stakeholders that the actors believed were easy targets so they would get away with it.

These two categories of stakeholders are impacted by many of the ethical lapses that occur. Examples are abundant. ABC News published an article titled "Former Female Inmates Speak about Widespread Sexual Abuse by

Prison Staff: Employees abused prisoners at 19 facilities, according to a Senate probe."[296]

Wikipedia reported,

> *During the early stages of the Iraq War, members of the United States Army and the CIA committed a series of human rights violations and war crimes against detainees in the Abu Ghraib prison in Iraq, including physical and sexual abuse, torture, rape and the killing of Manadel al-Jamadi. The abuses came to public attention with the publication of photographs of the abuse by CBS News in April 2004. The incidents caused shock and outrage, receiving widespread condemnation within the United States and internationally.*[297]

## The power of reversals

The idea of reversals is a powerful method to help increase awareness of unethical acts. You can understand various stakeholders' perspectives by reversing the situation and placing yourself in the other person's position or changing the stakeholders' roles.

### Reflection

- Identify stakeholders that belonged to the DNC and ET categories in part 1. Identify other stakeholders for which the same actions would not have occurred had they thought of reversals.
- Identify other examples of DNC and ET stakeholders.

---

[296] https://abcnews.go.com/Politics/senate-report-documents-widespread-sexual-abuse-female-inmates/story?id=95157791
[297] https://en.wikipedia.org/wiki/Abu_Ghraib_torture_and_prisoner_abuse

# Chapter 18

# Reasoning and Rationalization

*[W]e are more generous toward a stranger*
*if we have just found a dime;*
*a judge's decision to grant parole depends*
*on how long it has been since he or she had lunch.*

—Sarah Bakewell,
*New York Times* article Clang Went the Trolley
November 22, 2013

## What is ethical reasoning?

Ethical reasoning examines the logic used in making decisions. It ensures a decision-making process that captures the elements of ethical decision quality when making a decision. Most discussions of ethical reasoning focus on the logic used in analyzing an ethical issue: utilitarian (consequential), Kantian (deontological), and virtue ethics, among other well-known reasoning methods. Ethical reasoning requires additional considerations about the analysis of ethical issues. These include the ethics of the logic used in the analysis (whether flawed, outcome-predetermined, inconsistent, or purely deterministic) and the effects of uncertainty on ethical considerations, such as determining the benefit and harm when a decision leads to multiple outcomes. Ethical reasoning also requires identifying common rationalizations individuals use to rationalize unethical acts.

Ethical decision reasoning can be improved by training. This includes many aspects to ensure the following:

1. We understand our inherent limitations in decision-making under uncertainty and that these limitations can impede ethical reasoning.

2. There is a need for a sound decision-making method that avoids flawed methods of decision-making, outcome-predetermined analyses, methods that are subject to manipulation, and one that can incorporate uncertainty.

3. Several distinctions used in reasoning about ethical issues—including Kantian, utilitarian, and virtue ethics—should be consistent with this method.

4. Impediments to ethical reasoning exist and include intimidation, rationalizations, and biases that impede ethical decision reasoning.

## Recognizing that our mental abilities are limited when there is uncertainty

Decision-making is an area that is often difficult to teach because many people have already made a plethora of decisions in their personal and professional lives. In addition, many individuals have had successful careers without relying on a decision-making method and relying solely on intuition and experience. Any sound decision-making method will require you to rely on your experience. However, it has been shown on numerous occasions that our intuition fails quickly when there is uncertainty. This is why we need to rely on some machinery for ethical decision-making under uncertainty.

## How Benjamin Franklin made decisions: Pros and cons

Benjamin Franklin's approach is a simple and powerful way of visualizing preferences for possible scenarios. However, while this method provides insights, it cannot answer the simple *Let's Make a Deal* decision of whether to switch.

## Do we always have uncertainty in ethical decision-making?

As we discussed, there could be uncertainty about information—even about the validity of a written confession of wrongdoing by a suspect if it were coerced. Uncertainty also exists about the benefit or harm that could result from the actions. Ethical decision reasoning needs to take this uncertainty into account.

Examples include incorporating uncertainty when various levels of benefit or harm follow a decision or assessing the level of risk when there is a new technology and when we do not know for sure what the impact will be. In the article "Tesla Cars Will Not Be Approved as Fully Self Driving This

Year, Musk Says," US News & World Report said,

> *Chief Executive Elon Musk [indicated] that the company is not yet unable to satisfy authorities that its cars can be driven without someone behind the wheel.*[298]

## We need a sound method of decision-making

After recognizing the need for a decision-making system that can handle uncertainty, another requirement is that the decision-making method needs to be sound. This means it does not violate reasonable logic and adheres to some reasonable assumptions. For example, the analysis should not change by something that is irrelevant to the situation at hand. Further, the analysis should be repeatable when conducted by different people if they incorporate the same inputs.

Without relying on a sound method, we are subject to poor decision-making results. A coin toss to determine the best alternative would fail the consistency requirement because the outcome and recommendation for two similar situations might be different. This consistency requirement should not be taken for granted when the decision has ethical implications. Examples of how people make poor decisions abide.

The *New York Times* reports many real-life situations where

> *[w]e are more generous toward a stranger if we have just found a dime; a judge's decision to grant parole depends on how long it has been since he or she had lunch.*[299]

Would you want the outcome of court proceedings to depend on the mood or hunger level of the judge? No! We want a decision-making system that is not affected by things that are irrelevant to the decision. We also would like an analysis that is not outcome-predetermined. Conducting an analysis to come up with predetermined outcomes defeats the purpose of the analysis or the information gathering in the first place.

---

[298] https://money.usnews.com/investing/news/articles/2022-10-20/tesla-flags-its-cars-not-ready-to-be-approved-as-fully-self-driving-this-year

[299] https://www.nytimes.com/2013/11/24/books/review/would-you-kill-the-fat-man-and-the-trolley-problem.html

Many people make decisions using rules of thumb that apply regardless of the situation at hand:

> *I will first see which way the wind is blowing and then follow the strongest wind direction.*

In so doing, they wait to see the strongest political connections, the path of least resistance, or how others act; and then they follow that direction regardless of right or wrong. And of course, this may impact stakeholders.

Others make decisions by doing anything to repay the favors, selecting the alternatives that favor friends and family or the social club, winning the popularity contest, or jumping on the trending bandwagon, among other things.

Others may be influenced by biases, such as going with the flow, maintaining the status quo, or choosing subconsciously (such as Freud's defense mechanisms of projection).

## Recognizing that flawed methods and methods subject to manipulation exist

Many decision-making methods are widely used, but not all are sound. Further, some of them are subject to manipulation. So let us first understand the meaning of a flawed method.

> *A flawed decision-making method may contain an arbitrary algorithm or approach or violate reasonable rules of logic.*

An example of a violation of a reasonable rule of logic is rank reversal. This phenomenon happens with a decision-making method if removing an uninformative alternative changes the preference order for the remaining alternatives. For example, suppose you were considering the purchase of one of three houses: A, B, or C. You consider the price, location, size, commute time, view, and other important factors in this purchase. You then state that your preference would first be for house A, then house B, then house C. As you prepare to put in an offer on house A, you observe that house C is now off the market. No other information is revealed. Should this change your preference for the houses? Should you now say,

"I prefer house B to house A"? This would seem arbitrary. Your preference order should remain the same if you lost the alternative of house C and the removal of this alternative did not add any more information.

Some decision-making methods also use parameters or scales with no meaningful interpretation. Different decision-makers will have different interpretations of what the assessments mean. Yet their assessments are solicited and input into the analysis.

In my book *Foundations of Multiattribute Utility*, I present additional examples of flawed decision-making methods.[300] Examples include weight and rate and minmax regret.

## Example: Choosing the next CEO (by manipulation)

The following is another example of a flawed decision-making method. Don Saari presented it to show flaws in voting systems that may initially appeal to many. The text below is presented in *Foundations of Multiattribute Utility*.

## Using a Majority Vote to Please the Largest Number of Voters

Suppose your company is deciding on who will be the next CEO. It has six candidates in mind: A, B, C, D, E, F. The company conducts a survey to help with the selection process and asks employees about their preferences. The company had three departments (groups). Each group comprised ten people, and the response was coherent in each of the three groups. The preferences were as follows.

Group 1: Prefers candidate A to B to C to D to E to F.

Group 2: Prefers candidate B to C to D to E to F to A.

Group 3: Prefers candidate C to D to E to F to A to B.

Everybody prefers Candidate C to D to E to F. This might suggest that the company should immediately exclude candidates D, E, and F.

[300] A. E. Abbas, *Foundations of Multiattribute Utility* (Cambridge, UK: Cambridge University Press, 2018).

But let us design a "flawed" decision-making method that may appeal to many audiences. The CEO will be chosen by conducting a series of pairwise votes and sequential eliminations. The eliminations will be determined by a survey and a majority vote that starts by asking individuals in the company:

*Which Candidate do you prefer: Candidate D or E?*

The result of this vote would be Candidate D because everybody prefers candidate D to E. So candidate E is eliminated. Next, a new survey asks:

*Which Candidate do you prefer: Candidate C or D?*

The result of this vote would be Candidate C because everybody prefers candidate C to D. So candidate D is eliminated. Next, a new survey asks:

*Which Candidate do you prefer: Candidate B or C?*

From the survey results, two groups (20 people) would prefer candidate B and one group (10 people) prefers candidate C. The result of this vote would be that Candidate B has more votes, so candidate C is eliminated. Next, the company asks:

*Which Candidate do you prefer: Candidate A or B?*

From the survey results, two groups (20 people) would prefer candidate A and one group.

(10 people) prefers candidate B. The result of this vote would be that Candidate A has more votes, so candidate B is eliminated. Next, the company asks,

*Which Candidate do you prefer: Candidate E or A?*

From the survey results, two groups (20 people) prefer Candidate E, and one group (10 people) prefers Candidate A. The result of this vote would be that Candidate E has more votes, so candidate A is eliminated. Next, the company asks,

*Which Candidate do you prefer: Candidate F or E?*

From the survey results, two groups (20 people) prefer candidate F and one group (10 people) prefers candidate E. The result of this vote would be Candidate F, so candidate E is eliminated. They are left with Candidate F! Using this selection criterion, candidate F is selected as the next CEO, even though everybody prefers Candidate C to D to E to F.

*What happened? How was F elected?*

Well, the answer is that it is a flawed decision-making method subject to manipulation. To see why this method is flawed, note that the outcome of the analysis depends on the order we chose to eliminate the candidates. Had we chosen a different order, we would have ended up with another candidate.

## Outcome-Predetermined Analysis for Choosing a CEO

In the previous example, suppose that a member of the board wanted to eliminate candidate F. If the group had started by asking:

*Which Candidate do you prefer: Candidate E or F?*

Candidate F would have been eliminated at the start. Similarly, we can make any candidate win by changing the order that the polls are made. This method yields any desired (and predetermined) outcome by changing the order of the questions.

There are many similar situations where we eliminate candidates sequentially and then choose the finalist among the remaining candidates. Examples include sports, FIFA World Cup, and the NBA. The choice of finalist teams may change if the strongest teams were placed into one group at the beginning than if the strongest teams were divided amongst the different groups.

There are many other examples of flawed decision-making methods. Ethical decision reasoning requires you to identify and highlight flawed methods when you see them. An analyst's job is to identify those methods and not use arbitrary methods because of their simplicity.

## Using a sound method of ethical decision-making when there is uncertainty

Besides the possibility of having a flawed decision-making method, there is a need to incorporate uncertainty in the reasoning about alternatives. Since the days of Benjamin Franklin, the field of decision-making under uncertainty has changed significantly. The work of John von Neumann and Oskar Morgenstern has led to calculus and logic for making decisions. Despite the advancements made by von Neumann and Morgenstern, people still do not use this method in their decision-making, particularly for important ethical decisions that involve uncertainty. How do you rank decision alternatives that each have multiple consequences and that provide different levels of good and harm?

Recall Bill Gates's comment during his presentation at Stanford:

> *If you multiply a low probability by a big benefit of it happening, you get something great.*

Well, here is the more detailed version of that statement and the steps needed to make ethical decisions when there is uncertainty. This method is compatible with the various approaches for reasoning about ethical situations.

### Step 1: Consider all feasible alternatives and possible consequences

This step incorporates methods discussed in previous chapters, including "Ethical Formulation," "Ethical Alternatives," "Ethical Information," "Ethical Environment," "Ethical Motives," and "Cognitive Biases." Here, you should brainstorm alternatives and consider important uncertainties and unanticipated consequences. This step also identifies any environments that may impede the generation of alternatives.

The next step characterizes the relevant uncertainties for each alternative and some possible consequences. Suppose there is an alternative that you deem unethical through a Kantian perspective independent of the consequences (the morality of an act depends on the act itself, not on the consequences). In that case, you remove that decision alternative from consideration. After removing the alternative, you still need to decide what to do. So you continue with the following steps for the remaining alternatives.

### Step 2: Assign a probability to each consequence

Once you have characterized the decision alternatives and their possible consequences, the next step is to assign a probability to each consequence. As we discussed in the Information chapter, the elicitation of probability from individuals is well-studied and applied in practice. The assignment should minimize the effects of cognitive biases. It also incorporates any data that is available.

### Step 3: Order the prospects from best to worst using ethical theories

This step requires you to preferentially order the deterministic consequences (prospects) that may follow the alternatives. Different individuals can have different personal preferences in their ranking of prospects. Bill Gates, for example, noted that it is expensive to go to Mars if you can buy measles vaccines and save lives instead for $1,000 per life saved. Gates indicated a preference for spending money on the prospect of saving lives instead of going to Mars.[301]

Many ethical theories guide ordering the deterministic consequences of a decision. For example, sensitivity toward deception, harming, or stealing will impact the rank order of consequences that involve those acts. A rights approach would rank prospects where individuals' rights are not impinged upon higher in the list than those where rights have been violated. Consequentialism would order prospects providing "more good than harm" higher than those with "less good and a bit more harm." And if a prospect includes "more good in some aspects and more harm in others," ethical trade-offs are incorporated. A Kantian approach would judge the act by the act itself, not the consequence, and therefore remove consequences corresponding to certain acts from consideration or place them lowest on the list. Regardless of which ethical theory you follow, the result is consistent with the requirement of deterministic ordering in this step.

---

[301] https://www.businessinsider.com/bill-gates-elon-musk-rather-fund-vaccines-go-to-mars-2023-2

### Step 4: Assign a von Neumann–Morgenstern utility to each consequence

The next step is to assign a utility value to each prospect. Utility is not an arbitrary score nor a measure of happiness. It has a specific meaning provided by von Neumann and Morgenstern.[302] The utility of a prospect, B, is interpreted as follows: You are given three prospects (or consequences): A, B, and C. Suppose you prefer A to B and B to C. In that case, you can state a probability, $p$, that would make you indifferent to getting B for certain or a binary deal that gives you the best prospect, A, with probability, $p$, and the worst prospect, C, with probability $1-p$. The value of $p$ that you assign is the utility value of prospect B with respect to the best prospect A and the worst prospect C. This process is repeated for all prospects of a decision in terms of the best and worst prospects. If the prospects can be expressed as some value measure, a utility function can assign utility values to each prospect.

### Step 5: Choose the alternative with the highest expected utility

You multiply the probability of each scenario by its utility, and you add up the products for all consequences of your alternative. This defines the expected utility of a decision alternative, considering all positive and negative outcomes. The best decision alternative is the one with the highest expected utility.

**Reflection: Using this method in major decisions**

For the case where you are risk-neutral and outcomes are represented monetarily, you can multiply the probability by the money to determine the expected utility. And this is what Bill Gates was referring to in part 1 when he said,

- *If you multiply a low probability by a big benefit of it happening, you get something great.*

---

[302] J. von Neumann and O. Morgenstern, *Theory of Games and Economic Behavior* (Princeton, NJ: Princeton University Press, 1944).

**Consider also the following conversation with Elon Musk:**

- *Elon Musk: Well, I didn't really think Tesla would be successful. I thought we would most likely fail. But I thought that we at least could address the false perception that people have that an electric car had to be ugly and slow and boring like a golf cart.*
- *Scott Pelley: But you say you didn't expect the company to be successful? Then why try?*
- *Elon Musk: If something is important enough, you should try. Even if the probable outcome is failure.*[303]

The reasoning that was mentioned implies that the decision cannot depend solely on the probability of failure, which was low, but that it needs to balance the upside potential as well. Using the "expected utility" approach takes this notion into account by looking at the whole distribution and the utility of each prospect without looking only at the probability of failure.

## Implications of applying this method

There are many benefits to decide using the expected utility of the alternative in ethical decision-making:

1. This method relies on the rules of logic. There is a rationale for each step used in terms of desirable axioms.
2. This method incorporates uncertainty into the analysis of ethical decisions. For example, it enables you to rank the alternatives even when there are multiple possible prospects, each entailing different levels of benefit and harm.
3. This method looks at the whole distribution of the consequences and not just one outcome.
4. This method looks at the upside potential as well as the negative outcomes.

---

[303] https://www.businessinsider.com/elon-musk-thought-tesla-would-fail-2014-3

5. This method can reward based on the decision-making, not the outcome, to minimize the effects of the outcome bias. If you judge based on the consequences and those consequences are out of your control, you will be prone to falling into the "decision vs. outcome" trap.

6. This method is not subject to rank reversal: Removing an uninformative alternative does not change the ranking of the decision alternatives. Further, the outcome of this method is independent of the order by which you conduct the analysis.

7. This method captures your preferences, information, alternatives, and tolerance to risk.

8. This approach also helps you determine the value of information on any uncertainty and the value you need to be paid (or pay) to give up one alternative for another.

## Why do many people not use this method in their decision-making?

First, many people have yet to hear about it, and some do not realize that decision-making is taught or can be learned. Why do people pull out a spreadsheet when asked to choose between deterministic cash flows, and yet they assume they can make decisions under uncertainty without relying on tools? Because they were taught net present value and cash flows in high school, and it became a tool that they habitually relied upon to address these problems. They realized the answers they would get without relying on tools would be incorrect: it became second nature. Decision analysis still needs to be part of the high school (or college) curriculum. As a result, it is not second nature, and many people have had to make decisions based on intuition alone. Further, many flawed decision-making methods are still abundant, so there needs to be more clarity about what rational decision-making entails.

Second, many people have had successful careers without relying on this method. They have relied on their intuition, which may have led to successful careers. As a result, there is significant overconfidence about making decisions even with no formal studies because people have already made many decisions. And yet intuition fails when there is uncertainty. But many people still believe they can determine important decisions without analysis. Compare this to brain surgery. If you asked a person with no prior knowledge to conduct brain surgery on their friend, they would say,

> *I do not know how to do that, and you need to ask an expert.*

But this is not the case with decision-making. And as a result, they may make decisions with ethical implications for stakeholders without using a sound decision-making method.

Third, this method of decision-making is not simple: it involves "probability," a topic that might not resonate well with the greatest memories of many in school. The backlash against Marilyn vos Savant, even by university professors, indicates a problem we have with teaching probability in our educational system. But there is no way around using probability when making a decision that involves uncertainty.

It is descriptively true that people prefer simple explanations over complex ones and that people prefer "simple, but wrong answers" to "right, but complex answers." This is a descriptive phenomenon, but simplicity is not an excuse for making a bad decision. Albert Einstein once said,

> *It can scarcely be denied that the supreme goal of all theory is to make the irreducible basic elements as simple and as few as possible without having to surrender the adequate representation of a single datum of experience.*

This is often cited and rephrased as "Everything should be made as simple as possible, but no[t] simpler." Suppose we were making a decision and a prediction about an asteroid hitting the earth. Would we use a coin toss to determine the course of action? That would be simple, but it is also fraudulent and could result in the loss of lives. Instead, we would want to use our state-of-the-art tools and machinery to provide insights into this decision.

I mentioned the following in an earlier book:

> *Many flawed methods are motivated by Simplicity; the reluctance to use probability to describe uncertainty; and the reluctance to make explicit preferences and trade-offs in decisions. An often-cited argument is that making preference, value, or utility statements, and assigning probabili-*

*ties to the prospects is not easy. You will often hear statements motivating arbitrary decision-making methods along the lines of "Yes, this is not a perfect method, but it is approximate" Or even statements like "Expected utility is an academic exercise, but this is the real world."*[304]

But simplicity is not an excuse for making a bad decision or violating some stakeholders' rights. And with appropriate training, these individuals can rely on sound decision-making methods.

Fourth, this method of reasoning requires transparency. You must be clear about the information, preferences, frame, alternatives, trade-offs, and motives, among other aspects of decision quality. Some individuals and organizations do not want to reveal this information.

When I first met the chief risk officer of the TSA, I asked him two questions: The first was (1) what would you do if the analysis suggested that what you are currently doing is not the best strategy? I wanted to make sure this was not an outcome-predetermined analysis request. The second question was (2) what would you do with the report? He replied that he would much rather know the facts and change the system than try to save face. He also added that he would like to keep the analysis in case of a bad outcome to show the logic used. Both these answers provided reassurance that the individual was genuinely interested in an unbiased analysis.

## Understanding common rationalizations that support unethical reasoning

Understanding common rationalizations that impede ethical decision-making is important because they appear frequently and can be spotted on occurrence. Individuals and organizations often engage in unethical acts and rationalize to themselves, their employees, and the world why their actions were right. Sometimes rationalizations are presented to a group as "theater politics" without the individuals making them actually believing them. Their intent is to say something that resonates with a large group (subject to biases and motives) to gain their approval so that an unethical act is perceived as right instead of addressing the ethical issue.

[304] Abbas, *Foundations of Multiattribute Utility.*

Rationalization can take many forms, including the following:

1. What we are doing is in the best interest of the organization.
2. We are under no legal obligation to do anything differently.
3. I will be judged by the outcome. Better keep things safe and take no risk.
4. We know many things that they do not, and we have many more responsibilities than they have, and these responsibilities justify our actions.
5. These are major donors (and clients).
6. This is a small thing!
7. It will be okay.
8. Nobody will know, and it is a onetime thing.
9. I have been poorly treated, so this unethical act is justified.
10. All is fair in love and war.
11. Everybody does it.
12. This is the way things are done here.
13. Fake it till you make it.
14. It is above my pay grade.
15. I am minding my own business.
16. What's in it for me?
17. This is the real world, not an ethics class or a theory.
18. Keep it simple. No math!

19. I will just mind my own business.

20. Punch them before they punch us.

How would you respond to the rationalizations above?

**Reflection: *A Few Good Men***

The 1992 military drama *A Few Good Men* is an example of an environment wherein Colonel Nathan Jessep (Jack Nicholson) ordered a "code red," which led to the death of a marine named Santiago. In the classic script below, he is questioned by Daniel Kaffee (Tom Cruise) in court, and he provides his rationalizations for the act.

How many rationalizations can you identify in the following script?

### Colonel Nathan R. Jessep testifies in court: "You can't handle the truth!"

*Col. Jessep: I'll answer the question. You want answers?*

*LTJG Kaffee: I think I'm entitled to them.*

*Col. Jessep: You want answers?*

*LTJG Kaffee: I want the truth!*

*Col. Jessep: You can't handle the truth! Son, we live in a world that has walls, and those walls have to be guarded by men with guns. Who's gonna do it? You? You, Lieutenant Weinberg? I have a greater responsibility than you can possibly fathom. You weep for Santiago, and you curse the marines. You have that luxury. You have the luxury of not knowing what I know—that Santiago's death, while tragic, probably saved lives and my existence, while grotesque and incomprehensible to you, saves lives. You don't want the truth because deep down, in places you don't talk about at parties, you want me on that wall—you need me on that wall.*

*We use words like "honor," "code," and "loyalty." We use these words as the backbone of a life spent defending something. You use them as a punch line. I have neither the time nor the inclination to explain myself to a man who rises and sleeps under the blanket of the very freedom that I provide and then questions the manner in which I provide it. I would rather that you just said "Thank you" and went on your way. Otherwise, I suggest you pick up a weapon and stand the post. Either way, I don't give a DAMN what you think you're entitled to!*

*LTJG Kaffee: Did you order the code red?*

*Col. Jessep: I did the job—*

*LTJG Kaffee: Did you order the code red?*

*Col. Jessep: YOU'RE GODDAMN RIGHT I DID.*

**Reflection: Rationalizations**

Refer back to part 1 and identify rationalizations made by individuals for actions that were taken.

# Chapter 19

# The Acroynm for Ethical Decision Quality Sends a Global Message

*You may say I'm a dreamer*
*But I'm not the only one*
*I hope someday you'll join us*
*And the world will be as one*

"Imagine", John Lennon

We have completed the elements of ethical decision quality (EDQ). As you make your next decision, consider the strengths or weaknesses of each element. Use the elements of ethical decision quality as a checklist. Strengthen the weak elements, have an open conversation about them, and you will make a better decision.

We can now explain the acronym for the elements of ethical decision quality and observe that it sends a global message. Referring back to Dr. Benjamin Franklin's quote about the Constitution,

> *I doubt whether any other convention we can obtain may be able to make a better Constitution . . . for when you assemble a number of men to have the advantage of their joint wisdom, you inevitably assemble with those men all their prejudices, their passions, their errors of opinion, their local interests, and their selfish views. From such an assembly can a perfect production be expected?*

Imagine if there were a method to overcome this. Imagine a situation where people were instead working together for success. One possibility is to recognize the elements that impede the ethical quality of decisions in an assembly and speak openly about them. This was the initial motivation for the acronym and the elements fit precisely for a message to help with this call.

## AMERICA Working Together For Success

The eleven elements of ethical decision quality are as follows:

1. **A**wareness
2. **M**otives
3. **E**nvironment
4. **R**easoning and Rationalization
5. **I**nformation
6. **C**ognitive Biases
7. **A**lternatives
8. **W**ell-Being
9. **T**rade-Offs and Tolerances
10. **F**ormulation
11. **S**takeholders

## A Global Message

When I first presented this material to my colleagues in Europe, they asked for a version that would also include a call to action for Europe. Soon after, I decided that the acronym needs to be a global message. Using a simple permutation, the acronym works well with a similar call for Africa.

## AFRICA Working Together Even More Successfully

The eleven elements of ethical decision quality can be permutated as follows:

1. **A**wareness

2. **F**ormulation

3. **R**easoning and Rationalization

4. **I**nformation

5. **C**ognitive Biases

6. **A**lternatives

7. **W**ell-Being

8. **T**rade-Offs and Tolerances

9. **E**nvironment

10. **M**otives

11. **S**takeholders

## A EUROPE Working Together For Better

With some slight modifications, the elements of ethical decision quality also have an acronym that makes a call for action for Europe. If we use Uncertainty instead of Information, Objectives instead of Motives, People instead of Stakeholders, Ethical Awareness instead of Awareness, and Biases instead of Cognitive Biases. The elements of ethical decision quality can be represented as follows:

1. **A**lternatives

2. **E**nvironment

3. **U**ncertainty

4. **R**easoning and Rationalization

5. **O**bjectives

6. **P**eople

7. **E**thical **A**wareness

8. **W**ell-Being

9. **T**rade-Offs and Tolerances

10. **F**ormulation

11. **B**iases

I invite you to join me in sharing this global message so the "world will be as one."

# Part 3

# Some Organizational Impediments to Ethical Decision Quality

## Summary of Part 3

The elements of ethical decision quality can be used to assess the ethical quality of a decision either in real time or through an audit of past decisions. When a weak element is identified, it can be brought up, and its effects and remedies can be addressed. When dealing with organizational ethical decision-making, it is essential to consider inherent impediments to ethical decision quality within the organization. These impediments affect the elements of ethical decision quality and are repeatable. This part describes organizational impediments to ethical decision quality in the form of mindsets and corresponding decisions made by leadership and employees.

Organizational mindsets refer to actions justified by attitudes, beliefs, and rationalizations for unethical acts held by more than one individual at the leadership level of an organization. As a result, they affect organizational policies, decisions, and ethical decision quality. These mindsets are inherent within an organization in that they persist even with a leadership change. By themselves, these mindsets impede the ethical quality of decisions. But they also influence leadership actions and present barriers to employees' moral courage. Understanding and addressing the effects of mindsets and the corresponding leadership actions can help mitigate their impact and minimize the recidivism of ethical collapses.

The mindsets presented in this part have been gleaned from numerous organizations and media articles, including those in part 1. Although these mindsets are prevalent and describe what occurs in many organizations particularly those that end up in an ethical collapse, some organizations might have different mindsets that impact the elements of ethical decision quality. If this is the case, it will be essential to identify them. Once the concept of a mindset impeding ethical decision-making is clear, identifying additional mindsets and their implications on leadership and employee actions becomes easier. Part IV presents a survey to assess some prevailing mindsets that impede the ethical quality of decisions.

## Six organizational mindsets that impede ethical decision quality

Below are the six organizational mindsets that impede ethical decision quality gleaned from numerous organizations:

1. "Legally unethical" mindset: "If it is legal, then it is okay."
2. "Organizational transgression" mindset: "Transgressions in the organization's best interest are okay."
3. "Pendulum swings" mindset: "If the unethical act involves these particular stakeholders, then it is okay."
4. "Black hole" mindset: "If you can hide all information and ensure nobody finds out, then it is okay."
5. "Unethically fast and slow" mindset: "If we are slow to acknowledge and fast to cover up and deny, then it is okay."
6. "No decision process" mindset: "If there is no sound decision process or a decision trail, then it is okay."

### Reflection

Figure 3.1 demonstrates the mindsets impacting the elements of ethical decision quality. As you read through this part, identify which elements of ethical decision quality are impacted by each mindset.

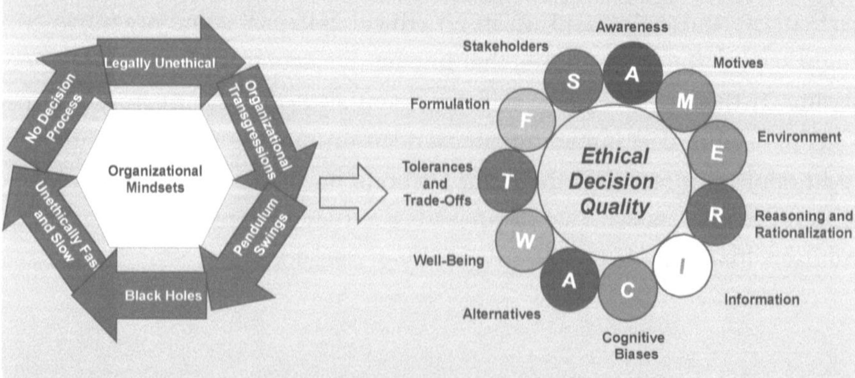


**Figure 3.1.** *Mindsets impacting the elements of ethical decision quality*

## Employee actions under the influence of the mindsets

Consider an employee at a certain rank in the organization operating under the influence of the mindsets. How do the mindsets impact decisions made by employees? Can they induce further ethical violations? This chapter describes decisions made by employees who observe violations. These actions include the following:

- Do nothing: ignore it or tolerate it (willingly or reluctantly).
- Cover liabilities by invoking more ethical violations.
- Use the situation to their advantage.
- Try to change it.
- Leave the organization.

## Managerial and leadership actions under the influence (DUI) of the mindsets

Finally, consider an organizational administrator operating under the influence of the mindsets. How do the mindsets impact their decision-making and the types of actions they choose? Can they lead to further ethical violations from leadership? And can they impede the formation of an organization's ethical decision culture?

The four main managerial/leadership decisions under the influence of the mindsets are as follows:

1. Often-fake top bottom slogans of the form "We are the champions of morality"
2. Using the media, politicians, and celebrities to enable misconduct
3. Erratic decision-making on a trending bandwagon
4. Surround yourself by friends, family, yes-men, and destructive confidants: It's all in the family

**Figure 3.2** shows actions common under the influence of the mindsets.

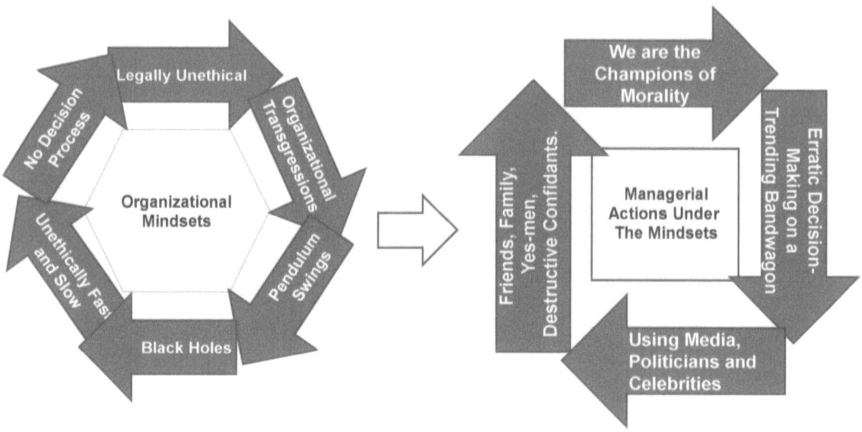


**Figure 3.2.** *Decision-making under the influence of the mindsets*

## Reflection

As you read through this part, identify which mindsets nurtured the decisions made by employees and the leadership of the organization. Identify the elements of ethical decision quality that are further impacted by these decisions.

# Chapter 20

# Six Mindsets Impeding Ethical Decision Quality

## Mindset 1: "Legally Unethical"

***If it is legal, then it is okay.***

*Arthur Andersen and our lawyers had taken a very hard look at this structure, and they deemed it appropriate.*

—Jeffrey Skilling of Enron,
who was sentenced to twenty-four years in jail
(Arthur Andersen lost its license.)

### Is your organization legally unethical?

The organizational leader or chief executive officer (CEO) makes many decisions on behalf of the organization. Decisions should be prudential (in providing value to stakeholders), legal and ethical, to avoid deception, stealing, or harm to stakeholders.

When making decisions on behalf of the organization, the leader sets the organization's ethical tone and draws on their own (and others') experience and domain knowledge. Note that the abbreviation CEO could just as well stand for "chief ethics officer." However, the leader need not be a legal expert and is guided on the legal front by the legal department.

The legal department provides one aspect of legal, ethical, and prudential decision-making, and is generally unaware of the entire technical context or domain knowledge of the decisions. Further, the legal team may consider only some of the ethical implications. The legal team's primary focus is to find (or approve) an action they perceive to be in the organization's best interest within the bounds of the legal system. And this motive generally leads to actions that score high on the legal front but may not score as high on the ethical front or even be in the organization's long-term interest.

Some organizational administrators, who may need to better grasp the difference between legal and ethical endeavors, delegate corporate matters exclusively to the legal department or even ask the legal department to find legal (even if unethical) loopholes in the legal system or try to lobby for legislation in their favor that may harm other stakeholders.

A legally unethical organization is one whose leadership is willing to engage in acts of deception, harming, or stealing if deemed legal or the legal department gives them the green light. The "legally unethical" mindset applies to both internal and external stakeholders of the organization. The standard rationalization for this behavior is that *"We were under no legal obligation (NLO) to do anything else."*

You might ask, *"Well, isn't it the precise job of the legal team to navigate the legal system and to take advantage of its benefits?"*

That is a fact. But the question is whether you want to navigate the legal system, take advantage of its benefits, and be ethical.

## Fundamental problems with the "legally unethical" mindset

There are some fundamental problems with the "legally unethical" mindset. First, it reduces sensitivity to unethical acts relying on the "green light" from the legal department. As a result of this and the potential desirability of these acts to organizational leaders, the organization will put less effort into exploring alternatives that might score higher on the ethical front, which could also be more consistent with the organization's "stated" core values.

If the first problem is not a deterrent for the "legally unethical" mindset, then the second problem might: the legal team can make legal and ethical mistakes! Many of the organizations presented in part 1 received advice from a legal team. As we discussed, the legal team can also get caught up in achieving their motives and often needs more training on decision-making under uncertainty, probability assignment, and belief updating. Like everybody else, the legal team is also prone to biases, fatigue, stress, depression, and many other factors contributing to their well-being.

The legal system is now catching up on ethical issues with attorney conduct. The *LA Times* reported about a change in the legal system in California, *"California attorneys must report misconduct by their peers."* Further, the State Supreme Court now obligates attorneys to notify the State Bar if they have *"credible evidence that another lawyer has committed a criminal act or has engaged in conduct involving dishonesty, fraud, deceit"* or other wrongdoing that *"raises a substantial question as to that lawyer's honesty, trustworthiness, or fitness."*[305]

And finally, the legal team may not be aware of the complete technicalities and domain knowledge of the decision and its long-term implications, rendering their recommendations legal, but not necessarily in the organization's long-term best interest.

The "legally unethical" mindset is so prevalent that it is often exhibited without attempts to cover it up, relying on its widespread acceptance and the confusion between what is legal and what is ethical. It is often exhibited as a first line of defense when problems arise. Examples abide:

- Enron's Skilling said in a televised interview, *"Arthur Andersen and our lawyers had taken a very hard look at this structure, and they deemed it appropriate."* The follow-up: Skilling was sentenced to twenty-four years in prison.

- The *New York Times* reported, *"The Times publicly fired Mr. Boies's law firm, which had been representing the newspaper, after learning that he had been personally involved in an undercover operation to smear Mr. Weinstein's victims and deceive Times reporters."*[306]

- The University of Southern California told the *LA Times* why it did not report George Tyndall, a gynecologist who had sexually abused women for years, once they found out about him. The *LA Times* stated, *"The university did not inform Tyndall's patients. Nor did USC report him at the time to the Medical Board of California. . . . USC told The Times in a statement that it was under no legal obligation to report Tyndall."*[307] The follow-up:

[305] https://www.latimes.com/california/story/2023-06-22/california-attorneys-must-now-report-misconduct-by-their-peers
[306] https://www.nytimes.com/2018/09/21/business/david-boies-pleads-not-guilty.html
[307] https://www.latimes.com/local/california/la-me-usc-doctor-misconduct-complaints-20180515-story.html

Pressure built up and USC paid over $1.1 billion in fines.

- Volkswagen: *"It is impossible for us to know exactly what legal advice VW received (Thank you, attorney-client privilege . . .), but it is interesting to speculate whether VW's internal response would have been different if outside legal counsel had simply said "there is no analog for this, it's uncharted territory" or "here's the worst thing we found, given our different facts, we could easily be facing penalties ten times greater (i.e., US$1 billion-plus)."*[308] The follow-up: billion-dollar fines and jail time.

Other manifestations of the "legally unethical" mindset occur when an organization discovers its procedures are unethical. What does it do when it finds out? What does it do if it believes it can "legally" get away with it? Would the organization take accountability or change its procedures or actions if they are perceived as legal? Once a "legally unethical" mindset is present, it persists in its downstream decisions. By this stage, cognitive consistency, sunk cost biases, and escalations of commitments affect the follow-up decisions. Consequently,

*[a] legally unethical organization will change its unethical procedures only if it becomes required by law to do so or if pressure builds up for it to change.*

The Volkswagen emissions scandal is an example of how a corporation changed its practices when it was finally required to by the legal system. When an unethical act is regarded as legal or they can get away with it, there is seldom further discussion about its ethics until pressure builds up for it to change. Examples of situations where corporations change their policies under pressure abide. The AP reported, *"Cloudflare has dropped the notorious stalking and harassment site Kiwi Farms from its internet security services."*[309] This occurred after pressure from an online campaign started by "transgender Twitch streamer Clara Sorrenti to pressure it to do so."

---

[308] W. Haak, "What Compliance Lessons Can We Learn from Volkswagen's Diesel Emissions Scandal?," EM, *The Magazine for Environmental Managers, AWMA,* June 2018.

[309] https://apnews.com/article/technology-gay-rights-7d64f7b71736e091a4b5d1b393 5551b5

**Reflection**

- Identify manifestations of "legally unethical" mindsets in organizations in the media and part 1.
- Identify instances where organizations' downstream decisions did not change until they were forced to change them by the legal system.
- Comment on the case of VW and the downstream decisions that occurred once the CARB and EPA learned about the defeat devices.
- Identify examples in part 1 where an organization lobbied for or used legislation in its favor in unethical ways.
- Identify other examples of "legally unethical" mindsets where actions were legal, but unethical.

## An everyday example of a "legally unethical" mindset: Befriending the arbitrator?

As a result of limited resources and to relieve the burden off the courts, the legal system allows (in fact encourages) organizations and employees to resolve civil disputes through a private arbitrator instead of litigation through the court system. Organizations embrace this act.

The American Association for Justice noted,

> *Forced arbitration is a rigged system that stacks the deck against millions of Americans. There is no right to a jury, no right to discovery, no transparency, no legal precedents to follow, no opportunity for group actions when it would be too difficult or costly to file a claim alone, and no meaningful judicial review. Without such checks and balances, the deck is stacked heavily against workers, patients, and consumers, and systemic misconduct can continue in secret.*

The *Washington Post* reported the following based on results from JAMS and American Arbitration Association (the largest arbitrators):

> *Employees were awarded money in just 1.6 percent of arbitration cases in 2020.*[310]

Consumers' win rate in arbitration cases in 2020 was slightly higher than employees, at 4.1 percent.

Stanford Business discussed the situation in the article "Why the Binding Arbitration Game Is Rigged against Customers: A new study documents how companies shop for sympathetic arbitrators, and how the arbitrators compete for their business":

> *Now, a new analysis of almost 9,000 arbitration cases from the securities industry confirms what many have long suspected: The system is biased against consumers—not just because big companies have more money to spend on lawyers. When it comes to arbitration, the study finds, companies have a big information advantage in fishing for arbitrators who are likely to rule in their favor. Making matters worse, the arbitrators themselves know that being pro-company in one case greatly increases their chances of being picked for future cases.*[311]
>
> *These statistics explain why*
>
> *very few people go through the forced arbitration process because it's so rigged, and the ones that do almost never get relief.*

The *New York Times* noted that a significant obstacle for consumers and employees is that payouts on individual arbitration judgments do not justify the costs of mounting an arbitration case.[312] Most arbitration agreements limit class action lawsuits.

In 2019, California governor Gavin Newsom wanted to take a step against potential bias in arbitration agreements in an assembly bill (AB 51[313]).

---

310 https://www.washingtonpost.com/business/2021/10/27/mandatory-arbitration-family-dollar/

311 https://www.gsb.stanford.edu/insights/why-binding-arbitration-game-rigged-against-customers

312 https://www.nytimes.com/2020/04/06/business/arbitration-overload.html

313 "This bill would prohibit a person from requiring any applicant for employment or any employee to waive any right, forum, or procedure for a violation of any provision of the California Fair Employment and Housing

However, it was met with resistance from organizations. Consequently, it did not go through.

**Reflection**

- Given the statistics of 1.6 percent of employees awarded money when pursuing arbitration, ask yourself the following:
    - Can this encourage organizations to engage in unethical acts that would be deemed legal by an arbitrator?
    - Do you believe this number would deter employees from opposing acts by the organization?
- Reflect on some acts of ethical violations that may escalate from organizations if they believed the arbitrator would favor them in case of a legal dispute.
- Reflect on the role of "obedience to authority" bias and its amplification in an organization with an exclusive arbitrator.
- If an organization had a relationship with the exclusive arbitrator, what disclosures would you expect the organization to have in its arbitration agreement to make this agreement ethical?
- Can you think of other examples of actions by organizations that are legal but involve aspects of deception, harming, or stealing?

Act (FEHA) or other specific statutes governing employment as a condition of employment, continued employment, or the receipt of any employment-related benefit." https://leginfo.legislature.ca.gov/faces/billNavClient.xhtml?bill_id=201920200AB51

# Mindset 2: "Organizational Transgression"

***Transgressions in the organization's best interest are okay.***

*I did not do anything that was not*
*in the best interest of the shareholders.*

—Jeffrey Skilling

The "organizational transgression" mindset rationalizes acts of deception, harming, or stealing that impinge on the rights of stakeholders (either internal or external) with the notion that

> *"what we are doing is in the best interest of the organization or its shareholders."*

An observer within an organization will have a hard time opposing these acts if they are perceived as being in the organization's best interest and if the legal department gives them the green light. Conformity bias, fear, and the need for job security are often too strong for individuals to oppose the acts. Opposers would be considered as going against the team, not playing the game, or as troublemakers (recall the case of Theranos' CFO who had issues with testing using a prototype that was not ready).

While organizational transgressions can start with something small, they escalate gradually due to unanticipated consequences and further cover-ups. When the media finds out, organizations end up in embarrassing situations of explaining how the actions were tolerated. This chapter aims to increase sensitivity toward the implications of this mindset and the environments that enable it.

## Environments enabling the internal "organizational transgression" mindset

The internal "organizational transgression" mindset enables transgressions on internal stakeholders within the organization. This mindset thrives on a culture of fear and coercion. Examples include the environment described at Theranos, which included NDAs, preventing people from communicating with others, firing and rehiring individuals who expressed concerns about the product, corporate policies that covered up procedures, and using attorneys to intimidate whistleblowers.

This mindset is enabled by individuals close to leadership who choose to follow the course for benefit, confirming expectations and roles (as in the Zimbardo experiment), or those who exhibit obedience to authority (as in the Milgram experiments).

Organizational transgressions can also be conducted by outside consultants or outside legal teams who justify the transgression by *"This is what I am paid to do."* At the same time, the organization can throw the moral blame on the outside teams and not the internal leadership if the transgressions are discovered and say, *"Company X had taken a very hard look at this structure, and they deemed it appropriate."*

## Environments enabling the external "organizational transgression" mindset

The external "organizational transgression" mindset enables transgressions on external stakeholders. This mindset is encouraged by corporate leaders feeling that they can get away with it for many reasons (such as connections with the media and politicians), they have a coercion edge (such as manufacturing an orphan drug), or they are too big to fail.

Organizational transgressions also rely on "us vs. them" biases. An example was Sunny Balwani's rally of employees at Theranos when an investigation was launched: "One, two, three, f— — you."

**Reflection**

- Identify "organizational transgression" mindsets in part 1 from internal leadership actions or outside consultants and legal teams.

- Conduct an internet search on examples of "organizational transgression" mindsets.

### Sample media and public record quotes

In the following, identify signs of the "organizational transgression" mindset, if applicable, and the corresponding rationalizations.

Hans Koberstein, the editor of *Frontal 21*, explained that every European manufacturer was using calibration strategies that had emissions up to 400–500 percent higher than those during the laboratory tests. But no government had intervened. He explained the rationale that any European government was thinking:

> *Should I harm my national car industry if others won't? No, I will not do this. I am not stupid.*[314]

In response to the federal investigation about Enron's practices, Jeffrey Skilling responded,

> *I did not do anything that was not in the best interest of the shareholders.*

In November 2006, Theranos CFO Henry Mosley was fired after questioning the reliability of its technology and the honesty of the company. Holmes fired Mosley for not being a "team player."[315]

NPR reported,

> *Apple on Wednesday agreed to pay $113 million to settle consumer fraud lawsuits brought by more than 30 states over allegations that it secretly slowed down old iPhones, a controversy that became known as "battery gate." Apple first denied that it purposely slowed down iPhone batteries, then said it did so to preserve battery life amid widespread reports of iPhones unexpectedly turning off*[316]

According to Canada's *Global Workplace Insider,*

> *Employer's egregious conduct in the course of a dismissal attracts both moral damages and human rights damages. . . . In* Doyle v Zochem, *both the trial judge and a unanimous Court of Appeal agreed that the*

---

[314] Hans Koberstein, editor of Frontal 21, from the Netflix documentary Dirty Money
[315] https://ctmfile.com/story/the-cfo-who-called-out-deception-at-theranos
[316] https://www.npr.org/2020/11/18/936268845/apple-agrees-to-pay-113-million-to-settle-batterygate-case-over-iphone-slowdowns

*employer's conduct clearly warranted moral damages. Among other things, [the employer] Zochem's inappropriate pre- and post-termination conduct included:*

- *instructing other employees to "dig up dirt" on Ms. Doyle;*
- *pressuring her to sign a release without advice from counsel; and*
- *taking Doyle's car keys from her purse and moving her car without even asking her permission on the day of her termination; and*
- *failing to respond appropriately to the plaintiff's sexual harassment complaints and instead responding in a way that the Court of Appeal described as "insensitive to the point of verging on cruel."*[317]

**The Air & Waste Management Association noted,**

*VW's troubles ultimately sprang from an all-in U.S. sales strategy that began in 2006 tied to "clean diesel" vehicles that apparently ran headlong into the unfortunate reality that VW had no idea how to manufacture a "clean diesel" vehicle. Shortly after the sales campaign was kicked-off, a senior VW official was filmed in 2007 complaining that compliance with CARB's diesel regulations was "impossible."*[318]

**According to US News & World Report,**

*Employees at Wells Fargo were given impossibly high sales goals that rose like clockwork from 2002 to 2016. But to meet these quotas, employees at the bank were incentivized to open fake accounts under customers' names—if a customer opened a savings account at the bank, employees might surreptitiously open a credit card under that customer's name as well. Short-term profits soared thanks to more than 2 million of these fake accounts, but it wasn't worth it in the long run. Wells Fargo will pay $3 billion in fines to the U.S. Securities and Exchange Commission and Department of Justice, and who knows when customers will be able to fully trust the bank again.*[319]

---

[317] https://www.globalworkplaceinsider.com/2017/03/employers-egregious-conduct-in-the-course-of-a-dismissal-attracts-both-moral-damages-and-human-rights-damages/

[318] https://pubs.awma.org/flip/EM-June-2018/haak.pdf

[319] https://wtop.com/news/2020/07/7-of-the-biggest-corporate-frauds-in-history/

## Mindset 3: "Pendulum Swings"

***If the unethical act involves these particular stakeholders, then it is okay.***

*LAPD captain led cover-up of sexual assault report against Moonves, Attorney General says.*

—Meg James and Richard Winton, writing for the *Los Angeles Times*, November 2, 2022[320]

### What are pendulum swings?

We shall define the term "pendulum swings" to refer to an environment that enables a double standard in tolerance for unethical acts across various stakeholders. The ethical tolerance in this environment depends on the stakeholders, not on the actual actions or the situation. The term "pendulum swings" does not refer to giving higher salaries or benefits to individuals of higher ranks or those of higher experience or qualifications. It relates specifically to the double standard in tolerance for unethical acts by various individuals.

For example, an organization might be tempted to have pendulum swings for individuals close to leadership or those that may have orchestrated organizational transgressions. Think of how Kenneth Lay, Jeffrey Skilling, and Andrew Fastow tolerated unethical acts throughout their time at Enron—even selling their stock once they felt a collapse was imminent. At the same time, they were advocating "integrity" to Enron employees. Pendulum swings may also occur with friends and family members. They may also occur with individuals who have compromising information and may coerce the leadership of the organization.

Pendulum swings are a form of double standards that relate specifically to a tolerance of unethical acts or the organization's ethical tolerance toward some individuals. They may occur for many reasons, including the following:

- Exchange of favors, differences in rank, beholden employees, entitlement, celebrity factors, "us vs. them" biases, significant donors, major clients, and the need to protect members of a social club or to favor friends or family members or politically connected employees

[320] https://www.latimes.com/entertainment-arts/business/story/2022-11-02/paramount-cbs-moonves-pay-million-ny-ag-settlement

- The desire to cover up for individuals who have engaged in organizational transgressions viewed as being in the organization's best interest. To enable an "organizational transgression" mindset, the organization must close its eyes on ethical violations if conducted by a particular group of stakeholders.

- Coercion, especially by individuals who have "dirt" on the organization and would pose a threat if exposed or by individuals who coerce leadership to get/give special treatment because of trending bandwagons or obedience to authority or fear from the board, among other things

- Pendulum swings may also occur against individuals who are perceived as "easy targets" or those who will not oppose the double standards.

Pendulum swings usually occur in an organization before the media finds out and often escalate. By the time the media finds out, some stakeholders (internal or external) will have their rights impinged upon, and the organization will have supported the impingement and the escalation that followed. Once the media finds out, the organization will find itself in an embarrassing position to have to explain to external and internal stakeholders how they occurred, and stakeholders will wonder how the acts were tolerated. This chapter aims to increase sensitivity toward the "pendulum swings" mindset and its implications.

## Pendulum swings in government, sports, and celebrities?

Allegations of pendulum swings abide not only in business organizations but also with the government.

The three most influential figures in the federal government under President Nixon were each sentenced to at least two and a half years in prison for their role in the Watergate cover-up. But Nixon, who was identified as a critical figure in the cover-up, was pardoned by President Ford.

- Allegations of pendulum swings are also widely used by politicians to attack another party. For example, allegations of pendulum swings were made by Republicans for Nancy Pelosi not investigating the travel expenses of Democrats. The *Washington Times* reported on behalf of Rep. Patrick T. McHenry, North Carolina Republican:

> *She demanded an investigation into [Majority Leader] Tom DeLay, but hasn't said a word about these Democrats who have done the same thing.*[321]

- Hunter Biden's laptop was also the subject of allegations of pendulum swings. CNN published the article titled "The Double Standard with Hunter Biden's Laptop Is Worse Than You Think."[322]

In a conversation with some individuals at NASA in 2006, the issue of how an organization places value on human life came up. They said that the value of an astronaut's life is perceived as higher than that of other individuals because of their training, the investment made in their development, and the public's interest in their success. My response, in relation to pendulum swings, was whether there would be a different standard in tolerance to unethical acts if an astronaut conducted them. There was little information about that then: there had been no prior incidents (or imagination) of astronauts being arrested. A year later, *Time* reported an incident in February 2007 involving NASA's astronaut Lisa Nowak.[323] She drove from Houston, Texas, to Orlando, Florida, in a diaper (to avoid restroom breaks) for fourteen hours nonstop to confront her former lover's new girlfriend. She was arrested for attempted kidnapping and burglary with assault. The legal system did not have pendulum swings in this case.

Pendulum swings are also a frequent topic of discussion with celebrities and athletes. Examples include O. J. Simpson's murder trial and allegations about whether the celebrity factor was invoked. And these types of allegations abide. The *San Diego Union-Tribune* published the editorial "SDSU Failed Students When Rape Allegation Involving Football Players Languished for Months."[324]

## Examples

In the following, identify pendulum swings if applicable.

The *LA Times* article "CBS, LAPD Captain Led Cover-Up of Sexual Assault Report against Moonves, AG Says" noted,

---

321 https://www.washingtontimes.com/news/2005/may/4/20050504-122024-4420r/

322 https://www.cnn.com/2022/03/30/opinions/garland-trump-hunter-biden-laptop-obeidallah/?hpt=ob_blogfooterold

323 https://time.com/5685017/lucy-in-the-sky-true-story-lisa-nowak/#:~:text=The%20film%20is%20loosely%20inspired,astronaut%20ever%20to%20be%20arrested

324 https://www.sandiegouniontribune.com/opinion/editorials/story/2022-06-08/opinion-sdsu-failed-students-after-rape-allegation

> *The New York attorney general's office released a sweeping report Wednesday that detailed an elaborate cover-up at the highest levels of CBS in late 2017 and 2018 to try to contain allegations of sexual harassment by former chief Leslie Moonves.*[325]

*LA Times* published another article called "Cal State Agreed to Keep Sexual Harassment Findings against Two Professors Under Wraps."[326]

An investigator within USC's investigative offices, who is also a licensed attorney, filed a federal whistleblower lawsuit alleging that within USC's investigative offices, "*investigations that may implicate members of the administration were curtailed.*"

The Daily Mail published an article titled "Law Firm Boies Schiller Flexner Has Seen Exodus of 'Dozens of Attorneys' amid Staff Anger . . . Over Son of Firm's Founder 'Caught Using the N-Word.'"[327] CNBC also covered the issue in "Boies Schiller Law Firm Loses Several Attorneys over Issues Involving Harvey Weinstein, Elizabeth Holmes, Founder's Kids."[328]

Fox News reported,

> *FBI officials told agents not to investigate Hunter Biden's so-called "laptop from hell" for months due to concerns about influencing the 2020 presidential election; whistleblowers told Sen. Ron Johnson, R-Wis. According to Johnson, "individuals with knowledge" of the Hunter Biden case told his office that the investigation was intentionally slowed on orders from "local FBI leadership."*[329]

**Reflection**

- Identify instances of pendulum swings in part 1.
- Identify further instances of pendulum swings in government and business enterprises.

---

[325] https://www.latimes.com/entertainment-arts/business/story/2022-11-02/paramount-cbs-moonves-pay-million-ny-ag-settlement

[326] https://www.latimes.com/california/story/2022-07-26/two-csu-san-marcos-professors-faced-no-punishment-after-sex-harassment-claims

[327] https://www.dailymail.co.uk/news/article-9980365/Top-law-firm-Boies-Schiller-Flexner-loses-100-attorneys-advised-Harvey-Weinstein.html

[328] https://www.cnbc.com/2021/09/10/boies-schiller-loses-lawyers-over-controversies-involving-theranos-harvey-weinstein.html

[329] https://www.foxnews.com/politics/fbi-officials-slow-walked-hunter-biden-laptop-investigation-until-after-2020-election-whistleblowers

## Mindset 4: "Black Hole"

***If you can hide all information and ensure nobody finds out, then it is okay.***

*I know that Madoff's company is very secretive about their operations, and they refuse to disclose anything. If my suspicions are true, then they are running a highly sophisticated scheme on a massive scale.*

—email received by the Office of Inspector General (Mr. Madoff was sentenced to 150 years in prison.)

### What is a black hole?

*"A black hole is a region of spacetime where gravity is so strong that nothing—no particles or even electromagnetic radiation such as light—can escape from it."*

Source *Wikipedia.*

The "black hole" mindset is associated with a lack of transparency and cover-up so that no information that reveals unethical behavior is leaked. This mindset is like a black hole in the sense that information, once entered, disappears and never comes out. There is a deliberate effort to ensure that no information showing that the organization is at fault is revealed internally or to the outside world.

The "black hole" mindset is not about concealing trade secrets or corporate know-how. It also does not mean you must tell everybody about your future plans for the organization. It is about deliberately withholding information about unethical acts and concealing information that, if other stakeholders knew, would have caused them to act differently toward the organization. The "black hole" mindset also contributes to the notion of "we can get away with it," contributing to rationalizing unethical acts.

Examples of control of unethical information in organizations are abundant and occur through various mechanisms. This chapter aims to increase sensitivity toward some of these practices.

## 1. Absence of documented procedures to cover up misconduct

The absence of (or vague) documented procedures is a form of the "black hole" mindset that enables an organization to conduct business for extended periods without worrying about "checks and balances." Theranos continued to remain secret about its procedures until the media found out. The *WSJ* first reported about Theranos not disclosing that most of its tests were conducted by Siemens machines.[330] And the list of companies that purposefully did not disclose their procedures to enable fraud goes on. Enron could not produce a balance sheet, and Valeant did not disclose its relations with Philidor.

The SEC reported about an email received regarding Bernie Madoff, who led a massive Ponzi scheme:

> *I know that Madoff's company is very secretive about their operations, and they refuse to disclose anything. If my suspicions are true, then they are running a highly sophisticated scheme on a massive scale.*[331]

## 2. Shredding evidence

The *Washington Post* wrote about the indictment of Arthur Andersen by federal prosecutors for their obstructing justice by destroying "tons" of records relating to its accounting work with Enron.[332] The firm was charged with fraud and criminal conduct.

The *Washington Post* also reported about how Uber's chief executive, Travis Kalanick, ordered that the company's computer systems in Amsterdam be cut off from Uber's internal network to make the data inaccessible to authorities when they raided its European headquarters.[333] This technique, referred to within Uber as the "kill switch," demonstrated how the company used technological tools to prevent authorities from investigating the company's business practices.

---

[330] https://www.wsj.com/articles/theranos-has-struggled-with-blood-tests-1444881901

[331] US Securities and Exchange Commission, Office of Inspector General, case no. OIG-509, *Investigation of Failure of the SEC to Uncover Bernard Madoff's Ponzi Scheme*, https://www.sec.gov/files/oig-509-exec-summary.pdf

[332] https://www.washingtonpost.com/archive/politics/2002/03/15/andersen-charged-in-shredding-probe/97880913-e1b9-4600-8755-c44c693a2036/

[333] https://www.washingtonpost.com/technology/2022/07/10/uber-europe-raids-kill-switch/

### 3. Deleting emails

There is a growing trend of organizations deleting emails after a certain period of about a year or two. TechCrunch noted that companies' reasons for deleting emails are not the real reason and that "The Only Reason Companies Delete Emails Is to Destroy Evidence."[334] The *Columbia Daily Tribune* said,

> *Deleting emails is an obstruction of justice.*

The Society for Human Resource Management stated,

> *A court imposed $3 million in punitive sanctions on a company this summer for an employee's destruction of tens of thousands of e-mails, which occurred even after the company issued a litigation hold and held training on what that means (GN Netcom v. Plantronics, No. 12-1318-LPS (D. Del. July 12, 2016). What made it worse was that the person who destroyed the e-mails was an executive . . . "who was very aware of the retention and litigation hold policies and violated them anyway," said Maribeth Meluch, an attorney with Isaac Wiles in Columbus, Ohio.*[335]

### 4. "Preemptive" and "postcomplaint" secret agreements that enable misconduct

Secret agreements by themselves need not be unethical or even illegal. For example, trade secrets or NDAs relating to a business with the consent of all parties are not unethical. However, secret deals become unethical when they enable the impingement of the rights of some stakeholders or when they enable fraud on the side of the organization.

Unethical secret agreements arise from numerous issues, including the desire to hide unethical acts or to protect individuals who have conducted unethical actions and who are either close to leadership or will leave quietly.

---

[334] https://techcrunch.com/2012/02/12/the-only-reason-companies-delete-emails-is-to-destroy-evidence/#:~:text=It%20is%20standard%20practice%2C%20but,avoid%20liability%20and%20future%20lawsuits.

[335] https://www.shrm.org/resourcesandtools/legal-and-compliance/employment-law/pages/company-must-pay-$3m-for-deleting-emails.aspx

Secret agreements can be preemptive to ensure secrecy before an issue is found out, or they can be postcomplaint.

Examples of preemptive secret agreements that ultimately led to significant legal scandals abide. The *New York Times* reported about Harvey Weinstein on October 5, 2017:

> *Mr. Weinstein enforced a code of silence; employees of the Weinstein Company have contracts saying they will not criticize it or its leaders in a way that could harm its "business reputation" or "any employee's personal reputation," a recent document shows. And most of the women accepting payouts agreed to confidentiality clauses prohibiting them from speaking about the deals or the events that led to them.*[336]

If such agreements were not in place, Weinstein may have been brought to justice earlier, or others would have been spared from his actions. In the Hulu documentary *The Dropout*, Ian Gibbons, a Theranos scientist, was troubled by an NDA he had signed when he got a subpoena and ultimately committed suicide.

Paying secret hush money payments for individuals to leave when they have impinged on the rights of others without informing the compromised stakeholders is an act of deception, harming, or stealing. Further, when this occurs and if people submit complaints about the individuals who left, the organization will find itself curtailing ethical complaints because they have already given a pass to the person who left the organization.

The problem with these shortsighted strategies is that they usually end up with unanticipated consequences and might even be unlawful. The BBC reported about Jeffrey Epstein, saying that in a 2009 secret settlement, "*Virginia Giuffre agreed not to sue anyone connected to Jeffrey Epstein*" in exchange for $500,000.[337] Nevertheless, despite the secret agreement and the payment, a judge ordered the lawsuit involving Prince Andrew to proceed until another settlement was reached.[338]

---

[336] https://www.nytimes.com/2017/10/05/us/harvey-weinstein-harassment-allegations.html
[337] https://www.bbc.com/news/uk-59861831
[338] https://www.bbc.com/news/uk-60393843

## The legal system catches up

The National Labor Relations Board recently changed laws regarding severance agreements and particularly noted those that impinge on other workers' rights:

> *A severance agreement will be deemed unlawful if it precludes an employee from assisting coworkers with workplace issues concerning their employer, and from communicating with others, including a union, and the Board, about his employment.*[339]

In particular, it will be illegal for companies to offer severance agreements prohibiting workers from making disparaging statements or disclosing details about the severance agreement. CNN published an article titled "Companies Can No Longer Silence Laid-Off Employees in Exchange for Severance."[340]

**Reflection**

- Reflect on how the "black hole" mindset impedes ethical decision quality.
- Identify manifestations of the "black hole" mindset in part 1. Identify how it influenced ethical decision quality.
- Identify other instances of the "black hole" mindset in your organizations and government enterprises.

---

[339] https://apps.nlrb.gov/link/document.aspx/09031d45839af64d

[340] https://www.cnn.com/2023/02/22/success/severance-agreements-rule-change-from-nlrb/index.html

## Mindset 5: "Unethically Fast and Slow"

***If we are slow to acknowledge and fast to cover up and deny, then it is okay.***

*"One week after the [WSJ] Journal report,*
*Holmes is interviewed on-stage at the outlet's*
*conference in Laguna Beach.*
*"We know what we're doing, and we're very proud of it."*

By Sara Ashley O'Brien, CNN Business, July 7, 2022.[341]

### What do you do when you find out?

Organizations may be unaware of ethical violations mainly because of the size of the organization and its bureaucracy. But the question is, what does the organization do when there is new information or when it finds out its actions were unethical to a group of stakeholders?

An essential aspect of ethical decision quality is the need to act upon the revelation of new information. Benjamin Franklin said,

> *I have experienced many instances of being obliged . . . to change opinions even on important subjects, which I once thought right but found to be otherwise.*

And Abraham Lincoln noted in his first political address,

> *[S]o soon as I discover my opinions to be erroneous, I shall be ready to renounce them.*

In contrast, the fundamental mantra of an "unethically fast and slow" organizational mindset is

> *Slow (if at all) to acknowledge ethical organizational violations, fast to cover up and deny them*

There are many reasons why organizations rationalize to themselves that it is appropriate to act slowly to acknowledge when faced with an ethical

341 https://www.cnn.com/2022/07/07/tech/theranos-rise-and-fall/index.html

dilemma, mainly when there is no pressure buildup and before the media has found out. One reason is the hope that the issue might go away or that they can get away with it. Other reasons include those that may limit the organization's legal liability such as, the affected stakeholders might get tired or exhausted with the complaint process mentally and financially and give up on the complaint or that the legal statute of limitations would expire.

In contrast, when there is a need to cover up unethical acts for specific individuals, organizations will act swiftly to modify procedures, and cover up their faults. On the other hand, if the media finds out or pressure builds up, the organization will swiftly condemn the behavior and make changes to show that a culture change is happening.

## Why is it an issue?

There are several problems with the "unethically fast and slow" mindset. The first problem is that other stakeholders might be harmed in the process of being slow to acknowledge or quick to deny and cover up.

The second problem is that the cover-up usually leads to an escalation of actions and more cover-up until the situation grows out of control, particularly when the media finds out or a whistleblower reports the actions. The escalation is often too much at that time; and so the individuals involved get fines, penalties, and prison time. People look back and wonder how organizations kept quiet about the acts that resulted in such considerable embarrassment and how nobody within the organization acted. The answer is simple: only a few mindsets—such as legally unethical, black hole, and unethically fast and slow—are sufficient to impede ethical decision quality.

My colleague Jim O'Toole noted,

> *The lesson is that the cardinal sin of management is not making a mistake but lying about it, or trying to hide it. Leaders who ignore that basic lesson about transparency soon find themselves attempting to explain embarrassing cover-ups: witness Nixon and Watergate, Regan and Iran Contra, Clinton and Monica Lewinsky, and Bush and WMDs.*[342]

---

[342] O'Toole, J. "Transparency: The What, How, and Why of Organizational Effectiveness and Ethics", in A. E. Abbas, ed., *Next-Generation Ethics: Engineering a Better Society* (Cambridge, UK: Cambridge University Press, 2019).

## Examples of "unethically fast and slow" mindsets

In the following, identify examples of "unethically fast and slow" mindsets:

- *Fortune* magazine reported,

  *Valeant Pharmaceuticals International's outgoing CEO, Michael Pearson, consented to be deposed by a U.S. Senate committee later this month after the panel threatened to hold him in contempt for failing to comply with a subpoena.*[343]

- According to *Automotive News Europe,*

  *After more than a year of stonewalling investigators, Volkswagen stunned two senior officials with the Environmental Protection Agency (EPA) and California's environmental watchdog by admitting the automaker hacked its own cars to deceive U.S. regulators about how much their diesel engines pollute.*[344]

- NPR wrote,

  *Apple first denied that it purposely slowed down iPhone batteries, then said it did so to preserve battery life amid widespread reports of iPhones unexpectedly turning off. Apple, the most valuable company in the world, acted deceptively by hiding the shutdown and slowdown issues, according to the court filing.*[345]

- History reported about Nixon's Watergate scandal:

  *When Dean realized that he was implicated in an illegal cover-up, he didn't do the right thing immediately. At first, he shredded incriminating files.*[346]

- According to the *Baltimore Sun,*

---

343 https://fortune.com/2016/04/13/valeant-pearson-contempt-senate/

344 https://europe.autonews.com/article/20150925/COPY/309259985/vw-stunned-u-s-regulators-with-diesel-cheat-confession

345 https://www.npr.org/2020/11/18/936268845/apple-agrees-to-pay-113-million-to-settle-batterygate-case-over-iphone-slowdowns

346 https://www.history.com/news/watergate-nixon-john-dean-tapes

*After denying culpability, [former vice president] Agnew, realizing he would be indicted and face prison if convicted, pleaded no contest to one charge of income tax evasion and resigned [from] the vice presidency on Oct. 10, 1973.*[347]

- CNN noted,

*Ernst & Young has been slapped with a record $100 million fine from the US government after regulators discovered that the company knew some of its auditors were cheating on exams for several years and did nothing to stop it.*[348]

- Following the Wall Street Journal article about Theranos, Holmes was asked whether they had launched too soon and therefore relied on testers made by other manufacturers. She replied

*We are the exact same company as we were last Wednesday before the article was published. Nothing has changed. When someone reports false stuff about us, it doesn't mean that it changes our business.*

**Reflection**

Identify other examples of the "unethically fast and slow" mindset in organizations in part 1 and the media.

[347] https://www.baltimoresun.com/opinion/op-ed/bs-ed-op-1109-agnew-remembered-20181107-story.html

[348] https://www.cnn.com/2022/06/28/business/ernst-and-young-sec-cheating-fine/index.html

## Mindset 6: "No Decision Process"

***If there is no sound decision process or a decision trail, then it is okay.***

*Our meetings were taking place in a curious atmosphere of assumed consensus, [and] not one spoke against it.*

—Arthur Schlesinger, Kennedy advisor and historian
(The result was the infamous Bay of Pigs Cuban invasion.)

### Benefits of having a decision process: Value creation

There has been a significant amount of work and literature demonstrating how having a decision-making process creates value in organizations. Decision quality is a framework that uses decision analysis methodologies and engages the most qualified parties in the decision process to achieve alignment and commitment to action.[349] My colleagues Ronald Howard, Carl Spetzler, Jim Matheson, and many others have spent decades showing the value of having a decision process within an organization. An example of the adoption of decision quality by Chevron is presented in a white paper by Carl Spetzler.[350]

There is also evidence about the loss of value incurred by not having a decision process. NBC News compiled a list of American organizations that made the worst decisions and the corresponding loss of value they incurred.[351] The list was compiled by identifying organizations on *Fortune* magazine's annual list of the largest one hundred companies ranked by revenue for at least ten consecutive years and then dropped off the top one hundred ranking for good. The list also identified the decisions that were made. Some of the companies mentioned include Motorola, Lehman Brothers, Firestone, and Digital Equipment Corporation.

---

[349] C. Spetzler, H. Winter, and J. Meyer, *Decision Quality: Value Creation from Better Business Decisions* (Hoboken, NJ: Wiley, 2016).

[350] C. Spetzler, "Chevron Overcomes the Biggest Bias of All" (working paper, Strategic Decisions Group, 2011), accessed May 8, 2022, https://sdg.com/wp-content/uploads/2015/06/SDG_-_Chevron_Overcomes_Biggest_Bias_of_All.pdf.

[351] https://www.nbcnews.com/businessmain/worst-business-decisions-all-time-1c6589327

### Why do organizational mindsets resist having a decision process?

There are many reasons why not having a sound decision-making process might appeal to some individuals in an organization; therefore, it becomes an organizational mindset. First, a decision process is not second nature; many executives have made numerous decisions in the past without relying on one. There is a sense that they have built their stars, so they get to call the shots, *"There is no need for a decision process, I have made it this far without one."* In addition, it might falsely be perceived that having a decision process slows down decision-making instead of improving it.

From an ethical standpoint, there are also reasons why organizations resist an ethical decision-making process: You will need transparency. You will need to be clear about the values, trade-offs, and tolerances made; the logic that was used; and the level of risk you bear. You need to be consistent in your decision-making. While you do not need to reveal all this information to the public, a decision process will document the decisions made on behalf of the organization.

If there is a transparent decision-making process, you will not be able to sustain the "legally unethical," "organizational transgression," "pendulum swings," "black holes," and "unethically fast and slow" mindsets. You will need to be clear about motives (short-term versus long-term), hidden agendas (including appeasing donors), why some stakeholders were favored versus others in their ethical conduct, and why some issues were ignored and others escalated.

On the other hand, if there is no transparent decision process, leadership will have the discretion to do and say whatever it wants. You can state whatever organizational values and top-bottom value slogans you want without checks or balances (think of Enron's Kenneth Lay talking about integrity). There is no trail for how decisions are made. Nobody will know the full details of the methodology used, the information, the preferences, the trade-offs used, or the quality of the process.

In an organization with no decision process, the facts and science do not matter because there is no process. Leaders can manipulate the process to achieve whatever decision they want. Without a decision-making process, they can also raise the "this is political" flag and motivate actions through political agendas. Politicians can make any statements and justify their actions (or inactions). Political opponents can also criticize decisions like shutting down the country or reopening it, shutting down schools, and enforcing curfews without providing decision-based reasoning.

Without an internal decision process, managers can selectively pick outside consultants to conduct outcome-predetermined analysis to suit their purpose or rubber-stamp procedures, as was the case with Arthur Andersen and Enron. In the event of an issue, managers can say that outside consultants looked closely at this and deemed it appropriate. Without a decision process, managers can say what they did "was in the best interest of the organization." Employees will be more prone to falling into obedience and authority biases and "us vs. them" biases, among others.

Because of this, it is tempting for (unethical) organizations to refrain from having a decision process or having any transparent procedures about how decisions are made despite the value that having a decision process can create.

## Why not having a decision process can be unethical

Relying purely on human intuition or flawed decision-making methods allows for judgment errors that may harm stakeholders or lose value. Even if there are no intentional acts of deception, harming, or stealing, you can deprive stakeholders of potential value by making poor decisions. You might also expose them to more risk than they are comfortable with.

Many organizational incentives reward based on the outcome, often with unanticipated consequences that interfere with good decision making. Wells Fargo incentives were an example. By not having a decision process, you judge by the outcome and incentivize individuals to meet their targets instead of questioning the incentives and whether those incentives impede the quality of the decision-making.

And even without incentives, judging by the outcome will induce decision-makers to minimize the chance of a bad outcome regardless of the upside potential. If you are worried only about avoiding a very low chance of a bad outcome, you can overspend to achieve that, even if there are better decisions. In TSA screening decisions, as an example, you can build a bulletproof plane with extremely tight security and multiple screening points at various gates. The result would minimize the probability of an accident, but you will have a flight system that nobody will want to go through or ride. Likewise, there would be no investments in the cure for cancer or Alzheimer's disease or in Tesla technology because there is a higher chance of a negative monetary outcome than a positive one regardless of the upside potential.

If there is no decision process to support a decision, nobody will make a decision that is unpopular with a group of influential stakeholders. Instead, they will rely on following the path of least resistance and winning the popularity contest.

Without a decision-making process, it would be easy to harm individuals and cause loss of lives without accountability. There would be no mention of how decisions involving life and death or going to war were made and no checks and balances. Theranos could not have justified introducing tests with low sensitivity if an ethical decision-making process were provided. And the examples of issues resulting from no decision-making process abide:

- The *LA Times* released the article "LAPD Officers Often Delay Providing Medical Aid after Shooting People."[352] This is not a rare incident in Los Angeles alone. In relation to Tyre Nichols, who was beaten to death by police officers in Memphis, CNN reported, "No One Rendered Aid in Critical Minutes after Tyre Nichols' Beating."[353]

- The *Guardian* released the article "BP Cost-Cutting Blamed for 'Avoidable' Deepwater Horizon Oil Sill: Disaster could have been prevented—White House. Complacency 'could lead to another catastrophe.'"[354]

---

[352] https://www.latimes.com/california/story/2022-04-05/lapd-officers-medical-aid-shootings

[353] https://www.cnn.com/us/live-news/tyre-nichols-memphis-news-1-28-23/index.html

[354] https://www.theguardian.com/environment/2011/jan/06/bp-oil-spill-deepwater-horizon

- Safety concerns were also ignored in a recent Florida condo collapse. NPR reported, *"Just weeks before Champlain Towers South collapsed, town officials in Surfside, Fla., were demanding immediate changes on the property—but all of their requirements focused on relatively minor concerns. . . . None of the town's orders urged a swift response to growing concerns about the building's structural soundness, identified in repeated warnings shared with Surfside officials beginning in 2018."*[355]

## How people make decisions in organizations with the "no decision process" mindset

### 1. Decision-making "around the table" or by intimidation or coercion

A widely used method of organizational decision-making is "decision-making around the table," where a group calls for a meeting and makes a decision. In many cases, a person of high rank hijacks the conversation and intimidates the others into following their required outcome. Obedience and authority biases, as well as the yes-man mentality, conformity, and groupthink biases, affect the decision quality and lead to predetermined outcomes—outcomes desired by the hijacker.

### 2. Path of least resistance and following the strongest wind direction

Following the path of least resistance is tempting if you do not have a decision process. You do not have analyses to support an opposing view, so you follow the strongest wind direction. The problem with this strategy is that it is a bet on who will win instead of considering ethical decision quality. The path of least resistance need not be ethical, as was demonstrated by large crowds gathering to watch Roman gladiators.

---

[355] https://www.npr.org/sections/live-updates-miami-area-condo-collapse/2021/06/30/1011670548/as-condo-warnings-mounted-town-officials-demanded-only-minor-changes

### 3. Cognitive consistency, projecting self-image, and saving face

Cognitive consistency is a theory in psychology that demonstrates how individuals strive to maintain consistency in their decision-making.[356] Quite often, decision-makers continue making the same decisions even in the light of new information, impacted by confirmation bias, sunk costs, the desire to save face, and to show consistency. Consistency in the reasoning method is a requirement in ethical decision-making. But consistency about the alternative you choose when you receive information showing you should be doing something else is not desirable.

### 4. Following a fad

When there is no decision process, new fads create bandwagon effects and a blind domino effect on organizations to follow a trend and be its pioneers. Management by objectives is a good idea in concept but can lead to poor decision-making if the incentives are not set appropriately, and rarely is the case when they are and do not conflict with decision-making. The quality movement also sounds interesting as a concept, but when followed blindly, it can deter from the goal of maximizing value. Motorola invented the Six Sigma quality improvement process in 1986, where you limit the variability of a product to enhance reliability. It quickly became a world-wide standard, but it needs to explain why there cannot be other decision alternatives besides improving variability that would yield better value to internal and external stakeholders. For one, the best decision might be to change the product because of new technologies rather than spend money to improve the variability of the current product.

**Reflection**

Identify decisions made in part 1 and decisions from the media that could have resulted in a different course of action if the organization had a decision process.

---

[356] Robert P. Abelson, *Theories of Cognitive Consistency: A Sourcebook* (Skokie, IL: Rand McNally & Company, 1968).

# Chapter 21

# Implications of the Mindsets: Employee Actions

*FBI Whistleblower Testimony Highlights Government Abuse, Misallocation of Resources, and Retaliation.*

—Interim Staff Report, Subcommittee on the Weaponization of the Federal Government U.S. House of Representatives, May 18, 2023

## Common patterns of employee actions under the influence of the mindsets

Consider an employee at a certain rank in the organization operating under the influence of the mindsets. How would that employee respond if they observe ethical violations? The mindsets impact the elements of ethical decision quality. Employees operating under these mindsets have different levels of ethical tolerances, different states of well-being (security, despair, fear), and different feasible alternatives (some may be independently wealthy and pursue other ventures, while others may not). Some of the actions lead to further ethical violations.

This chapter presents some actions employees undertake within an organization operating under the mindsets and cautions organizations about common actions that have been taken in response. These actions ultimately enabled violations to continue. The employee actions presented were gleaned from media articles and the case studies in part 1. As you read through the following actions, identify similar actions that occurred from part 1. Identify weaknesses in elements of ethical decision quality that contribute to these actions. Identify their implications for ethical decision quality.

### 1. Do nothing: Tolerate or ignore ethical violations

The "do nothing" alternative can result from many factors. In some instances, employees choose to consciously ignore the issue and do nothing about it, with the rationalization that it does not affect them. Others may seek the route of "willful blindness" and choose not to want to know anything else about the situation. This is amplified if they are gaining benefits from the organization. In other cases, the "do nothing" strategy results from knowing about the issues, but they are within the ethical tolerances of the individuals involved. As we discussed, there is a higher tendency to tolerate unethical acts in an atmosphere of fear and insecurity. And others might tolerate the situation uncomfortably, especially if they feel they cannot change it.

### 2. Minimize liability and do whatever it takes to keep your job

In some situations when ethical violations are involved, employees operate in "survival mode." They are likely to do whatever it takes to cover up any liability or wrongdoing they have done and do whatever it takes to keep their job. In the process, they conduct more ethical violations, and an escalation of commitment occurs. Examples of these actions involve shredding evidence, hiding documents, blaming others, scapegoating, and making false accusations.

### 3. Use the situation to their advantage

While some people in an organization that operates under these mindsets are stressed and insecure about their jobs, others may use the situation to their advantage. Examples of these actions include setting up personal companies to profit from the situation, manipulating employees and exploiting their cognitive and motivational biases, and acting as destructive confidants and yes-men to the administrators.

> *Harvard Business Review described a destructive confidant as a trusted colleague with whom the CEO develops a close relationship and feels free to share their thoughts and fears. Further, "many confidants end up hurting, undermining, or otherwise exploiting CEOs when they are at their most vulnerable. These confidants rarely make the headlines, but*

*behind the scenes, they do enormous damage to the CEO and to the organization. What's more, the leader is often the last one to know when and how the confidant relationship became toxic."*[357]

## 4. Try to change it

One common decision alternative is to try to change the situation. Recall that a legally unethical organization will not change its unethical procedures unless pressure builds up for it to change or if it is required to by law. Attempts to change the situation include confronting leadership, whistleblowing, leaking documents, conducting interviews with the media, filing lawsuits, or sending anonymous emails to authorities. And quite often these attempts are met with retaliation from the organization.

When Theranos' CFO expressed concern about the integrity of the product, he was fired because *"he was not a team player."*

U.S. House of Representatives notes that within the FBI, retaliation occurred against those who spoke up.[358] *"FBI Whistleblower Testimony Highlights Government Abuse, Misallocation of Resources, and Retaliation."*

CNN reports[359] about a Wells Fargo employee who witnessed the acts conducted by the bank, *"I called the Wells Fargo ethics line and was fired."*

KCET reported about the University of Southern California (USC) in August 2020:

*USC faculty members are pushing their leadership to demand an independent investigation into allegations that university administrators maintained "shadow files" on employees and utilized their accountability office to retaliate against professors who spoke out against them. Particularly because there are specific claims that faculty members were targeted and smeared with manufactured complaints and secret files, the allegations in*

---

[357] https://hbr.org/2004/02/worse-than-enemies-the-ceos-destructive-confidant

[358] https://judiciary.house.gov/sites/evo-subsites/republicans-judiciary.house.gov/files/evo-media-document/2023-05-17-fbi-whistleblower-testimony-highlights-government-abuse-misallocation-of-resources-and-retaliation-sm.pdf

[359] https://money.cnn.com/2016/09/21/investing/wells-fargo-fired-workers-retaliation-fake-accounts/index.html

*the lawsuit deserve a full and impartial investigation by someone independent of the University Administration," the letter said.*[360]

## 5. Leave the organization

Another common alternative is to leave the organization upon observing unethical stances. This occurs for many reasons, including employees who are tired of the organization's ethical violations, those who receive payments to leave and be quiet about the violations, and even administrators who would like to jump ship before being held responsible for their actions.

**Reflection**

- Identify instances in part 1 where individuals chose each previous action.
- Which of these actions do you believe members of your organization are more likely to do if they observe ethical violations or mindsets impeding ethical decision quality?
- What do you believe are the possible implications of these actions on ethical decision quality?
- Can you think of rationalizations that individuals may have to support each of these actions?
- Can you think of other actions that individuals may conduct when faced with ethical issues under organizational mindsets that impede ethical decision quality?

[360] . https://www.kcet.org/shows/socal-connected/usc-faculty-pushes-for-independent-investigation-into-allegations-of-shadow-and-dirt-files-on-colleagues

# Chapter 22

# Implications of the Mindsets: Managerial Actions

## Action 1: "We are the champions of morality"

*We are the only lab company that is actually really focused on leading with transparency.*

—Elizabeth Holmes on Theranos

Managers operating in an environment with mindsets that impede ethical decision quality have many feasible courses of action to take. Some of these actions include taking steps to address the mindsets. When these mindsets are prevalent, however, many organizational managers instead resort to a different strategy : covering up and presenting a different image of the organization than what really exists. In so doing, they engage in additional actions that impede ethical decision quality. Examples include often-fake or exaggerated top-bottom value slogans that portray themselves and their organization as "champions of morality" and even use virtuous actions in some areas (such as philanthropy) for self-promotion to appease to individuals and justify harm to others. In other cases, individuals who claim they champion morality feel the need to find a "punching bag" to smear, often with false allegations, so that their morality leadership is manifested. These tactics are often used in politics or in backstabbing in the organizational workplace.

In principle, there is nothing wrong with saying that you are a champion of morality if it is accurate and if there is no element of deception or cover-up or harm involved. But if it is not true, and if saying it further enables ethical violations, then this becomes a problem. Exaggerated morality statements can enable fraud, deter complaints, and lead to a sense of hypocrisy and corporate distrust.

This chapter aims to increase sensitivity toward the misuses of statements and actions about morality and to caution organizational leaders about their potential misuse.

## What do you do when you champion a cause?

Suppose that there is an ethical cause that you feel strongly about. You can express your views about the cause and dedicate time and effort to increasing awareness about it and fixing it. The focus is on the cause, not the organization or the individuals. Rosa Parks, Martin Luther King Jr., Nelson Mandela, Helen Hulick (who went to jail for wearing slacks in court and later had the ruling overturned),[361] and many others all expressed views about ethical issues they encountered. Their message was never that they were the "champions of morality," that they were great, or that their moral code was better than everybody else's. Their statements were about the cause itself.

## Do organizations involved in ethical violations use fake morality statements?

In part 1, we saw examples where individuals advocated morality amid extensive fraud. These statements helped deviate suspicions about their organizations and may have enabled further deception or fraud. In an interview with Charlie Rose, Elizabeth Holmes said the following about Theranos:

> *We are the only lab company that is actually really focused on leading with transparency.*[362]

And this strategy worked to deter complaints and erase doubts about the company. In an interview with Ken Auletta, General Mattis was asked about the first words that came to his mind when he thought of Elizabeth Holmes. He responded,

> *First, is integrity, uh, competence, and competence is both technical, scientific, but also focused on human rights in the most classical sense of what human rights are about.*

*The Vision & Values of Wells Fargo* brochure noted,

> *Our ethics are the sum of all the decisions each of us makes every day. If*

[361] https://www.latimes.com/local/california/la-me-california-retrospective-20141023-story.html
[362] https://www.youtube.com/watch?v=PvznWSEKoEE

*you want to find out how strong a company's ethics are, don't listen to what its people say. Watch what they do. This is even more important in our industry because everything we do is built on trust.*

And at the same time, employees were opening bank accounts and charging customers without their knowledge.

Enron's Kenneth Lay mentioned in an interview:

*Enron is a company that deals with everyone with absolute integrity. We want people to leave the transaction with Enron thinking that they've been dealt with in the highest possible way as far as integrity and truthfulness.*

An *MIT Sloan Management Review* article by Sull, Turconi, and Sull (2020) surveyed the stated core values of numerous organizations. The study found that 65 percent of organizations tallied included "integrity" as a core value. They also found that "*Volkswagen, Wells Fargo, and Barclays each included ethics or integrity among their core values in the years before their wrongdoings were discovered, while Boeing hit the trifecta by listing integrity, quality, and safety among its 'enduring values.'*"[363]

**Reflection**

Identify instances from the media where organizations used top-bottom value slogans that they were champions of morality when the organizational leaders had engaged in acts of deception, harming, or stealing. In your view, what were the motives for the morality statements?

### Using morality to cause excessive harm?

Under the morality flag, individuals have abused their power and caused excessive harm relying on their "morality" authority. In so doing, they hurt others along the way. It was a fake $20 bill used by George Floyd that led a Cup Foods convenience store to call 911 and the ultimate arrival of Derek Chauvin, the former Minneapolis police officer who killed Mr. Floyd. Jerry

[363] https://sloanreview.mit.edu/article/when-it-comes-to-culture-does-your-company-walk-the-talk/

W. Blackwell, the prosecutor, told jurors during opening statements, "*The police officers could have written him a ticket and let the courts sort it out. This was a call about a counterfeit $20 bill.*"[364]

Countries have launched wars and have rationalized the act to their citizens that they are championing morality. Some people also raise the "morality" flag to coerce or intimidate others or to enforce actions in their interest. Iran's ironically named "morality police" arrested and detained Mahsa Amini outside a metro station in Tehran for not abiding by the dress code imposed by the government. Witnesses claimed she was beaten while being transported to a detention center. She died three days later. Following mass protests, news broke that "Iran Has Abolished Morality Police."[365]

## Using morality for self-promotion and cover-up?

Some people might want to capitalize on an opportunity to promote themselves as the champions of morality for self-promotion. These actions are used frequently in politics, where individuals use morality statements for self-promotion and attack and smear other candidates.

In other cases, organizations pursue virtuous causes to gain public or political support and cover up their own ethical violations.

Philanthropy News Digest reports,[366]

> *Enron CEO Kenneth Lay exemplified the company's philanthropy, endowing several professorships at the University of Houston and Rice University, while the company itself was known for its generous gifts to arts groups, scholarship funds, and the Texas Medical Center*

[364] https://www.nytimes.com/2021/04/19/us/george-floyd-bill-counterfeit.html
[365] https://www.nytimes.com/2022/12/04/world/middleeast/iran-morality-police.html
[366] https://philanthropynewsdigest.org/news/enron-s-philanthropy-will-be-missed

## Reflection

- Search for organizations with core values that include "integrity" and those that have "transparency." Which core value do you believe is more prevalent? Why?
- List some consequences that may occur within organizations that use exaggerated morality statements.
- How do exaggerated morality statements impact distrust or a sense of corporate hypocrisy?
- What environmental factors and biases may contribute to the "We are the champions of morality" statements?

## Action 2: Using the Media, Politicians, and Celebrities to Enable Ethical Violations

*I have no wealthy or popular relations to recommend me.*

—Abraham Lincoln in his first political address

### Benefits of the association with the media, celebrities, and politicians

Many of the large organizational scandals presented in part 1, or others we hear about in the news daily, have associations with the media, politicians, and celebrities. Of course, not every organization with close ties with the media, politicians, and celebrities must be involved in ethical lapses or fraud. But these connections have been used to enable fraud and to further ethical violations. This chapter highlights actions associated with these connections that may impact the ethical quality of decisions and increases sensitivity toward inappropriately using these relations.

### Hey, media, we have a great story for you!

There are many ways that organizational leaders use the media to enable a corporation that may be rocked by scandals to survive. One way is if you are a famous symbol representing a great message or cause. You become the story everybody wants to hear, get free advertising, and create a win-win situation for yourself and the media.

CBS News reported that Elizabeth Homes duped the media. Katy Textor of *60 Minutes* said,

> *I think using the media was part of the Theranos strategy.*

The *WSJ* posted a glowing image of Holmes following the Walgreens partnership. The *Guardian* published the article "How Theranos Used the Media to Create the Emperor's New Startup."[367]

And *Inc.* magazine reported on "*how the media helped create the legend of Eliz-*

[367] https://www.theguardian.com/commentisfree/2018/jun/03/theranos-elizabeth-holmes-media-emperors-new-startup

*abeth Holmes, and enabled her fraud in the process."*[368]

Holmes was named *Glamour*'s "Woman of the Year," *Time* put her on its list of one hundred luminaries, and she made the front covers of *Fortune, Forbes, Inc.*, and *T* magazines.[369]

The media did not intend to enable the fraud, but their involvement lay in publicizing a story without validation.

From the perspective of media companies, just like any other organization, the media can be coerced. Transparency International discussed three ways to fight corruption in the media: (1) media ownership, (2) funding and nontransparent advertising where media companies searching for revenue streams agree to publish advertisements disguised as op-eds, and (3) integrity of journalists' work associated with the need for ethics training for journalists.[370] The article also notes that whether the outlet is state run or privately owned is a crucial factor for the independence and integrity of the media. When the state formally owns media companies, the government can censor stories, stifle investigations into high-profile cases, and compromise the neutrality of reporting. Privately owned media companies, on the other hand, *"can become beholden to certain public figures, individuals or corporate interests, who use them to promote a certain image of themselves, their opponents, or a certain issue or product."*

Since his purchase of Twitter, Elon Musk noted how the state could influence media and introduced "state-affiliated" media labels:

> *State-affiliated media is defined as outlets where the state exercises control over editorial content through financial resources, direct or indirect political pressures, and/or control over production and distribution.*[371]

Elon Musk also noted in a tweet,

> *Elon Musk @elonmusk*

[368] https://www.inc.com/dustin-mckissen/elizabeth-holmes-was-a-massive-fraud-our-click-driven-media-helped-create-her.html
[369] https://www.nytimes.com/2021/11/18/technology/elizabeth-holmes-theranos-trial.html
[370] https://www.transparency.org/en/news/three-ways-to-fight-corruption-in-the-media
[371] https://help.twitter.com/en/rules-and-policies/government-media-labels

> *Most people don't appreciate the significance of the point Matt was making:*
>
> **Every* social media company is engaged in heavy censorship, with significant involvement of and, at times, explicit direction of the government. Google frequently makes links disappear, for example.*

Even without coercion, the focus of government officials often shifts from doing their job to ensuring they get positive media press with the motive of getting reelected. Britain's former prime minister Boris Johnson deemed the trend so prevalent that his advice to an incoming prime minister in his last speech was "*It's not Twitter that counts.*"[372] It is not clear whether the incoming prime minister followed this advice, but she did not last long.

## Welcome, former politicians! Please join our board

Corporate administrators involved in massive fraud will likely benefit from connections with current and former politicians. These connections provide a sense of security to the organization's administrators and increase the feeling of "we can get away with it," amplifying the "organizational transgression" mindset. Current politicians are lobbied for regulation or asked for help. In return, such organizations can also offer perks to political figures, such as board membership positions, and make them feel they are supporting a cause. But having these connections can also help deter or coerce whistleblowers and complainants who would otherwise have stood up against the organizational actions when they first started.

The *Washington Post* questioned what makes a former elected official an attractive board member.[373] Of all the factors, including insight into lawmaking, the status and reputation, and the connections they had while in office, the article concluded that what matters most is the networks the former politicians have.

CBS News wrote about a leak of one hundred thousand records that showed that

---

[372] https://www.independent.co.uk/tv/news/boris-johnson-pmqs-final-advice-b2127436.html

[373] https://www.washingtonpost.com/news/monkey-cage/wp/2015/02/01/how-and-why-retired-politicians-get-lucrative-appointments-on-corporate-boards/

*Uber used stealth technology to ward off regulators and lobbied political leaders around the world to help the startup undermine worker rights, avoid taxes and expand its global footprint.*[374]

The *Guardian* also reported on the same topic:

*The files suggest pro-business Macron, who was re-elected French president in April, was close enough to Uber's managers during his two years in the economy ministry from 2014–16 for them not to think twice about contacting him for possible help when their premises were raided by tax and other authorities.*[375]

The same article reported, "*Emmanuel Macron went to extraordinary lengths to support Uber's lobbying campaign to help it disrupt France's closed-shop taxi industry.*" He even told the tech company that he had brokered a secret "deal" with its opponents in the French cabinet.

According to *New York* magazine, Jeffrey Epstein was known to say,

*I invest in people—be it politics or science, it's what I do.*

Indeed, Jeffrey Epstein had affiliations with Bill Clinton, Donald Trump, Bill Gates, Larry Summers, Woody Allen, and Prince Andrew.[376] "*Epstein was arrested on July 6, 2019, on federal charges for the sex trafficking of minors in Florida and New York.*" He was found dead in his prison cell on August 10, 2019, awaiting trial on federal sex trafficking charges.

PBS reports about Harvey Weinstein,[377]

*Weinstein and his family have given more than $1.4 million in political contributions since the 1992 election cycle, nearly all of it to Democratic lawmakers, candidates and their allies*

---

[374] https://www.cbsnews.com/news/uber-files-investigation-ride-share/

[375] https://www.theguardian.com/news/2022/jul/10/emmanuel-macron-secretly-aided-uber-lobbying-drive-france-leak-reveals

[376] https://nymag.com/intelligencer/2019/07/jeffrey-epsteins-rolodex-famous-friends-and-acquaintances.html

[377] https://www.pbs.org/newshour/politics/democrats-give-political-donations-harvey-weinstein-away-charities#:~:text=Weinstein%20and%20his%20family%20have,nonpartisan%20Center%20for%20Responsive%20Politics.

And the associations between political figures and organizations with ethical scandals continue. In part 1, we discussed Theranos board members were high-ranking political figures. Following the Wall Street Journal article about Theranos technology, Holmes was quick to note in an interview, *"We have an amazing relationship with our board and our investors. I have been incredibly privileged to be able to have incredible people who really understand what it means to build a great business for the long-term as shareholders and on the board."*

## Celebrities, please join us!

The celebrity factor brings the desire of many stakeholders to associate themselves with an organization. Celebrities also bring their fan base, which helps with sales and fundraising opportunities. Even politicians rely on celebrities during their campaigns. Even some religious entities desire the association with celebrities. The *Mercury News* reported how Scientology Church leaders were eager to welcome Tom Cruise into the fold and how they have long been known to recruit celebrities to raise the organization's profile.[378] The article alleged that Scientology even auditioned girlfriends for Mr. Cruise.

The association with celebrities can also deter complaints and enable ethical violations. Business Insider reported about "12 Famous Actors Who Have Publicly Praised and Thanked Harvey Weinstein, and What They Are Saying Now."[379]

**Reflection**

Identify organizations that have used the media, politicians, and celebrities to enable deception, fraud, or harm, or to gain an unfair advantage.

Can you identify other individuals, groups, or tools that organizations use to enable ethical violations?

---

[378] . https://www.mercurynews.com/2018/12/03/tom-cruise-absolutely-had-scientology-audition-girlfriends-for-him-says-defector/

[379] https://www.businessinsider.com/hollywood-stars-who-have-praised-harvey-weinstein-in-the-past-2017-10#gwyneth-paltrow-1

## Action 3: Erratic Decision-Making on a Trending Bandwagon

*The CEOs of nearly 200 companies*
*just said shareholder value is*
*no longer their main objective.*

—Maggie Fitzgerald,
writing for CNBC, August 19, 2019[380]

When an organization has a "no decision process" mindset, there is no mechanism or analysis to support unpopular decisions or to oppose fads that may impede quality decision-making. Within this environment, organizational administrators—particularly those who may feel the need to show fast improvement or those who feel insecure about their job—often embrace a fad or follow the path of least resistance or that of a trending bandwagon in their decision-making. It is not about how good or bad a decision is, how it affects stakeholders, or whether it makes sense. It is about following the trending bandwagon and overdoing it with erratic actions to show that you are on board. Those actions may hurt stakeholders and even any valuable aspects of the actual cause of the bandwagon. We refer to these actions as "erratic decision-making on a trending bandwagon." The purpose of this section is to increase sensitivity toward these actions. As you read through this section, identify examples of erratic decision-making on a trending bandwagon from the media, particularly those that may have hurt other stakeholders.

### Endorsements for Theranos: Was it a bandwagon? Did it hurt the cause?

Elizabeth Holmes received praise from highly sophisticated. They offered their endorsements excessively and without verification. Could it have been the case of following the trending bandwagon of what other board members were saying? Or could it have been individuals who wanted to support a cause—a bright young female entrepreneur who started a company at the age of nineteen? General Mattis noted what comes to his mind when he hears about *"First, is integrity, uh competence, and competence*

[380] https://www.cnbc.com/2019/08/19/the-ceos-of-nearly-two-hundred-companies-say-shareholder-value-is-no-longer-their-main-objective.html

*is both technical, scientific, but also focused on human rights in the most classical sense of what human rights are about."*

The excessive endorsements, however, hurt stakeholders, may have damaged the cause, and also caused harm to other stakeholders. Many female entrepreneurs in Silicon Valley have suffered as a result and are compared to Holmes when seeking funding. The *New York Times* stated,

> *A generation of female entrepreneurs—particularly those in life sciences, biotechnology and health care—is still operating in the shadow of Ms. Holmes.*[381]

And *Fortune* magazine reported about how female entrepreneurs are stereotyped by venture capitalists in the article "Silicon Valley Is Learning the Wrong Lesson from Elizabeth Holmes's Trial Verdict."[382] There are many other examples of dancing on the trending bandwagon with different interpretations and rationalizations. Try to identify some. Below are some stories that may fall under this category.

## Is shareholder value no longer a main objective?

Following numerous ethical scandals about "corporate greed" (including Enron, Valeant, and others), it is natural to have bandwagons discussing how maximizing profit for shareholders is harmful.

CNBC published the article "The CEOs of Nearly 200 Companies Just Said Shareholder Value Is No Longer Their Main Objective."[383] The CEOs of two hundred companies issued a statement:

> *While each of our individual companies serves its own corporate purpose, we share a fundamental commitment to all of our stakeholders. We commit to delivering value to all of them, for the future success of our companies, our communities and our country . . . investing in employees, delivering*

---

[381] https://www.nytimes.com/2021/08/24/technology/theranos-elizabeth-holmes.html

[382] https://fortune.com/2022/01/04/elizabeth-holmes-trial-guilty-verdict-legacy-female-founders-investors-silicon-valley/

[383] https://www.cnbc.com/2019/08/19/the-ceos-of-nearly-two-hundred-companies-say-shareholder-value-is-no-longer-their-main-objective.html

> *value to customers, dealing ethically with suppliers and supporting outside communities are now at the forefront of American business goals.*

There is nothing wrong with this statement if it is accurate and represents what the shareholders want and the fiduciary responsibility that the CEOs have toward them. It also reminds people of the importance of ethical stances with various stakeholders.

What is the problem then? First, it may not be true; and if so, it would not be the first time that statements like these were made. Many others have championed morality for marketing purposes or self-promotion. Enron's Kenneth Lay mentioned,

> *Enron is a company that deals with everyone with absolute integrity. We want people to leave the transaction with Enron thinking that they've been dealt with in the highest possible way as far as integrity and truthfulness.*

Second, why is shareholder value not a main priority? Are shareholders not stakeholders? Can this statement impede thinking about new technologies that could result in much larger profits for shareholders while simultaneously serving the stakeholders? Does being ethical mean that you should give less priority to decisions that would increase shareholder return, even if they simultaneously serve the needs of other stakeholders? Can a more profitable organization not contribute more to philanthropy? Or contribute more to the development of its employees? Or contribute more to ethical causes? Recall that "it is the love of money that is the root of all evil," not the money itself.

Suppose you had the choice of investing in two firms: both were legal and ethical, but one would generate a 20 percent return and the other a 1 percent return. Which would you invest in?

Even not-for-profit and government organizations should care about money. With money, they can help more people, further their cause, be better prepared for an emergency, advance science and exploration, or better manage a pandemic. NASA could launch more missions, motivate more teens toward science, and enhance scientific discovery. Nonprofit universities could offer more scholarships or even offer free education. If money was not a priority or a problem, then the government could return the tax money to the American people or even not collect it in the first place.

Third, will managers know how to make decisions with this statement? Or will it create confusion? What is it that you need to do to make this statement hold? There needs to be a mention of trade-offs: How much loss of corporate value is the organization willing to incur to support the outside communities? Is it okay that an organization spends all its money, for example, helping outside communities, giving them shelters, and not having sufficient funds to pay its employees their salaries? Further, if there is a need for layoffs, will these organizations incur loss and keep their employees?

Disney decided to lay off seven thousand employees when it faced tough times. CNN published the article "Disney Plans to Cut 7,000 Jobs and Reward Shareholders."[384] How does this coincide with the notion that shareholder values are not a main priority? Unless the trade-offs are specified, the statement would provide little guidance into decision-making and might be viewed as hypocritical, therefore even hurting corporate social responsibility's actual cause.

## Is Starbucks in America a public toilet?

Is Starbucks the public toilet of America, or is it not? Nobody knows the answer to that question—at least not in America. But the question would sound nonsensical if asked overseas. Why did this topic come up in the first place?

The actions presented here are of course not an indication that the six mindsets impeding ethical decision quality exist at Starbucks, but as we shall see, they do resemble the actions of erratic decision-making around a trending bandwagon.

Fox Business reported that in 2018, two men were denied access to the store's bathroom because they had not bought any merchandise.[385] They refused to leave the store and were subsequently arrested. In response

---

[384] https://www.cnn.com/2023/02/08/business/disney-earnings/index.html
[385] https://www.foxbusiness.com/politics/starbucks-pressured-keep-toilets-open-public-restroom-nonprofit-let-people-go

to this incident, Starbucks's CEO at the time, Kevin Johnson, apologized and shut down all Starbucks locations in the United States for a day so that employees would undergo antibias training. Of course, training is a welcome act. But then Starbucks officially informed its employees that its bathrooms were open for everyone. This might sound like a joke to coffee shops in Europe who would only allow you to use their facilities if you are a paying customer or perhaps if you pay 2 Euros to use the restroom.

A research study published a year later showed that attendance at Starbucks decreased by 6.8 percent compared with other coffee shops and restaurants. Further, the decrease was more prominent (about 84 percent) for Starbucks locations near homeless shelters.

In June 2022, Starbucks's CEO, Howard Schultz, floated the idea of revisiting its open-bathroom policy and banning people who do not purchase anything from using its facilities, citing safety and health considerations. Shortly after, Starbucks was under pressure from nonprofit foundations and the American Restroom Association (ARA), who urged the coffee chain against the rhetoric from Schultz and insisted on the full use of restroom facilities to the public.[386]

**Reflection**

- What was the original cause that Starbucks wanted to pursue?
- Must a restaurant or coffee shop allow people who are not customers to use its restrooms for it to be ethical?
- What would you do if someone you did not know went into your house to use the restroom?
- What would you have done in Kevin Johnson's place? Are there other alternatives that could have been explored?
- Who are the stakeholders in this situation?

[386] https://www.foxbusiness.com/politics/starbucks-pressured-keep-toilets-open-public-restroom-nonprofit-let-people-go

## The cost of erratic decision-making at Starbucks?

After writing this section, and before sending the manuscript to the publisher, more news about this incident was revealed. Following the incident, Starbucks fired a regional director, Shannon Phillips. On June 13, 2023, a jury voted unanimously after a six-day trial that Starbucks pay $25 million for punitive damages and $600,000 in compensatory damages.

CNN reports,

> *Shannon Phillips, who worked for Starbucks for about 13 years and managed a region of stores, was fired after the arrest of two Black men at a Philadelphia Starbucks in 2018. In a lawsuit first filed in 2019, Phillips alleged Starbucks "took steps to punish White employees who had not been involved in the arrests, but who worked in and around the city of Philadelphia, in an effort to convince the community that it had properly responded to the incident.*[387]

**Reflection**

- Did Starbucks's action help or harm the cause?
- What would you do if you were Starbucks's CEO today?

[387] https://www.cnn.com/2023/06/14/business/starbucks-manager-racial-discrimination/index.html?utm_term=1686826538943511 6ffbe0b07&utm_source=cnn_Five+Things+for+Thursday%2C+June+15%2C+2023&utm_medium=email&bt_ee=8MXQgXZnJJpG6Gfj23IFjPTw%2FXhCh2zw4NMJlKrShiQ9p63Pu3cDx-l278tYKHlUN&bt_ts=1686826538946

## Action 4: Bring on Friends, Family, Yes-Men, and Destructive Confidants

*We thank you for the opportunity and the blessing that you've given us to serve your agenda,*

— Former President Trump's Chief of Staff

### It's all in the family and the social club: Why is it an issue?

When an organization has an abundance of pendulum swings and organizational transgressions, many individuals choose to side with leadership in their actions instead of opposing them. The pursuit of benefits or job security amplifies this support. Within this environment, corporate and government administrators surround themselves with friends, family, and yes-men.

Decisions are systematically dictated in a top-down approach. Rarely do people provide input during the decision-making process or challenge the decisions made. A decision team (which could be members of the C-suite, VPs, executive committees, or academic senate members in the case of universities) then rubber-stamps the decisions amid an atmosphere of mutual admiration, conformity, flattery, fear, and reaping benefits enjoyed by a particular group of stakeholders strongly affiliated with the leadership.

Individuals who agree with the leadership decisions are rewarded or are offered repeat business, while those who disagree or express opposing views are diluted or retaliated against. The group conformity, groupthink, false consensus, and obedience and authority biases are highly manifested. Within this environment, everything leadership says or does is deemed fabulous. This includes setting impossible sales targets and announcing products like clean diesel engines or single-drop blood-testing devices whose technical feasibility is nonexistent or using deceptive accounting methods to increase the stock price.

In terms of impacts on stakeholders, administrators end up being isolated, receive less input, incur less innovation and creativity, and make worse decisions than they would have made if they were exposed to direct input from the organization at large. Examples at the government level include launching a war. At a corporate level, many employees within this environment are deprived of opportunities to engage or to get a promotion, even if they are more qualified than others who receive the perks and are close to the leadership. Within this environment, there is also room for destructive confidants. An example of a destructive confidant was the character of Frank Underwood (Kevin Spacey) in *House of Cards*.

**Reflection**

- Identify organizations in part 1 where friends, family, and yes-men surrounded leadership.
- What biases, mindsets, and environmental factors may contribute to the friends, family, and yes-men environments?

## Examples of friends, family, and yes-men environments: Mr. President, thank you for the blessing

The Guardian reported about former president Trump's cabinet in the article "The Cabinet Takes Turns Lavishing Trump with Praise."[388] The article also highlighted how some cabinet members mentioned, "We thank you for the opportunity and the blessing that you've given us to serve your agenda," while others mentioned "This is just the greatest privilege of my life." A former Whitehouse communications director also mentioned "I just love the President."

These comments did not go unnoticed on social media, *Chris Lu @ChrisLu44*

> *I ran 16 Cabinet meetings during Obama's 1st term. Our Cabinet was never told to sing Obama's praises. He wanted candid advice not adulation*

## Laplace's letter to Napoleon "the Grand"

If you think that friends, family, and yes-men actions are recent, think again. Laplace wanted Napoleon to appoint him as minister of interior. Napoleon did appoint Laplace as minister (for a short while). Before that, Laplace sent the following letter (translated from French into English), dedicating his treatise on the calculus of probabilities to Napoleon:

---

388 https://www.theguardian.com/us-news/2017/jun/12/donald-trump-first-cabinet-meeting-praise

*To Napoleon-the-Grand. Sire,*

*The benevolence with which Your Majesty has deigned to greet the homage of my Traité de Mécanique Céleste, has inspired me to desire to dedicate to You this Work on the Calculus of the Probabilities. This delicate calculus extends to the most important questions of life, which are in effect, for the most part, only some problems of probability.*

*It must, under this relationship, interest Your Majesty of whom the genius knows so well to appreciate and so deservedly to encourage all that which can contribute to the progress of knowledge and to the public prosperity.*

*I dare to implore He to accept this new homage dictated by the most lively appreciation, and by the profound sentiments of admiration and of respect, with which I am, Sire, of Your Majesty, The very humble and very obedient servant and faithful subject,*

*Laplace*

## Addressing a yes-man decision culture

A textbook example of a decision made without a good decision process and the effects of groupthink and the yes-man environment was demonstrated in the 1961 Bay of Pigs decision to send poorly trained Cuban exiles to overthrow Castro. As noted in the *Wall Street Journal* article "All the President's Yes-Men: JFK remade his decision-making process after the Bay of Pigs debacle," the decision went through partly because nobody among JFK's advisors was willing to speak up or play devil's advocate.[389] Arthur Schlesinger, a historian and aide, wrote of the decision process: "*Our meetings were taking place in a curious atmosphere of assumed consensus, [and] not one spoke against it.*"

After that decision, JFK created the Executive Committee of the National Security Council, which could openly express its ideas and debate national security decisions. Further, it met with and without the president to minimize the effect of obedience to authority and the yes-man environment. Robert Kennedy later recalled, "*There was no rank, and in fact, we did not even have a chairman . . . the conversations were completely uninhibited.*"

[389] https://www.wsj.com/articles/president-decision-making-biden-kennedy-johnson-taliban-afghanistan-bay-of-pigs-vietnam-saigon-blinkin-sullivan-11629641380

# Chapter 23

# Implications of the Mindsets: Predictable Recidivism of Ethical Concerns

*[T]here is no panacea, and I think we will continue to see abuses and excesses—but hopefully fewer.*

—Mary Driscoll, an analyst with Standard & Poor's

## Why is it important to address the impediments?

Ethical lapses will continue at various magnitudes. Following are some predictions for organizations operating with the six mindsets identified in part 3.

**Prediction 1:** *In organizations operating with the six mindsets, the occurrence of large ethical scandals associated with politicians and celebrities should be an expectation, not a surprise.*

If you have an organization operating with mindsets that impede ethical decision quality, an ethical scandal should be an expectation, not a surprise. And suppose you have managers making decisions under the influence of these mindsets. The following should not come as a surprise: These scandals will have associations with the media, politicians, and celebrities. The managers would have championed morality along the way; and they would have surrounded themselves with friends, family, yes-men, and destructive confidants.

Further, if the mindsets are present, then lapses will occur despite a change in leadership. New leadership will also make decisions under the mindsets. The biases and affected elements of decision quality remain.

**Prediction 2:** *A change in leadership that does not change the mindsets will not resolve the recurrence of scandals or the pileup of complaints.*

If the biases remain, a third prediction is that whistleblowers will continue to blow. Remember that if there were no "black holes" mindset, there would be nothing for whistleblowers to blow the whistle about. Whistleblowers would be out of business. But with the "black holes" and "organizational transgression" mindsets, the whistleblowers will remain.

**Prediction 3:** *An organization operating with the six mindsets will continue to have whistleblowers.*

And whistleblowers may also be from within the circle of friends and family. It was Bernie Madoff's son who called the FBI to arrest him. CBS News reported on November 5, 2011,

> *"We knew that we couldn't live with this information and not do something about it." That's what Andrew Madoff, son of Bernard Madoff, told Morley Safer about his decision to call in the FBI after his father revealed to the family that he had been running the world's largest Ponzi Scheme.*[390]

*"Theranos was exposed by a few courageous employees and a rather obscure pathologist blogger."*[391] One of the whistleblowers was George Shultz's grandson. Shultz was a close friend and supporter of Holmes.

**Prediction 4:** *When faced with an ethical issue, organizations with the six mindsets are likely to do the following:*

1. Inaction and silence until the media finds out: If they receive a complaint before the press finds out, they will do nothing or retaliate against or coerce the complainants and then follow up with top-bottom value slogans about morality.

2. If the media finds out, but they feel they can get away with it, they will deny the incidents. If there is a whistleblower, they may attack the whistleblower and follow up with top-bottom value slogans about morality.

3. If the media finds out and they feel they cannot get away with it,

[390] https://www.cbsnews.com/news/sons-called-in-fbi-to-arrest-bernie-madoff/

[391] https://www.centerconsulting.org/blog/10-things-deceptive-leaders-do-to-fake-their-way-to-success

but pressure has not built up for a change in leadership, they may change some procedures and follow up with top-bottom value slogans about morality.

4. If the media finds out, they cannot get away with it; and if the pressure has built up, they will change leadership and follow up with top-bottom value slogans about morality.

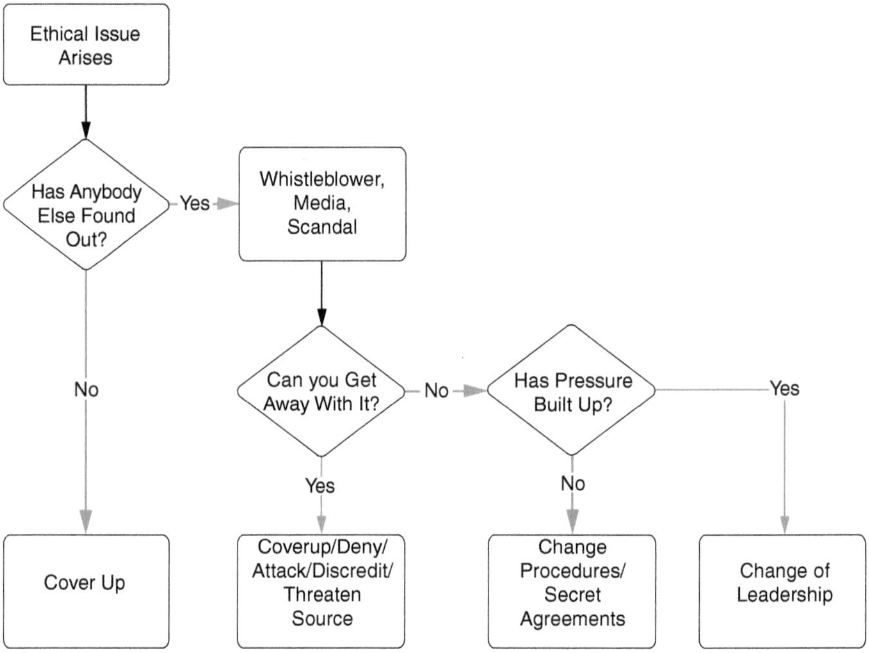


**Figure 3.3.** *Flowchart of descriptive organizational reactions to an ethical concern*

## Reflection

Identify instances in part 1 where this response model was incorporated.

# Chapter 24

# Over and Over and Over Again: FTX—a Familiar Story?

*His actual support of Dem elections is probably over $1B. The money went somewhere, so where did it go?*

—Elon Musk via Twitter

As I finished the first draft of *Ethical Decision Quality*, news about FTX broke. And so I looked into some of the patterns described by the media to see if new insights could be added. The patterns are listed below. As you read through them, identify if they are consistent with the patterns already discussed.

## Introduction: Fast growth due to an arbitrage opportunity

Sam Bankman-Fried (SBF), a Stanford graduate, was able to capitalize on arbitrage opportunities by buying cryptocurrency on one exchange and then quickly selling them for a higher price on a different exchange.

## Friends and family: It's all in the family

Following his passion, SBF convinced some altruistic friends to provide funds to help found the trading firm Alameda Research. The firm was so profitable that in 2019, SBF launched his exchange, FTX. At the age of twenty-nine, Bankman-Fried was worth $22.5 billion.[392] Caroline Ellison, who was SBF's girlfriend, was also a top executive.[393] She ran the trading firm.

---

[392] https://www.vox.com/the-goods/23458837/sam-bankman-fried-ftx-sbf-downfall-explained

[393] https://nypost.com/2022/11/14/meet-caroline-ellison-sam-bankman-frieds-rumored-ex-girlfriend/

## Politicians

SBF was a generous donor to political campaigns. He spent around $40 million during the midterm election cycle of 2022 and pledged up to $1 billion if it meant blocking Donald Trump from running again for reelection. Elon Musk believes that the donations he made were actually higher.

> *Elon Musk @elonmusk*
>
> *That's just the publicly disclosed number. His actual support of Dem elections is probably over $1B. The money went somewhere, so where did it go?*

## Celebrities

Fox Business reported about the sports and celebrity investors associated with FTX in the article "FTX Bankruptcy Embroils Its Sports, Celeb Investors."[394] Examples of celebrities related to FTX included Naomi Osaka (who wore the company's logo during her matches) and Shaquille O'Neal (who appeared wearing a wig in a promotional Twitter video). Other celebrities included quarterback Tom Brady, Brazilian fashion model Gisele Bündchen, and basketball star Stephen Curry, who filmed commercials for FTX. Trevor Lawrence also became a partner and ambassador for FTX. Other celebrities including Shohei Ohtani, David Ortiz, and Udonis Haslem also became ambassadors/partners.

## Media

SBF graced the cover of *Fortune* magazine. The media portrayed him as a nerdy person with messy hair and a Toyota Corolla. The fact that he played *computer games during pitch meetings* was taken as proof of his unique genius.

**Lobbying politicians about the amazing things that can be done!**

The *LA Times* reported about the young crypto billionaire's political agenda and how he had become a familiar sight on Capitol Hill, meeting with

---

[394] https://www.foxbusiness.com/markets/ftx-bankruptcy-embrols-sports-celebs-investors

lawmakers. SBF told the *Times,*

> *I am spending a lot of time talking with members about what constructive things would be on crypto policies and about what can be done to provide federal oversight of it. And so when I go to D.C., that is often what I'm doing.*[395]

**Reflection**

Does this sound familiar with Enron's and Theranos's statements made to encourage deregulation and to change legislation?

## We are the champions of morality!

FTX's core values (posted on its web page) used to be integrity (of course), honesty, accountability, and passion. But those were not enough, and the firm announced their core values needed expansion. In a statement on their web page (still posted as of January 2023), FTX notes, "*We've expanded our core values of integrity, honesty, accountability, and passion to encompass the current real-life challenges.*"[396] The expanded set includes "Cultured," "Honesty," "Excellence," "Integrity" (of course), "Teamwork," and "On-time Delivery."

## Investment banks dancing on the trending bandwagon? SBF walks on water

In an interview, Elon Musk mentioned, "*I got a ton of people telling me [that] he's got, you know, huge amounts of money that he wants to invest in the Twitter deal.*" He added, "*Then I was like, man, everyone including major investment banks—everyone was talking about him like he's walking on water and has a zillion dollars.*"[397] Musk rejected SBF's offer of $8 billion to $15 billion to partner in Twitter.

---

[395] https://www.latimes.com/politics/story/2022-08-12/sam-bankman-fried-ftx-political-donations

[396] https://ftxglobal.com/ftx-global-company/ftx-global-story/

[397] https://www.dailymail.co.uk/news/article-11420189/Elon-Musk-says-FTX-founder-set-BS-meter-offered-Twitter-purchase.html

### "Organizational transgression" mindset: Cover Alameda's risky bets using FTX customer funds

Cryptonews.com reports that SBE siphoned billions of dollars of customer funds and deposits from his FTX exchange into political contributions, buying luxury real estate in the Bahamas, and financing trading at Alameda.[398] Some transactions at Alameda were risky, and allegations were that funds were transferred from FTX to cover them up.

### Rationalization: "It will be okay"

Two managers had voiced concerns about client fund use and deficits in FTX before the collapse. SBF, while concerned, mentioned that a rise in cryptocurrency prices would be sufficient to cover the deficit.

### Unethically fast and slow: Fast to cover up and deny

On November 7, 2022, SBF tweeted that "*FTX is fine. Assets are fine*" and that "*FTX has enough to cover all client holdings.*" In another tweet, he wrote, "*We don't invest client assets (even in treasuries).*" The tweets have since been deleted.

### Whistleblower

Two days later, on November 9, 2022, Ryan Salame, cochief executive of FTX's Bahamas entity, informed the country's securities commission that FTX Digital had transferred funds to Alameda Research. On the same day, the commissioner of the Royal Bahamas Police Force (RBPF) was notified and asked to conduct an investigation. A day later, Binance withdrew an offer to buy FTX.

### Media finds out

On November 11, the *Wall Street Journal* reported that "FTX Tapped into Customer Accounts to Fund Risky Bets" and that Bankman-Fried may

---

[398] https://cryptonews.com/news/ftx-bosses-voiced-their-concerns-about-client-fund-use-court-papers-show.htm

have illegally taken about $10 billion from FTX customers' funds for his trading firm, Alameda Research.[399]

## Unanticipated consequences?

After an explosion of customer withdrawals that occurred shortly after, the Bahamas-based FTX filed for bankruptcy. On December 13, 2022, the SEC charged Samuel Bankman-Fried with orchestrating a scheme to defraud equity investors in FTX Trading Ltd. and that the *"[d]efendant concealed his diversion of FTX customers' funds to crypto trading firm Alameda Research while raising more than $1.8 billion from investors."*[400] The SEC also charged Caroline Ellison and Gary Wang with defrauding investors.[401]

## Feeling you cannot get away with it: Caroline Ellison confesses to fraud

*Forbes* published the article titled "Caroline Ellison Admits She and Bankman-Fried Conspired to Deceive FTX Customers and Investors."[402] Further, both Caroline Ellison and Gary Wang have pleaded guilty to several fraud charges and are cooperating with federal prosecutors. Bankman-Fried lost his $16 billion fortune overnight, one of the largest-ever single-day collapses among billionaires, according to Bloomberg. On December 22, 2002, the *WSJ* released the article "Sam Bankman-Fried Likely to Plead Not Guilty to Fraud Charges."[403] He has pleaded not guilty and currently remains on house arrest with a bond of $250 million. We have yet to see what happens.

[399] https://www.wsj.com/articles/ftx-tapped-into-customer-accounts-to-fund-risky-bets-setting-up-its-downfall-11668093732

[400] https://www.sec.gov/news/press-release/2022-219

[401] https://www.sec.gov/news/press-release/2022-234

[402] https://www.forbes.com/sites/jonathanponciano/2022/12/23/caroline-ellison-admits-she-and-bankman-fried-conspired-to-steal-from-ftx-customers-and-mislead-investors-reports-say/?sh=63ef016b5cde

[403] https://www.wsj.com/articles/sam-bankman-fried-likely-to-enter-plea-of-not-guilty-11672431309

# Part 4

# Building an Ethical Decision Culture: If You Build It, He Will Come

# Summary of Part 4

Part 4 presents a framework for building an ethical decision culture. This framework entails identifying weak elements of ethical decision quality and strengthening them through training, restructuring, and minimizing the effects of the common impediments.

The steps needed to build an ethical decision culture are as follows:

## Step 1: Conduct an ethical decision quality audit

The first step in building an ethical decision culture is to become aware of weaknesses in the elements of ethical decision quality that impact decision-making. Conducting an ethical decision quality audit can help achieve this purpose. This step can be achieved by several means, including surveys and examining past decisions. An example of a survey is presented. It can be modified and tailored for specific organizations.

## Step 2: Identify and minimize organizational impediments

This step requires identifying inherent mindsets and actions impeding ethical decision quality. The mindsets and leadership actions presented in part 3 were gleaned from common impediments obtained from numerous media articles. Although these mindsets are common, some organizations might have different mindsets and structures that impede the quality of the decisions. These additional mindsets can also be determined by an audit. An example of a mindset audit is presented.

## Step 3: Restructure for legal, ethical, and prudential decision-making

This step requires restructuring the decision-making process to ensure decisions are given ethical considerations as well as legal and prudential considerations. This step advocates mobbing from compliance to ethics.

## Step 4: Beef up the elements of ethical decision quality

This step identifies training requirements on both the decision-making and the ethical aspects of a decision and increases awareness about the ethical implications of decisions. This step also builds organizational trust by identifying and minimizing actions inconsistent with the organization's core values. This step also requires that an organization identify and set its ethical code, which is not a compliance code, but one that determines its ethical trade-offs and tolerances. This step is not a marketing tool, but a way to build an ethical culture—the effects of which will be observed naturally: "If you build it, he will come."

## Step 5: Give yourself an ethics nudge

This step occurs at the individual level and requires individuals to have a general ethical awareness and knowledge of ethical decision quality and to set their ethical tolerances in advance. It helps individuals reflect on their (and their organization's) ethical tolerance.

# Chapter 25

# An Ethical Decision Quality Assessment

*It should first be decided whether we are honest.*
*If we are not honest, everything stays as it is.*

—Oliver Schmidt, former VW executive to the board
who was sentenced to seven years in prison

## Assess the elements of ethical decision quality

The elements of ethical decision quality can be used to determine the ethical quality of decisions on an individual or organizational level in real time while making a decision. They can also be used to assess the quality of the ethical decision culture of an organization through a survey or an audit of past decisions.

This chapter presents an ethical decision quality assessment that may help assess the ethical quality of a decision on either an individual or an organizational level. The following are sample questions that may be offered to individuals, administrators, and employees to assess the elements of ethical decision quality. On an individual level, this assessment can be conducted in real time while making a decision. When performed on an organizational level to assess the ethical decision culture, they apply to the perception of employees about the elements of ethical decision quality within their operating environment.

This assessment provides a general framework that can be tailored or modified for various organizations. Some sections of this assessment might be more relevant to a particular organization or individual. As with any evaluation, the purpose is not to blame or point fingers.

## Awareness

- Does the decision at hand involve acts of deception? Is there information that would lead to different reactions from stakeholders if revealed?

- Does the decision at hand involve aspects of harming or stealing?
- Does the decision at hand impinge on the rights of some stakeholders?
- Are individuals involved in the decision aware of legal versus ethical distinctions?
- Are individuals involved in the decision aware of ethics versus compliance?
- Are there company policies that involve (or can lead to) deception, harming, or stealing and are impacting the current decision you are about to make?

## General organizational awareness questions

- Will employees/leaders in the organization identify an ethical issue that is illegal?
- Will employees/leaders in the organization identify an ethical issue if it is legal?
- Will employees/leaders in the organization identify an ethical issue if it does not violate a corporate policy?
- Are employees in the organization sensitive to deception, harming, or stealing for either small or large amounts (e.g., Would employees charge extra on reimbursement reports? Would individuals on an hourly rate take extra hours off [unnoticed] after lunch? Would they leave the office early if they could do it quietly and unnoticed?)?
- Does the organization have an ethics officer? If so, is the ethics officer a compliance or legal officer or an ethics officer? Are they beholden to the legal team and to the leadership? How much power do they have in expressing opposing views?
- Are there any instances where individuals opposed unethical actions in the past? What was the response from organizational administrators?
- What venues do you have to oppose leadership decisions?

- If someone received no response for a complaint they filed, what other venues are there to pursue the issue further?

## Motives

- Do you have any personal motives that may impact the ethical quality of the decision you are about to make?
- For those involved in the decision-making in the current decision (or in your organization), are there individuals with particular motives that may impact the quality of the decisions? Can you identify the individuals and their possible motives?
- Are organizational incentives impacting the quality of the current decision?

## Environment

- Is the operating environment affecting your current decision?
- Does the environment entail any of the following?
  - Coercion, intimidation, or manipulation
  - Does obedience to authority impact the decision-making culture?
  - "Us vs. them" or group polarization
  - Politics
  - Lack of transparency
  - Exchange of favors
  - Friends and family aspects
- Are there recognizable trending bandwagons that individuals are pursuing?
- How dominant is the "winning the popularity contest" factor in the operating environment? Is that factor impacting decision-making?

- Are there external environmental factors that impede the ethical quality of decisions (e.g., requests of significant donors or clients or government contracts)?
- Are there things that you would not do in a different environment, but you are doing in your current environment?
- Can you identify situations where other individuals involved in the decision-making would have made different decisions on an individual level than they would have made in the current organizational environment?
- How dominant is the "do whatever it takes to get things done" culture in your decision-making environment?
- How dominant is the "desperate to show improvement" culture within your environment?
- How dominant are the effects of "social clubs beholden to each other" on decision-making?
- How dominant are the effects of the "exchange of favors" aspects on decision-making?

## Reasoning and Rationalization

- How are decisions made in your organization? Do you have a decision-making process? Does it allow for uncertainty about the consequences and the need to act in the light of new information? Are you using a sound decision-making method in your reasoning?
- Are you consistent in your reasoning about ethical issues? Which approach for reasoning about the ethical issue are you using? What type of reasoning about ethical issues are you using to rank the prospects? Kantian, utilitarian, virtue, rights, fairness, common good, other?
- Are you rationalizing any unethical acts in the current decision? What are the common rationalizations in your organization that people use to justify unethical actions toward themselves or others?

- How often is the expression "This is in the organization's best interest" used to justify acts?
- How frequent are top-bottom decisions? How often are employees told about new policies without being informed beforehand?
- How frequently are the expressions "This is politics" and "This is above my pay grade" used?
- Would individuals express opposing views to leadership or an opposing opinion if an act is unethical but perceived as legal and in the organization's best interest?

## Information

- Have you assessed the credibility of the information in the decision you are about to make?
- Have you considered the role of uncertainty and assigned appropriate probabilities?
- Have you considered the role of confirmation bias in your assessments?
- Have you identified possible unanticipated consequences?
- Are unintended consequences frequent? Does the organization spend enough time thinking about them in advance?
- Can you gather more information before making the decision?
- How would you rate the overall transparency of the organization? Are procedures spelled out clearly?
- Is information that is relevant to individual decision-making accessible?
- Is there transparency about procedures? Are relevant files hidden?
- Is there a habit of inaction and silence about inquiries from employees?

## Cognitive biases

- Have you considered the effects of the following biases in your current decision?
    - Confirmation bias
    - Overconfidence
    - Cognitive dissonance
    - Sunk costs
    - Escalation of commitment
    - Obedience to authority
    - Conformity
    - Groupthink
    - False consensus
    - Group polarization
- How would you rate the organization's awareness of the impacts of cognitive biases on ethical decision-making?
- List the top three biases that impact the ethical quality of decisions in your organization.
- How dominant are each of the following biases in your organization?
    - "Us vs. them" bias from leadership toward internal or external stakeholders
    - "Obedience to authority" bias
    - Conformity bias
    - Groupthink and group polarization

## Alternatives

- Does your organization spend enough time exploring ethical alternatives to achieve its objectives?

- Does your organization spend enough time thinking about uncertainties that may impact the decision, the consequences of its alternatives, and their ethical implications?

- Does the organization analyze the possible consequences (intended and unintended) and brainstorm in advance to avoid the escalation of commitment?

- Does the organization spend enough time identifying downstream decisions in the event of new information?

## Well-being

- Are you (or the people involved in the decision) facing any elements of SSSSFFDDAAMCC (Survival/Security/Safety/Stress/Fatigue/Fear/Despair/Depression/Addiction/Anxiety/Mental Health/Coerced/Compromised)?

- How would you rate the overall well-being of individuals in your organization?

- How prevalent is operation under fear, stress, fatigue, and insecurities?

- Does leadership coerce individuals to achieve particular outcomes?

- Is leadership compromised?

- Is leadership (or are individuals) operating with the "desperate to show improvement" mentality?

- Are individuals operating under stress or fear? Do incentive structures and employee review processes cause regular anxiety or fear?

- Are individuals operating under fatigue?

- Have the operating conditions affected the well-being or contributed to any unethical behaviors from employees?

## Trade-offs and tolerances

- Are you clear on the trade-offs you are making?
- Are you clear on your ethical tolerance?
- Has your tolerance for unethical acts changed because of commitment biases?
- Through a survey, identify how respondents rate the ethical tolerance of (1) individuals they work with, (2) the ethical tolerance of leadership, and (3) the ethical tolerance of the organization's past decisions.
- What are your organization's trade-offs and tolerances? Are they clear? Would managers know how to make decisions relying on the stated core values?
- How often are trade-offs and tolerances inconsistent with leadership decisions?

## Formulation

- How much of the "scope of a frame" is dictated to you before making a decision?
- Are you given the flexibility to challenge "what is taken as given," "what is to be decided now," and "what is to be decided later"?
- Are you given enough information or authority to change the frame?
- Are you operating with one perspective? Have you considered others?
- Does your organization explore different perspectives of a frame?
- Does your organization consider "being legal" as a "taken as given" in its scope?

- Does your organization consider "being ethical" as a "taken as given" in its scope?
- Does your organization consider "being prudential" as a "taken as given" in its scope?
- Are there situations where ethical issues are deferred till later?
- Are there situations where legal issues are deferred till later?
- Are there situations where prudential issues are deferred till later? Either for the absence of a process or for some mindsets?

## Stakeholders

- Are there powerful individuals dictating policies for their personal motives that impinge on the rights of other stakeholders?
- Does your organization spend enough time identifying the stakeholders affected by its decisions?
- Does your organization provide a forum for different stakeholders to be heard?

## General questions

- How do you rate the impacts of each element of ethical decision quality on your organizational decision-making?
- Can you identify the three weakest elements of ethical decision quality in your organization?
- Identify the top three organizational actions, structures, or policies that contribute to weakening the elements of ethical decision quality.
- Is there a general trust in organizational structure and its leadership?
- What is the general sense that employees have about reporting? About leadership actions? About top-bottom value slogans? Is there

a general sense of corporate hypocrisy?

## Raising the issues and giving examples

- If you identify weak elements of ethical decision quality as you make a decision or when you conduct a survey, then it is essential to raise the issues before the decision is made.
    - For example, if you can identify the personal motives of individuals involved in the decision-making that may impact the decision, it would be essential to raise the issue.
    - If you can consider better alternatives or different ways of acting that align better with your ethical values, then it would be essential to raise them.
    - If organizational issues impede the ethical quality of the decision, then it would be essential to bring them up.
    - If individuals are operating under fatigue, stress, or coercion, then bring this issue up and discuss it.
- It is also helpful to bring examples from the media covering the consequences of weaknesses in each element of decision quality. Parts 1, 2, and 3 of this book provide extensive examples from the media.

## Using elements of ethical decision quality in an audit of past decisions

The elements of ethical decision quality can also be used to audit past decisions. Through an analysis of past decisions, identify common factors that contributed to weakness in a particular element before an unethical decision was made. These factors can be filtered and analyzed to understand organizational impediments in ethical decision quality.

### Reflection

For each case in part 1, you can check for the weak elements of ethical decision quality and the subsequent ethical collapse. For example, was there a need for more awareness? A need for thinking about better alternatives? An issue with the reasoning or rationalization? The environment? Others?

# Chapter 26

# Identify and Minimize the Inherent Impediments to Ethical Decision Quality

*Someday, and that day may never come,*
*I will call upon you to do a service for me.*
*But until that day, accept this justice as*
*a gift on my daughter's wedding day.*

—Don Vito Corleone from the movie *The Godfather*

## Understanding organizational structures and impediments

The next step in building an ethical decision culture is minimizing impediments to ethical decision quality. This step includes identifying the common weaknesses in the ethical decision quality audit, the mindsets, and organizational structures and environments that impede ethical decision quality.

## Mindset audit

The mindsets identified in Part 3 were gleaned from recurring patterns in media articles and public records. Although these mindsets are prevalent in many organizations, different mindsets can be specific to your organization.

Identifying additional mindsets in an organization becomes easier once the concept of a mindset that impedes ethical decision quality is identified. This can occur through surveys. In addition, weaknesses in elements of decision quality surveyed across the organization can determine prevailing mindsets. Further, when these common issues are raised, they may be met with rationalizations, black holes, and organizational resistance. The response of the organization by itself determines some of the prevailing mindsets.

The following survey questions help identify the six mindsets identified in part 3.

## Legally unethical

- How often does the legal team dictate the decisions to the leadership?
- How do you rate the legal quality of decisions made by your organization?
- How do you rate the ethical quality of decisions made by your organization?
- How do you rate the prudential quality of decisions made by your organization?
- Does your organization spend enough time considering the ethical implications of its decisions as it does the legal implications?
- Can you identify acts conducted by your organization that were legal, but in your view were unethical?
- Do you believe your organization would engage in unethical acts to gain a legal advantage?
- Does the organization have "legally unethical" practices toward either internal or external stakeholders?
- Does your organization have arbitration agreements? Does your organization have an exclusive arbitrator? Does your organization have a financial or professional relationship with the arbitrator? What are the statistics of outcomes of previous arbitration cases?

## Organizational transgressions

- Can you identify policies or actions that are "in the best interest of the organization" that impinge on the rights of stakeholders?
- Do stakeholders feel empowered to speak up against organizational transgressions?
- How often are there retaliatory actions from your organization when confronted with unethical acts?

### Pendulum swings

- Is there a perception of fairness in the organization?
- Is there an "elite" social club that is treated differently in making decisions affecting other stakeholders?
- Is there a group that may be treated with a different ethical tolerance than others regarding unethical acts?
- Are some individuals coerced or compromised or beholden to others for past favors?
- Are there organizational actions contradicting the stated organizational core values?

### Black holes

- How do you rate the level of transparency within your organization?
- Are organizational procedures transparent?
- Are there checks and balances for the specifications of products?
- Are there actions that could impact decisions made by others that you believe the organization intentionally keeps hidden?
- How often do employees leave quietly with hush money payments?
- Does your organization need to be more transparent?
- How often are there no responses from your organization when confronted with unethical acts?

### Unethically fast and slow

- Does the organization admit mistakes when they occur?
- Is the organization fast to acknowledge and remedy unethical acts?

- Does the organization resolve a problem ethically if new information about its transgressions is revealed?

## No decision process

- How are decisions made in the organization?
- Does the organization incorporate a sound decision-making process?
- Are decisions made with a top-bottom approach?
- Are decisions made by an isolated group?
- Is there transparency about the decision process?
- Are there many surprise decisions?
- How would you rate ethical decision-making at the individual level of the organization?
- How would you rate the ethicality of the decision-making at the leadership level?
- Do the expressions "This is politics" or "This is above my pay grade" often appear when justifying why things have to stay as is?
- Is the decision-making process impacted by significant clients, donors, or individuals who desire repeat business from the organization?

## General survey questions

- Are there organizational policies impacting ethical decision quality?
- Can you identify the most common organizational mindsets (beliefs and preferences held by more than one individual at the leadership level) that impede ethical decision-making?
- If your organization has been through an ethical collapse, identify the primary mindsets and factors that enabled the transgressions to occur.

### Leadership actions audit

Following a mindset audit, the following audit concerns leadership actions operating under the mindsets and impacting ethical decision quality. Some general questions about leadership actions may help identify those pertaining to a particular organization. Examples include the following:

- Can you identify some common leadership actions that impede ethical decision quality?
- Can you identify common leadership actions that lead to distrust or are perceived as hypocritical?

### We are the champions of morality!

- Is there a perception that leadership overdoes it with top-bottom value slogans about morality?
- Is there a perception of a "wink-wink" or "non-nod" culture?
- Do you trust leadership's ethics?

### Erratic decision-making on the trending bandwagon

- Can you identify leadership actions of following a trending bandwagon without considering the implications for different stakeholders?
- What are the top three actions that employees would want leadership to do less of because they impede ethical decision quality?
- What actions do employees wish leadership would do more to improve the ethical decision-making culture?

## Friends, family, yes-men

- Can you identify any yes-men and yes-women in your organization?
- Does leadership surround itself with friends and family?

- Are there individuals in the organization who get different treatment regarding tolerance for unethical acts? Does the organization close an eye on its transgressions?
- Does leadership engage in exchange of favors that may impact stakeholders?
- Are there yes-men individuals who appease leadership and who rubber-stamp and impede the ethical quality of their decisions?

### Inappropriate use of the media, politicians, and celebrities

- How far does your organization go to make connections with the media?
- How far does your organization go to make connections with celebrities?
- How far does your organization go to make connections with politicians?
- Can you identify incidents of relations with the media, celebrities, or politicians that were perceived as mechanisms for deterring complaints against the organization or its leadership?
- Can you identify political connections in your organization that may deter complaints?
- Do you believe leadership is using any media politicians or celebrities to deter complaints?

## Working on the mindsets

If you have identified mindsets or leadership actions that impede ethical decision quality, then it is essential to highlight them. The first step is to increase awareness of the implications of mindsets on the decision-making process. Give examples of how similar mindsets have had drastic effects on decision-making. Explain the impact of the prevailing mindsets on stakeholders and how they can lead to the recidivism of ethical concerns. Sometimes training will be required. In other cases, particularly for deeply embedded mindsets, restructuring and change of processes are needed.

# Chapter 27

# Restructure for Legal, Ethical, and Prudential Organizational Decision-Making

*"In civilized life, law floats in a sea of ethics"*

—Earl Warren, Chief Justice U.S. Supreme Cort

## Three aspects of organizational decisions

There are three aspects of an organizational decision:

1. The prudential aspects consider value for the organization and its shareholders. The prudential aspects rely on having a good value-creating decision-making process, and they capture the expertise of individuals and leadership in making decisions on behalf of the organization.

2. The ethical aspects of the decision and their implications to the various stakeholders. These aspects identify elements of deception, harming, or stealing in decisions.

3. The legal aspects of the decision. These aspects investigate the compliance of the organizational decisions with the legal system.

## Responses from polls

In seminars, I ask participants which aspects of decision-making they believe their organizations place the most emphasis on and which they place the least on.

- Almost all of them respond that their organization places the most emphasis on the legal aspects.

- About 85 percent say the prudential aspects would come in second place and that the ethical aspects would come third.

- About 10 percent say that the ethical aspects would be second over the prudential aspects.

- About 5 percent say that the ethical and prudential aspects are equally emphasized in the decision-making after the legal aspects.

Achieving ethical decision quality requires vetting all three aspects and creating an environment that nurtures ethical decisions to be made. It is not sufficient to conduct a few virtuous causes for society, for example, while not working on the interests of the shareholders or closing an eye on ethical violations by the organization. Conducting legal, ethical, and prudential decision-making requires commitment from organizational leaders and may require restructuring the decision process.

**Reflection**

- Are your organizational decisions vetted on all legal, ethical, and prudential components?

- Are there organizational structures that impede ethical decision quality within your organization?

- Does the organization use a good decision process in making important decisions?

- Are there incentive structures and reward systems that impede the quality of the decisions?

- Do employees trust the ethical code of organizational leadership and the ethicality of their decisions?

## A commitment from organizational leaders

To implement ethical decision quality, you will need to restructure the decision-making process to enable the three aspects of decision-making to be included in organizational decisions. This process will require a commitment to ethical decision quality from organizational leaders and a commitment to minimizing mindsets and policies that impede ethical decision quality. For example, the organization will need to operate with transparency. It will need to be clear about its values, as well as its ethical trade-offs and tolerances, and minimize its pendulum swings. The organization might also end up rejecting decisions that are legal and perceived as in the organization's best interest but are unethical toward stakeholders. The organization might also need to acknowledge wrongdoing or make reparations to stakeholders who were harmed by previous decisions.

## Restructuring for legal, ethical, and prudential organizational decision-making

This step aims to ensure an atmosphere within the organization that enables ethical decision quality and that organizational decisions are vetted on all three aspects of the decision. This step might require some restructuring to achieve some considerations for reasoning about a decision.

### 1. Considerations for the legal aspects

There are two main elements to consider in your organization's emphasis on the legal aspects of a decision:

- First, are important decisions vetted by a legal team? Or is the organization exposed to legal risk? You want to avoid exposing the organization to legal risk, so it is essential to vet decisions by a trusted legal team.

- Second, is the legal team focusing too heavily on only the legal aspects of the decision in a way that overlooks the ethical aspects? Are organizational structures listening solely to the legal team? Do the chosen alternatives need to be vetted on the ethical aspects? If so, then this is an element that requires restructuring, as we discuss below.

### 2. Considerations for the ethical aspects: From compliance to ethics

Is there an entity within the organization or an outside ethics counsel that vets the ethical aspects of significant decisions? This entity is not merely a compliance team, but an independent ethics counsel not beholden to leadership or influenced solely by legal counsel. The ethics counsel should have, in the least, equivalent influence on the decision-making as does the legal counsel. The ethics counsel should have sufficient authority to be approached by employees within the organization without fear of retaliation from leadership.

### a. Assess the ethical quality of important decisions

The ethics counsel can assess the ethical quality of current or past decisions or situations that arise using the elements of ethical decision quality. The ethics counsel must comment on the ethical implications of the alternatives and endorse/sign that they approve of the ethicality of each alternative considered. The comments provided should include the ethical issue at hand, the elements of ethical decision quality, whether there is an environment that is impeding the ethical quality of the current decision, the affected stakeholders, any deception, any follow-up decisions that are needed, implications of decisions for stakeholders, which values of the organization are being emphasized and which are being overlooked, any short-term vs. long-term goals, and any conflicts of interest. Then the ethics counsel must identify the ethical reasoning in the decision (Kantian, utilitarian, or other approaches of ethical reasoning). The CEO or other members of leadership must sign and acknowledge that they have read the ethics report and are aware of the ethical implications of each alternative.

### b. Engage in the decision-making process

The ethics counsel needs to be involved in the decision-making in real time when it relates to important decisions. The counsel should also be included during framing and facilitation. The ethics counsel should not be used to merely rubber-stamp the alternatives once a decision has already been made. The ethics counsel may raise issues, such as follows: Are hidden motives impacting the decision? Is the information credible? Are we subject to groupthink or group polarization? Are there friends, family, and yes-men affecting the decision-making process? Are we consistent with our core values? The ethics counsel may also comment on the ethical implications of various alternatives being considered or omitted and on the decision-making process itself.

### c. Increase awareness about elements of ethical decision quality

The ethics counsel may also suggest training modules for particular (or all) aspects of ethical decision quality that may be most relevant for the organization. For example, training and debiasing practices could be recommended if there has been much escalation because of cognitive biases. If aspects related to well-being affect employees' ability to make ethical decisions, the ethics counsel may bring them to leadership. And if the organization needs to spend more time identifying feasible alternatives that could score higher on the ethical front, it should bring the issue up.

#### d. Identify ethical issues and mindsets within the organization

The ethics counsel may also conduct an ethical decision quality assessment and identify the significant impediments. The counsel may recommend restructuring to minimize the mindsets and impediments. Restructuring for an ethical emphasis might also entail actions to reduce the effects of pendulum swings, black holes, or other mindsets that impede the ethical quality of decisions if they are prevalent.

### 3. Considerations for the prudential aspects

There is also a need to vet major decisions and the organization's decision-making on a prudential aspect. Dictionary.com defines "duty of care" as *"a requirement that a person act toward others and the public with the watchfulness, attention, caution and prudence that a reasonable person in the circumstances would use."*[404]

It is essential to capture the expertise and qualifications of various individuals to make prudent decisions for the organization (not just the legal staff). It is also necessary to identify factors affecting the quality of decision-making and the prudence of the decisions made. Does the organization use a flawed decision-making method that impacts the quality of its decisions? Are decisions made with a top-bottom approach? Is leadership surrounded by yes-men approving decisions in a "mutual admiration" environment? If so, the organization must also restructure the decision-making process. This process would need to minimize the effects of a yes-man decision-making culture, "decision-making around the table," or groupthink and escalation.

---

[404] https://dictionary.law.com/Default.aspx?selected=599

This restructuring could also benefit from training individuals on sound decision-making methods so they may observe flawed methods once detected. Training can also involve sound methods to incorporate uncertainty into the decision.

Chevron is an example of a corporation that has restructured and embraced a rigorous decision-making process and training from within. Intel Corporation and many others have also restructured to include sound decision-making methods. The Society of Decision Professionals is an example of a society of professionals working on advocating quality decision-making practices in organizations.

### Example of a legally ethical organizational decision-making process

A situation that requires a decision is identified. A decision team, an ethics counsel team, and a legal team are identified. The decision-makers who will approve the decision are identified.

The ethics team may identify any weaknesses in the elements of ethical decision quality that may impact the decision-making process. After the team is selected, the analysis of the decisions begins.

The decision and ethics teams ensure that a sound decision process will be conducted—one that considers the various motives, environment, well-being of individuals involved, and other aspects that may affect the ethical quality of the decision.

In collaboration with the ethics and legal teams, the decision team conducts a proper facilitation, framing, perspectives, and scope analysis of the situation—identifying biases, motives, groupthink, group polarization, the environment, implications to stakeholders, and other aspects of ethical decision quality. The frame identifies the ethical implications of the scope, what is to be decided now versus later, and the various perspectives involved. The decision-makers then approve the frame.

An initial set of alternatives is explored. The alternatives are commented upon by the legal and ethics teams and then forwarded to the decision-makers. The legal team weighs on the legality of the alternatives, throws in some alternatives, and removes others due to their compliance with the legal system. The ethics team weighs in on the ethical implications of the alternatives to stakeholders, adds some alternatives, red-flags some alternatives based on the organization's ethical trade-offs and tolerances, and throws in some new alternatives that may have less ethical implications even if they are legal and less profitable. The decision team may facilitate a session with the legal and ethics teams and develop new or hybrid alternatives. The decision-makers then vet the feasible, legal, and ethical alternatives.

The critical uncertainties are identified; and a discussion about the different beliefs, biases, and credibility of the information is had. The teams recommend a decision based on the values, alternatives, stakeholders, and information as well as a sound decision-making method that considers the elements of ethical decision quality. The teams also ensure that choices are made consistent with the organization's core values and trade-offs. If a strategy favors short-term gain, the team can quantify the value lost due to the focus on short-term versus long-term gain.

**Reflection**

Refer back to part 1 and play the role of an ethics counsel present in the room during the discussion of the crucial decisions.

Comment on the role of the ethics, legal, and decision analysis teams in the following conversations that may arise during the decision-making process.

The CEO and legal team approve of a decision and say the following:

- "We are legally okay."
- "We are not legally obliged to do so."
- "We need to be clear that shareholder return is not our top priority. Instead giving back to society." Let's send an email to employees that *"our work environment has the highest integrity in the industry and that we are the champions of morality. We will all take a pay cut to contribute to society."*

- *"Mr. Clarke from our federal funding agency wants to see this person in this role. They are good friends. Even though Clarke's friend does not inform individuals about projects and keeps all information to himself to increase his power, Clarke wants to see him in this role."*
- *"Mr. Sebastian in the mayor's office wants his son to have a job within this project. It will give us a significant advantage over our competitors and significant opportunities for future funding. Nobody will know."*

# Chapter 28

# Beef Up the Elements of Ethical Decision Quality

*Without action, the best intentions in the world are nothing more than that: intentions.*

—Jordan Belfort from the movie *The Wolf of Wall Street*

## 1. Ethical decision quality training

Ethical decision quality can be effectively improved by training, particularly when the impediments to ethical decision quality have been minimized. This training involves several modules, such as the following:

- Awareness of ethical implications of decisions; understanding the ethical implication of deception, harming, or stealing; understanding distinctions about the ethicality of an act versus its consequence; understanding the difference between ethics and the legal system or ethics and corporate compliance; understanding the ethical implication of deception, harming, or stealing

- Identifying various motives and understanding the effects of motives on ethical decision-making

- Recognizing environments that impede ethical decision quality

- Understanding the implications of cognitive biases and their effects on (both individual and group) decisions and training on debiasing methods to minimize the effects of cognitive biases

- Training on improving the generation of ethical decision alternatives and recognizing the need for follow-up decisions upon discovering new information

- Training on identifying the main uncertainties that affect the ethical quality of the decision, on the ethics of information gathering, and on thinking about possible unintended consequences

- Training on incorporating uncertainty into modeling decisions, updating beliefs, and identifying flawed methods and rationalizations that impact ethical decision quality.
- Training on using rational decision-making methods
- Training on characterizing ethical trade-offs and tolerances in decisions involving multiple objectives and incentive structures
- Understanding the effects of the frame on ethical decision quality
- Identifying the stakeholders and impacts of the decision
- Recognizing the effects of well-being on ethical decision quality

## 2. Setting organizational ethical tolerances

A worthwhile endeavor would be for an organization to set its ethical trade-offs and tolerances. The organization can form its ethics code. This code should have precise specifications about what the organization is willing to do or not do or tolerate and whether or not it can be "taken as given" that they would implement ethical decision quality in their decisions. The ethics code can set guidelines for ethical decision-making and identify situations and mechanisms by which individuals can receive help if they encounter weak elements of ethical decision quality. The ethics code should not be a marketing tool or a forum to advocate that you are the champion of morality. Instead, build your ethical culture, and it will happen naturally: *If you build it, he will come.*

## 3. Incentive structures: Rewarding based on decision-making, not the outcome

The organization will also need to examine the incentive structures, targets, and their impacts on decision-making. Part 1 illustrated the case of Wells Fargo and the consequences of setting almost impossible-to-meet targets.

The reward should also move to be decision-based and not outcome-based when there is uncertainty and should consider long-term interests. Cures for cancer or Alzheimer's disease would not have been pursued if incentive structures required short-term profit. The focus on short-term gain and the desperate desire to show improvement can induce organizational leaders to act unethically.

Trade-offs should also be incorporated into the goals. Otherwise, attempts to exceed some targets or goals independently can impact the quality of decisions and can yield results that rank lower on the corporate value function.[405]

## 4. Attending to the organization's wave-particle dualities

Wave-particle duality is a concept in quantum mechanics that explains how quantum-scale objects (such as atoms, photons, and electrons) cannot be described individually as either a "particle" or a "wave."[406] At times, they exhibit the properties of a particle; and at others, they exhibit the properties of a wave. Albert Einstein wrote,

> *It seems as though we must sometimes use the one theory and sometimes the other, while at times we may use either. We are faced with a new kind of difficulty. We have two contradictory pictures of reality; separately, neither of them fully explains the phenomena of light, but together they do.*

Similarly, there is often an observed paradox between stated organizational core values and actions conducted by its leadership, particularly with organizations that have top-bottom slogans about being champions of morality. The core values–leadership actions paradox refers to the inability of the organization's stated core values to describe the behavior of its leadership. Sometimes leadership exhibits actions consistent with core values; at other times, it does not. If Albert Einstein were alive today, he would almost surely have described this phenomenon as follows:

---

405 A. E. Abbas and J. E. Matheson, "Normative Decision-Making with Multiattribute Performance Targets," *Journal of Multi-Criteria Decision Analysis* 16, nos. 3–4 (2009): 67–78.

406 https://en.wikipedia.org/wiki/Wave%E2%80%93particle_duality

*It seems as though we must sometimes use one set of core values to describe leadership actions and sometimes the other, while at times we may use either. We are faced with a new kind of difficulty. We have two contradictory pictures of reality; separately, neither of them fully explains the phenomena of leadership actions, but together they do.*

There are many reasons why some corporate administrator actions may be inconsistent with the stated core values. Examples include not really believing in the stated core values, the feeling that they can get away with it, the rationalizations that what they are doing is an exception in the best interest of the organization, and the entitlement; and often, it can be due to recommendations of a legal team that was not involved in setting the core values.

There is a need to minimize the core values–leadership actions paradox partly because they lead to distrust, and they also lead to confusion in the organization's values used in decision-making. Following the oil spill incident in the Gulf, as an example, many oil, gas, and energy companies launched initiatives to improve decision-making. I was invited to give a seminar in the headquarters of a large organization, and so I decided to talk about values. I asked what values their organization cares about when making decisions. Immediately, everybody responded, "Safety." I asked if there were any other values, and after some discussion, they said, "Having a clean environment." I asked if there were any other values, and no hands were raised. There was a pause. After about ten minutes, a participant sitting at the back of the room raised their hand hesitantly and said, "Profit." He seemed embarrassed by saying it. I replied, "Of course. If you aren't interested in profit, you can achieve those values of safety and environmental effects by shutting down your operations. You would have a stellar safety record and have minimal impact on the environment." It was evident that leadership had provided top-bottom messages that "it was all about safety." But in so doing, they may have provided statements that are at odds with the company's actual operations, which can confuse individuals making decisions.

## Resolving the core values–leadership actions paradox

An acid test that may be useful in helping to minimize the core values–leadership actions paradox and the "We are the champions of morality" slogans within an organization is that if the administrator violates core values, then they should do one of the following:

1. Change the core values to account for the inconsistency, acknowledging that there was an inconsistency when setting the core values.

2. They should leave to help rebuild trust in the organization.

### Reflection

- Can you think of core values–leadership actions paradoxes in part 1 or the media?

- Can you identify acts wherein leadership or the organization contradicted its stated values?

- How often does the organization engage in acts (either internally within the organization or externally toward other stakeholders) that contradict its stated values? If so, are internal or external violations more prominent?

- Can you identify actions that are perceived as organizational hypocrisy?

# Chapter 29

# Give Yourself an Ethics Nudge

*Dr. Teddy Oglethorpe: A man's always got choices, Randall! Sometimes you just gotta choose the good one!*

From the movie *Don't Look Up*

## 1. Get into the habit of using the elements of ethical decision quality

There are three levels of learning. One level is to take a class on a topic, pass an exam, and then forget the material after the class is over. Another level is to learn a topic to develop a skill that you use when called upon. A third level is to learn the material in such a way that it becomes second nature and is incorporated into your everyday activities. This is the level that you can incorporate the material in this book.

The elements of ethical decision quality can be used on an individual level in day-to-day decision-making. Examples include becoming more aware of the effects of biases and hidden motives, spending more time brainstorming alternatives that improve the ethical implications of decisions, exploring uncertainties and unintended consequences (give yourself a consequences nudge), recognizing various stakeholders, recognizing that false information exists and that it affects the ethical quality of decisions, understanding the impacts of the environment on ethical decision-making, understanding the role of the frame, understanding the effects of the environment and the mindsets on ethical decision quality.

## 2. Recognize and improve your personal limitations

You can do many things on an individual level to improve the ethical quality of decisions. Once you become aware of the confirmation bias, for example, it is up to you to take steps to minimize its impact on your personal decisions. It is up to you to work on calibrating your probability assessments to better represent your belief and on using debiasing techniques to minimize the effects of biases. It is also up to you to understand your motives and know when they are kicking in and impeding the ethical quality of decisions. It is also up to you to recognize stressful environments that may affect well-being and lead to unethical acts. And it is up to you to validate the information and act in light of new information. It is also up to you to recognize groupthink and group polarization and to stop jumping on the trending bandwagon.

## 3. Anticipate in advance ethical scenarios and set your ethical tolerance

It is up to you to set (and think in advance about) your ethical tolerance and trade-offs before an issue arises and escalates. You can do that by reflecting on past experiences and determining whether your tolerance was too low or too high. Howard and Korver (2008) advocate writing a personal ethical code that describes in advance how you will react when an ethical issue arises.[407] As you make your next decision, use the elements of ethical decision quality to determine weak elements that need to be rectified before the decision is made.

**Reflection**

Refer back to Part 1 and determine what you would do in each of the decisions faced as an organizational leader or as an employee witnessing the acts. Identify the uncertainties, preferences, environment, and other elements of ethical decision quality that you would consider. Identify alternatives including whistle-blowing or other attempts to change the system.

[407] Howard, R.A. and Korver, C, Ethics for the Real World. Harvard Business Press (2008).

www.ingramcontent.com/pod-product-compliance
Ingram Content Group UK Ltd.
Pitfield, Milton Keynes, MK11 3LW, UK
UKHW041643031026
15587UKWH00001B/459

9 781804 412206